JAPANESE FASHION CULTURES

Dress, Body, Culture

Series Editor: **Joanne B. Eicher**, *Regents' Professor*, *University of Minnesota*

Advisory Board:

Djurdja Bartlett, *London College of Fashion, University of the Arts*
Pamela Church-Gibson, *London College of Fashion, University of the Arts*
James Hall, *University of Illinois at Chicago*
Vicki Karaminas, *University of Technology, Sydney*
Gwen O'Neal, *University of North Carolina at Greensboro*
Ted Polhemus, *Curator, 'Street Style' Exhibition, Victoria and Albert Museum*
Valerie Steele, *The Museum at the Fashion Institute of Technology*
Lou Taylor, *University of Brighton*
Karen Tranberg Hansen, *Northwestern University*
Ruth Barnes, *Ashmolean Museum, University of Oxford*

Books in this provocative series seek to articulate the connections between culture and dress, which is defined here in its broadest possible sense as any modification or supplement to the body. Interdisciplinary in approach, the series highlights the dialogue between identity and dress, cosmetics, coiffure and body alternations as manifested in practices as varied as plastic surgery, tattooing, and ritual scarification. The series aims, in particular, to analyse the meaning of dress in relation to popular culture and gender issues and will include works grounded in anthropology, sociology, history, art history, literature and folklore.

ISSN: 1360-466X

Previously published in the series

Helen Bradley Foster, *'New Raiments of Self': African American Clothing in the Antebellum South*
Claudine Griggs, *S/he: Changing Sex and Changing Clothes*
Michaele Thurgood Haynes, *Dressing Up Debutantes: Pageantry and Glitz in Texas*
Anne Brydon and Sandra Niessen, *Consuming Fashion: Adorning the Transnational Body*
Dani Cavallaro and Alexandra Warwick, *Fashioning the Frame: Boundaries, Dress and the Body*
Judith Perani and Norma H. Wolff, *Cloth, Dress and Art Patronage in Africa*
Linda B. Arthur, *Religion, Dress and the Body*
Paul Jobling, *Fashion Spreads: Word and Image in Fashion Photography*
Fadwa El Guindi, *Veil: Modesty, Privacy and Resistance*
Thomas S. Abler, *Hinterland Warriors and Military Dress: European Empires and Exotic Uniforms*
Linda Welters, *Folk Dress in Europe and Anatolia: Beliefs about Protection and Fertility*
Kim K.P. Johnson and Sharron J. Lennon, *Appearance and Power*
Barbara Burman, *The Culture of Sewing*
Annette Lynch, *Dress, Gender and Cultural Change*
Antonia Young, *Women Who Become Men*
David Muggleton, *Inside Subculture: The Postmodern Meaning of Style*
Nicola White, *Reconstructing Italian Fashion: America and the Development of the Italian Fashion Industry*
Brian J. McVeigh, *Wearing Ideology: The Uniformity of Self-Presentation in Japan*
Shaun Cole, *Don We Now Our Gay Apparel: Gay Men's Dress in the Twentieth Century*
Kate Ince, *Orlan: Millennial Female*
Nicola White and Ian Griffiths, *The Fashion Business: Theory, Practice, Image*
Ali Guy, **Eileen Green and Maura Banim**, *Through the Wardrobe: Women's Relationships with their Clothes*
Linda B. Arthur, *Undressing Religion: Commitment and Conversion from a Cross-Cultural Perspective*
William J.F. Keenan, *Dressed to Impress: Looking the Part*
Joanne Entwistle and Elizabeth Wilson, *Body Dressing*
Leigh Summers, *Bound to Please: A History of the Victorian Corset*
Paul Hodkinson, *Goth: Identity, Style and Subculture*
Leslie W. Rabine, *The Global Circulation of African Fashion*
Michael Carter, *Fashion Classics from Carlyle to Barthes*
Sandra Niessen, **Ann Marie Leshkowich and Carla Jones**, *Re-Orienting Fashion: The Globalization of Asian Dress*
Kim K. P. Johnson, **Susan J. Torntore and Joanne B. Eicher**, *Fashion Foundations: Early Writings on Fashion and Dress*
Helen Bradley Foster and Donald Clay Johnson, *Wedding Dress Across Cultures*
Eugenia Paulicelli, *Fashion under Fascism: Beyond the Black Shirt*
Charlotte Suthrell, *Unzipping Gender: Sex, Cross-Dressing and Culture*
Irene Guenther, *Nazi Chic? Fashioning Women in the Third Reich*
Yuniya Kawamura, *The Japanese Revolution in Paris Fashion*
Patricia Calefato, *The Clothed Body*
Ruth Barcan, *Nudity: A Cultural Anatomy*
Samantha Holland, *Alternative Femininities: Body, Age and Identity*
Alexandra Palmer and Hazel Clark, *Old Clothes, New Looks: Second Hand Fashion*

Yuniya Kawamura, *Fashion-ology: An Introduction to Fashion Studies*
Regina A. Root, *The Latin American Fashion Reader*
Linda Welters and Patricia A. Cunningham, *Twentieth-Century American Fashion*
Jennifer Craik, *Uniforms Exposed: From Conformity to Transgression*
Alison L. Goodrum, *The National Fabric: Fashion, Britishness, Globalization*
Annette Lynch and Mitchell D. Strauss, *Changing Fashion: A Critical Introduction to Trend Analysis and Meaning*
Catherine M. Roach, *Stripping, Sex and Popular Culture*
Marybeth C. Stalp, *Quilting: The Fabric of Everyday Life*
Jonathan S. Marion, *Ballroom: Culture and Costume in Competitive Dance*
Dunja Brill, *Goth Culture: Gender, Sexuality and Style*
Joanne Entwistle, *The Aesthetic Economy of Fashion: Markets and Value in Clothing and Modelling*
Juanjuan Wu, *Chinese Fashion: From Mao to Now*
Brent Luvaas, *DIY Style: Fashion, Music and Global Cultures*
Jianhua Zhao, *The Chinese Fashion Industry*
Eric Silverman, *A Cultural History of Jewish Dress*
Karen Hansen and D. Soyini Madison, *African Dress: Fashion, Agency, Performance*
Maria Mellins, *Vampire Culture*

JAPANESE FASHION CULTURES

Dress and gender in contemporary Japan

MASAFUMI MONDEN

Bloomsbury Academic
An imprint of Bloomsbury Publishing Plc

B L O O M S B U R Y
LONDON · OXFORD · NEW YORK · NEW DELHI · SYDNEY

Bloomsbury Academic
An imprint of Bloomsbury Publishing Plc

50 Bedford Square	1385 Broadway
London	New York
WC1B 3DP	NY 10018
UK	USA

www.bloomsbury.com

Bloomsbury is a registered trade mark of Bloomsbury Publishing Plc

First published 2015
Reprinted by Bloomsbury Academic 2015, 2016

© Masafumi Monden, 2015

Masafumi Monden has asserted his right under the Copyright, Designs and Patents Act, 1988, to be identified as Author of this work.

British Library Cataloguing-in-Publication Data
A catalogue record for this book is available from the British Library.

ISBN: HB: 978-1-4725-3621-1
PB: 978-1-4725-3280-0
ePDF: 978-1-4725-8673-5
ePub: 978-1-4725-8672-8

Library of Congress Cataloging-in-Publication Data
Monden, Masafumi.
Japanese fashion cultures : dress and gender in contemporary Japan / Masafumi Monden.
pages cm – (Dress, body, culture)
Includes bibliographical references and index.
ISBN 978-1-4725-3280-0 (paperback) — ISBN 978-1-4725-3621-1 (hardback) —
ISBN 978-1-4725-8673-5 (epdf)   1. Fashion–Japan–History.   2. Clothing and dress–Japan–History.   3. Clothing and dress–Social aspects–Japan.   I. Title.
GT1560.M63 2015
391.00952—dc23
2014010741

Series: Dress, Body, Culture

Typeset by RefineCatch Limited, Bungay, Suffolk
Printed and bound in Great Britain

CONTENTS

ILLUSTRATIONS

Figures

Tables

ACKNOWLEDGEMENTS

This book is like a personal diary, a memory lane leading to the people I have met and known throughout my life. It is therefore such a delight to thank the people who have inspired me and made this book possible.

Foremost, I am deeply grateful to my excellent supervisors, mentors and friends, Professor Meredith Jones and Professor Peter McNeil. This book would not have been possible without their continued guidance, enthusiasm and encouragement.

It is important to acknowledge both the Australia Postgraduate Award Scheme and the Faculty of Design, Architecture and Built Environment (DAB) at the University of Technology, Sydney, for offering me funding and facilities that were quite vital to the completion of this book. I would like to thank Ms Ann Hobson and the staff of the Faculty. I am indebted to my former fellow students and friends in both the Faculty of Arts and Social Sciences and DAB, who are too many to name here, for sharing this incredible journey and making it such a convivial experience. It is also my pleasure to acknowledge the support, generosity and advice of many individuals, who have, whether directly or indirectly, ensured the completion of this book. I would like to give special mention to Professor Jaqueline Berndt, Dr Tim Edwards, Dr Lucy Fraser, Professor Alisa Freedman, Ms Tiffany Godoy, Dr Olivier Krischer, Professor Vera Mackie, Ms Patricia Mears, Dr Yumiko Mikanagi, Professor Laura Miller, Professor Brian J. McVeigh, Mr Dominik Mohila, Dr Fuyubi Nakamura, Dr Ronnie Zuessman and two anonymous readers for their valuable suggestions, encouragement and feedback. I would also like to thank Dr Valerie Steele and the Museum at FIT (Fashion Institute of Technology) team, Professor Toby Slade for offering me memorable opportunities to present portions of this book in New York and Honolulu, and my friends in Japan to whom the foundation of my knowledge and experience in Japanese fashion and popular culture is largely indebted.

I also thank the Whitehouse Institute of Design, Sydney, especially Dr Melissa Laird and the wonderful design students for their kindess and inspirations.

I thank Professor Joanne Eicher, editor of the Dress, Body, Culture series, for her encouragement in developing this book. The Bloomsbury editorial team deserves my heartfelt thanks for their tireless effort and assistance. I am thankful to Ms Kathryn Earle, Ms Anna Wright, Ms Abbie Sharman, Miss Noa Vázquez, Ms Kim Muranyi, Ms Chloe Darke, Ms Emily Ardizzone, and especially Ms Hannah Crump.

I am grateful to Ms Hitomi, Mr Shingo Yasuda and especially Mr Kenji Hiraoka of Milkboy for allowing me to use the splendid images for the cover and inside illustrations. My thanks also go to Ms Kaori Hayashi (Hearst Fujingaho Co., Ltd), Mr Ide (Adams), Mr Rui Ishizu, Ms Rikako Nakahara (Himawariya Co., Ltd), Mr Daisuke Ota (Kyodo News International), Ms Mariko Sato (Suzuki), Ms Mai Sakamoto (Innocent World), Ms Asako Takabatake (The Kasho Museum) and Ms Shizue Uchida (The Yayoi Museum), for their generosity in sourcing wonderful images for this book.

Lastly, I wish to thank my family, particularly my grandparents Noriko and Masaichiro, my mother Kazuyo and my sister Izumi for always believing in me. This book is dedicated to Lino, Alise, Claire, Luca, Marius and the one and only Norina. My new journey has just begun, and I am very excited about what the future holds for me.

M.M. July 2014
Sydney

Note

A portion of Chapter 2 was published in Joanne Eicher (ed.), *Berg Encyclopaedia of World Dress and Fashion* (2012). A portion of Chapter 3 appeared in *Fashion Theory* (16(3), 2012). Parts of Chapter 4 appeared in the journal *Japan Forum* (Taylor and Francis, 2014), and parts of Chapter 5 were published in Fuyubi Nakamura, Morgan Perkins and Olivier Krischer (eds), *Asia Through Art and Anthropology* (2013). An earlier version of Chapter 6 appeared in Patricia Mears (ed.), *Ivy Style: Radical Conformists* (Yale University Press, 2012).

1
INTRODUCING JAPANESE FASHION, PAST AND PRESENT

There is a certain enigmatic air surrounding the images of Japanese fashion culture conceptualized by those 'outside'. On one hand it is a culture ruled by regimental uniformity and patriarchal values, perhaps best exemplified by the figures of the 'salaryman' or the 'high school student', where freedom of individual expression is a luxury.[1] On the other hand, however, there is a recurrent flowering of youth adorned in vivid, flamboyant fashion styles, showcasing their creativity and individuality in such fashion magazines as *FRUiTS*. The kaleidoscope of these enthralling images might mirror certain aspects of Japanese culture. But understanding the culture only through such extreme binaries signals a danger of creating and sustaining an imagined 'distance'. They are so different that they seem to be of no relevance to non-Japanese culture. Is a fleeting trace of Orientalist ideas, which predominantly appreciate the 'exotic', the 'authentic', and by implication, the 'different' qualities of foreign culture, still present? Or are these images and perceptions fruit of Japan's conscious construction of pure 'Japaneseness' in order to differentiate the culture from any non-Japanese cultures?[2] Even as far back as 1891, Oscar Wilde wrote that '[t]he Japanese people are the deliberate self-conscious creation of certain individual artists' and thus 'the whole of Japan is a pure invention'.[3] In either case, clothes play a crucial role in the construction of such images and the workings of visuality.

In our contemporary world with its advanced media technologies, the increased presence of Japanese popular culture outside Japan is evident. A number of excellent studies of Japanese fashion and beauty practices have also been published. Works such as Brian J. McVeigh's *Wearing Ideology: State, Schooling and Self-presentation in Japan* (2000), Laura Miller's *Beauty Up: Exploring Contemporary Japanese Body Aesthetics* (2006), Toby Slade's *Japanese Fashion: A Cultural History* (2009) and Valerie Steele's *Japan Fashion Now* (2010) are scholarly indications of a growing desire for a more accurate picture of the intellectual history of the subject, while Tiffany Godoy's *Style Deficit*

Disorder: Harajuku Street Fashion (2007) offers a vivid picture of what is happening in the streets of Japan's most dazzling fashion district. Despite this notability, however, only a selected portion of the cultural and art objects of everyday Japan have received comprehensive scholarly attention in the English-speaking world.[4] How clothes are represented in contemporary Japanese culture, such as films, magazines and music videos, for example, remains to be studied in great detail. This 'absence' has contributed to the further flow of the clichéd images of the culture mentioned above.

With the intention of ameliorating this situation, what I demonstrate through this book is that individuals in Japan engage with fashion in culturally significant ways. These ways might differ from how individuals are assumed to engage with clothes in European and American mainstream cultures. Not only that, I argue that using the lens of fashion reveals the complexities of gender relations in Japan. Four contemporary case studies position this argument: young men's fashion publications, female performers' use of Lewis Carroll's Alice in music videos, *Lolita* fashion and Tetsuya Nakashima's film *Shimotsuma monogatari* (*Kamikaze Girls*, 2004), and the continuing remarking of 'Ivy League' style in Japan. These four examples are notable for their adoption of historic European and American clothing forms. Their relatively 'mainstream' stature in contemporary Japanese culture comes with a 'twist' or unconventional characteristics. The 'mainstream' standing of these types of popular culture indicates their reach, consumed by a great number of individuals within Japan. Certain qualities they manifest, on the other hand, impose a subtle, almost delicate kind of revolt against a set of *idées fixes* surrounding the relationship between clothes and gender. Sociologist Diana Crane has argued that mainstream texts, which are generally directed toward large and heterogeneous audiences, tend to be stereotypical, unlike texts with smaller audiences. This is because 'more stereotyped products are communicated more readily to heterogeneous audiences with diverse backgrounds and outlooks'.[5] The subtle combination of mainstream and atypical characteristics of the selected texts for this research is thus significant.

What needs to be recognized here is that we should avoid falling into a simple orientalist idea that 'they' are 'different' and hence are of minor, if any, importance to non-Japanese culture. This is because, as global anthropologist Jan Nederveen Pieterse has convincingly argued, an anthropological definition of culture narrates that there are no territorial limitations of culture. It is both sharable and learnable. According to him:

> Culture refers to behaviour and beliefs that are learned and shared: learned so it is not 'instinctual' and shared so it is not individual. Sharing refers to social sharing but there is no limitation as to the boundaries of this sociality. No territorial or historical boundaries are implied as part of the definition. This

understanding of culture is open-ended. Leaning is always ongoing as a function of changing circumstances and therefore culture is always *open*. To sharing there are no fixed boundaries other than those of common social experience, therefore there are no territorial limitations to culture. Accordingly culture refers as much to commonality as to diversity.[6]

Perhaps more cautiously than Nederveen Pieterse, dress historian Margaret Maynard argues that, to a certain extent, clothes are 'a form of informational exchange'.[7] If clothes operate as a form of informational exchange, certain experiences and aesthetics of dress might be transmitted, shared or understood cross-culturally. Japanese fashion is a good example for looking at this hypothesis because this is where, particularly since the country's re-engagement with Euro-America in 1868, European sartorial styles have been actively promoted, both politically and aesthetically.[8] Consequently, Japan has become an ethnographically unique space where the subtle marriage of European dress style and Japanese aesthetics has taken place.

The theory of 'format' and 'product', as articulated by sociologist Keiko Okamura, also reinforces the relevance of the study of Japanese fashion to other cultures. This theory allows a cultural form to be seen as a 'format' when becoming transculturally accepted.[9] This standardized 'format' becomes a carrier of a local culture, making its qualities visible and hence comparable with those of other cultures. This theory, when applied to the study of Japanese fashion, demarcates characteristics both culturally specific to and shared by Japanese and non-Japanese cultures. In other words, a critical examination of a range of cultural representations of fashion and gender identity in contemporary Japan can underscore how conceptions and representations of fashion and gender identities are circulated in other cultures, including those of Europe, North America and Australia. As illustrator Kazuo Hozumi states in his now classic *IVY Illustrated* (1980), there is a certain degree of universality ascribed to fashion and clothes.[10] Thus, how clothes are worn, represented and understood in the Japanese cultural context is important for understanding non-Japanese cultures, and vice versa.

One of the prominent aspects of dress as an object of study is its ability to amalgamate with other research matters. It could be used in order to calibrate the ways in which our conceptions of gender manifest, or to interpret the psychological state of a character in literature. The significance of academically examining fashion is enhanced by 'the cultural stereotype that suggests that fashion has always been more closely connected with the domain of women'.[11] This cultural stereotype then renders fashion to be 'almost automatically judged as less important, less worthy, less "great" than more "masculine" kinds of art'.[12] However, dress is, as feminist scholar Elizabeth Wilson beautifully puts it, 'the cultural metaphor for the body, it is the material with which we "write" or "draw" a representation of the body into our cultural context'.[13] Indeed, representations of gender within the four cultural arenas that this book analyses largely manifest through, and are intertwined with, clothes. The discourses of dress in the case studies selected for this book are, then, a vehicle for understanding constructions of gender, identity and the Japanese cultural milieu.

Layers of Japanese aesthetic history

Dress is a useful instrument in order to calibrate Japanese cultural and aesthetic history. For example, in the Heian court (794–1185), the art of matching colours was especially important in men's and women's dress, and a woman's skill in selecting clothes, and particularly in combining colours, was considered a fundamental measure in determining her character and charm, much more important than the physical features with which she was born.[14] The colour combination of layers called 'cherry blossom', for instance, was created by wearing a white kimono over a red kimono, the layers of 'rose plum' consisted of a pink kimono over a lavender or crimson one, and the layers of 'lavender' had a light-green kimono beneath a pale lavender kimono.[15] This cult of beauty is well narrated in Lady Murasaki's *The Tale of Genji* (eleventh century), often noted as one of the oldest romance novels in the history of literature. In one scene, Prince Genji becomes the centre of attention when he attends a flower festival and demonstrates his immaculate sense of fashion:

> He went to his apartments and dressed. It was very late indeed when at last he made his appearance at the party. He was dressed in a cloak of thin Chinese fabric, white outside but lined with yellow. His robe was of a deep wine-red colour with a very long train. The dignity and grace with which he carried this fancifully regal attire in a company where all were dressed in plain official robes were indeed remarkable, and in the end his presence perhaps contributed more to the success of the party than did the fragrance of the Minister's boasted flowers.[16]

Fusae Kawazoe, the scholar of Japanese literature and expert on *The Tale of Genji*, writes that it would have been as mesmerizing as a beautiful young man making his attendance to a social event wearing a pale pink dinner jacket while the other men were dressed in sober black.[17]

In more recent times, schoolgirls in urban areas came under intense attention when they started commuting by bicycles or trains to newly established women's schools at around the turn of the twentieth century. With their long-sleeved arrow-feathered patterned kimono, maroon-coloured *hakama*, European-style boots, and their long hair swept back and tied with single big ribbons, these young women were dressed in a typical, privileged schoolgirl style.[18] Both the *hakama* and European-style shoes were regarded as masculine items at the time, and while the government issued an edict to prevent women from wearing men's clothes, the modified version of this odd combination of Japanese and European men's attires became the 'uniform' of schoolgirls in that era.[19] Most of the schoolgirls of the beginning of the last century were wealthy daughters of elite families, and like schoolgirls today, they were typified as personifications of purity and blossoming sexual maturity.[20] On the one hand, these 'social princesses' were the symbols of 'ethereally sweet and innocent' girlhood. On the other hand, however, they were criticized for being embodiments of 'moral degeneracy', 'sexual promiscuity' and 'unfavourably masculine attitudes'.[21] The latter conception was largely predicated on their progressive and liberated behaviours, which gave them the name *haikara-san*, Miss High-collar.[22] Her deployment of *onna-bakama* (female *hakama*) moreover gave these women a sense of mobility adequate for them to ride a bicycle or play tennis without compromising their modesty.

In the Meiji (1868–1912) and Taisho (1912–26) periods, it is argued that adoption, appropriation and restyling of European-style clothes 'remade' the Japanese people.[23] This imposes a series of questions: can clothing 'perform' a particular role in contemporary Japan? Does it represent 'identity', as art philosopher Llewellyn Negrin proposes – 'the way one adorns oneself should reflect one's values and beliefs'?[24] Historians like Ken'ichiro Hirano and Toby Slade have suggested that Japanese women and men in the late nineteenth and early twentieth centuries adopted European-style clothes at different rates. Does this suggest, then, that Japanese women and men have profoundly different relationships to fashion? This book implies something more subtle than simple yes or no answers to these questions.

Dress and gender

Fashion defines and redefines the boundaries between two gender categories, 'masculinity' and 'femininity'.[25] Clothes can also be understood 'as the boundary between body, self and society' and they can be used to show acceptance, conformity to, and refusal to social expectations of gender.[26] In this reading, not only 'masculine' or 'feminine' clothing styles, but 'genderless' or 'androgynous' styles, too, are placed on the poles of a continuum of 'gendered' looks, for they are defined against the two gender categories.[27] In a converse reading, this points to the 'constructed' and 'crafted' nature of what we come to understand as 'masculinity' and 'femininity'. The theory of gender performativity, made famous by post-structuralist philosopher and scholar Judith Butler, comes immediately to mind. Gender, this theory argues, is not a stable fact but something we imagine and construct. Butler considers gender as a collective performance that is designed primarily to sustain the legitimacy of heterosexuality, punishing those who fail to perform their 'gender' roles correctly.[28] Conventional masculinity and femininity, or the 'gender reality' as Butler calls it, are therefore created through sustained and repeated social performances. This means that:

> [t]he very notions of an essential sex and a true or abiding masculinity or femininity are also constituted as part of the strategy that conceals gender's performative character and the performative possibilities for proliferating gender configurations outside the restricting frames of masculinist domination and compulsory heterosexuality.[29]

The theory of gender performativity therefore denounces the absolute distinction between the two gender categories. It might be too extreme, and in a sense too simplistic, to reduce the whole existence of gender identity to a construction and fabrication. Biological differences between men and women, for example, should not be disregarded when examining gender.[30] In relation to socio-biological perspectives on 'masculinity', social work scholar Bob Pease also states that '[i] n rejecting biological determinism, we have to be careful not to replace it with cultural determinism'. Thus, gender identity could be much more complex than either thoroughly biologically determined or culturally constructed. Accordingly, dress anthropologist Joanne B. Eicher is right in saying, '[o]bviously, both men and women have sexed bodies and gendered dress in every society.'[31] That being said, Butler's idea that (the conventional ideas of) gender is *largely* performative, and indeed relies on collective performances, is highly useful. This is particularly so when we consider that in reality, not every male acts or behaves strictly according to the conventional idea of 'masculinity', while not every female acts or behaves accordingly to the conventions of 'femininity'. Dress is, quite patently, one of the most crucial elements both supporting and revealing the performance of gender.

Clothes are a fundamental component in the sustenance of 'gender' performance because they are 'one of the most immediate and effective examples of the way in which bodies are gendered, made "feminine" or "masculine"'.[32] Indeed, children and even adults tend to distinguish gender not by individuals' actual biological gender, but by their dress or appearance.[33] The sartorial distinctions between men and women are moreover not always kept transparent in the European history of dress.[34] Modern sartorial distinctions between men and women in Europe were increasingly accentuated in the Victorian period, when 'the renunciation of decoration on the part of men is contrasted with the increasing fussiness of women's dress'.[35] Anne Hollander offers a possible explanation – that the early nineteenth century witnessed the emergence of the Romantic movement, which required patent differences between the two gender categories. She also suggests that fashion in the periods when male and female sartorial styles were kept distinct from each other (e.g. in 1380 or 1680, 1850 or 1950), illuminates two points.[36] Firstly, men and women in such periods were compelled to express 'a very clear sense of distance from the other one', which was often endorsed by laws and penalties.[37] Secondly, and more importantly, this would usually emerge 'when the visual differences between men's and women's clothes [were] actually in a new state of confusion, and fashion [was] beginning to bring the sexes closer together after having sharply divided them'.[38]

Hollander's theory endorses the cultural and socio-psychological proposition that gender is a cultural or social construction, an imaginative necessity for which clothes are used as a primary device to demarcate such differences. Since the subjects of this book are Japanese, it is useful and logical to see how sartorial distinctions between the two gender categories have been manifested in the history of Japanese clothing. The Japanese history of dress before the country 'reopened' to Euro-America in the 1860s also demonstrates the instability of gender differences. The rich history of Japanese clothes would require no less than a whole book to explore fully, and thus I refer briefly to only a portion of it in the present setting.[39]

Wearing gender in Japan

The Chinese-influenced clothing styles for men and women in the seventh century did not differ significantly. 'Men and women wore a similar upper body garment and ceremonial skirt. Beneath this skirt, men wore trousers, while women wore another long skirt that Japanese call a *mo*.'[40] In the Heian court when Japan closed its door to Chinese influences, sartorial differences between noble men and women, let alone between social classes and ranks, became relatively more visible.[41] Although sartorial sensibilities were a requirement of both men and women in the period, men's clothes were less elaborate in shape than women's.[42] Court ladies' ceremonial robes consisted of several layers of unlined kimono worn one over the other, taking great sensitivity to 'match and contrast the colors of each layer, which were visible at the neck, sleeve ends and lower skirt . . . Worn underneath were an under-kimono and a *hakama*.'[43] Further difference was marked by the great length of women's hair.

Anthropologist Liza Dalby's work on kimono still gives some useful insights into the intricate relationship between gender and kimono. Dalby argues that the most significant historical change in the kimono form occurred during the Muromachi period (1336–1573), when women ceased to wear trouser-like *hakama* altogether, triggering the refashioning of *kosode* from calf-length to ankle level.[44] Once a Japanese version of chemise, *kosode* now became a prototype of today's kimono. The shape of *kosode* in the early Edo period was identical for both sexes.[45] But the first stylistic ramification of *kosode* seemingly occurred in the late 1660s, when the sleeves of women's *kosode* grew longer. A sleeve of eighteen inches (approximately 46 cm) was considered *furisode* (women's *kosode* with long 'fluttering' sleeves) in the late 1660s. They reached more than thirty inches (75 cm) long in the Genroku period (1688–1703), after only two decades since the lengthening of the *kosode*'s sleeves began, possibly showcasing the luxurious aspects of life in this period.[46]

It seems that the Japanese history of kimono *per se* tells the defining and redefining process of gender boundaries, sometimes closing and sometimes demarcating the distinction. Significantly, sartorial distinctions between social class and age were as important as gender in the Japanese history of kimono. These distinctions were manifested through not only forms but also colours, patterns and textiles. Fabrics seem to have attracted the strongest interest throughout Japanese history.[47] In the Edo period, however, people in the merchant class would incorporate the styles embraced by either court people, kabuki actors or courtesans, making dress further complicated. Any discussion of dress in the Edo period needs to take into account the existence of sumptuary laws, which were issued primarily to maintain status distinctions in the period, especially in order to distinguish the samurai class from *chōnin* (townsmen, often used to describe both artisans and merchants), who were often richer than but socially inferior to samurai.[48] The laws were difficult to enforce. Scholar of Japanese literature and culture Donald H. Shively notes that the sumptuary laws in the early Edo period possibly received respect only for a short period after their issue, and that infractions slowly became more patent and more radical.[49] Apart from overtly infracting the laws, it was a secret pleasure for both men and women to wear fancy, expensive loincloths throughout the Edo period, and for merchants to use finer silk materials for the linings of otherwise simple kimono, as ways of subterfuge.[50]

Dalby alludes to a significant aspect of the relationship between garments and gender in the Genroku period. According to her, the mixing of male and female in the world of fashion was a facet of Genroku culture, where 'men borrowed styles from women just as women copied fads from men'[51] – for example, the on-and-off stage styles of kabuki actors specializing in women's roles:

> served as showcases for original kosode patters, hairstyles, and ways of tying the obi.[52] These styles in turn inspired the wardrobes of townswomen. In effect, women strove to copy men who were mimicking women. Furthermore, certain female dancers . . . and a specialized subset of prostitutes called *wakashū jorō* played on the popularity of the stylish young men by reproducing their mode as faithfully as possible. These creatures were women taken for men who wished to be taken as women.[53]

Dalby assures us that there would have been subtle cues for the contemporary Genroku dwellers in order to distinguish the gender of these people. This also indicates that as in the European history of dress, the Japanese history of fashion has alluded to the rather precarious affairs of gender and fashion.

Keeping in mind this delicate relationship between gender and clothes, this book poses a series of arguments, namely: that the sense of ambivalence attached to the relationship between men and fashion reflects the unstable nature of 'masculinity'; representations of (young) women through established multiple binaries of sexualization, subservience and (masculinist) assertiveness allude to the regulation of women's fashion; and that senses of autonomy and independence are likely to be woven into female sartorial ornamentation, thus repudiating the idea that such a style is symbolic of dependency and subservience. Through reviewing these points, I hope to unearth a set of paradigms concerning gender and clothes, which might invert or even subvert these preconceptions.

Cultures concerning Japanese youth are an ideal site to investigate this proposition. This idea is reinforced by a survey conducted by the Japan Youth Research Institute in 2004, in which around 1,000 high school students each from China, Japan, South Korea and the United States participated.[54] This survey indicated that contrary to participants of the other nations, about 40 per cent or less of Japanese participants answered either 'strongly' or 'somewhat' agree to the questions of 'Do you think women should be feminine?' and 'Do you think men should be masculine?'.

It is too early to draw a conclusion from one survey, and the aim here is not to read this survey result as reflecting general social attitudes. What 'masculine' and 'feminine' attributes connote could moreover be different across cultures. However, the results seem to suggest that Japanese young people may be affected by conventional gender expectations and restrictions, perhaps much less significantly than they are assumed to be. Representations of gender in aspects of mainstream Japanese culture further endorse this perspective.

In their studies of girls' *manga* culture, Japanese literature and cultural studies scholars Susan J. Napier and Anne Allison articulate a possibility that (girlish) femininity, asexuality and agency could be compatible. Napier suggests that 'all aspects of the female persona have a far wider play in Japanese popular culture than they do in the West'.[55] As for young men, linguistic anthropologist Laura Miller, in her observation of male beauty practice in contemporary Japan, finds that they appear considerably 'androgynous' and are sensitive towards the female gaze and evaluation of their appearance.[56] Although they may not automatically indicate the flourishing of gender egalitarianism in Japan, such interpretations of gender representations should contribute to our picture of the culture. If contemporary Japanese popular culture can offer 'innovative' representations of gender, as authors such as Napier and Miller have demonstrated, can they also offer new ways in which clothes and gender are represented?

Table 1.1 Data from the Survey of the Lifestyles and Consciousness of High School Students by the Japan Youth Research Institute (2004, Survey period: September to October 2003)

Women should be feminine

	Japan	USA	China	South Korea
Completely agree	5.8	17.3	34.0	16.5
Somewhat agree	22.6	40.7	37.4	31.2
Somewhat disagree	45.0	28.1	21.2	36.9
Completely disagree	26.5	6.4	5.8	15.0
No Response	0.1	7.5	1.4	0.6

Men should be masculine

	Japan	USA	China	South Korea
Completely agree	13.2	21.2	44.8	21.6
Somewhat agree	30.2	42.4	36.3	33.3
Somewhat disagree	35.0	24.6	13.1	31.1
Completely disagree	21.6	4.6	4.0	13.6
No Response	0.0	7.3	1.7	0.5

Interlaced flows of culture: seeing Japanese fashion globally

The book pays particular attention to the relationship of past and present. It examines contemporary Japanese fashion trends that adopt and restyle European and American historical clothing forms: the Edwardian dandy style, Victorian little girls' dresses, the rococo and Romantic dress typical of the eighteenth and nineteenth centuries, and Ivy style. It needs to be acknowledged that there is another important way of looking at the Japanese adaptations of those styles. For instance, these clothing forms may refer to Japanese cultural texts such as *manga* and animation, which are already circulating within Japanese cultural discourse, rather than directly to specific period and clothing models of European and American histories. It is arguable, however, that these cultural examples *per se* indicate, at least to a certain degree, the influences of these Euro-American clothing styles.[57] This highlights the importance of investigating the relationship between Euro-American clothing forms from the past and contemporary Japanese fashion culture. Looking at the appropriation process of European and American clothing styles in a Japanese cultural context, it is almost inevitable that the issue of cultural globalization arises. This is a diverse and complex area of study, needing dedicated research that I cannot offer here. Thus, my reference to it in this present book is rather limited.

When the presence of Japanese culture becomes known outside the East Asian context, its 'Japanese' qualities are often emphasized. This is particularly visible in the world of high fashion, as dress curator Patricia Mears highlights. In her study of Japanese designers Rei Kawakubo and Yohji Yamamoto, Mears writes that when they address international audiences, Japanese designers tend to be perceived as sharing identical aesthetic visions, for 'modern Japanese fashion has often been viewed less as the result of individual designers' efforts than as a form of collective expression'.[58] This emphasis on the 'Japaneseness' relates to the process of 'othering'. By articulating the complexity of cross-cultural influences present in high fashion scenes, fashion sociologist Lise Skov argues that:

> It is especially ironical that the 'Japanese fashion' has been interpreted with reference to simplistic ideas of Japanese culture, because of the way the style was worn, exactly as a marker of individualism. Hence, one of the meanings of 'Japan' in Western consumer culture seemed to be an 'otherness' inside people's minds, made visible through austere dress.[59]

This 'othering' theory is closely associated with the field of postcolonial theory. Leela Gandhi, in her postcolonial studies, argues that 'othering' of culture is important for Orientalist theorists. Those theorists often accuse formerly colonized countries of being too 'modernized' and 'Westernized'. This is because these countries are, for them, no longer 'otherable'.[60] Japan is another culture that is frequently subjected to this 'othering' process by Euro-American perspectives. This is because Japan has frequently been regarded as the first 'non-Western' culture to have achieved a degree of 'modernity'. Modernity is generally believed to be only achievable by 'the West', and 'if the Japanese are able to achieve modernity, then the distinction between "the West" and "non-West" will disappear'.[61] Therefore, Japan 'can no longer be handled simply as an imitator or mimic of western modernity'.[62] Needless to say, the 'othering' process may also be initiated by 'non-Western' cultures, too.[63] In any case, this 'us' versus 'them' logic is often constructed in order to serve a particular purpose, to define their identity and achieve a feeling of 'superiority' over other cultures. As the works of Mears and Skov suggest, the difficulty of 'non-Western' cultures in being understood and accepted globally without a sense of 'otherness' is highlighted.

As theorists of social-cultural approaches have indicated, 'global' and 'local' cultures interact instead of one infiltrating the other.[64] Cultural globalization is about cross-cultural interaction, appropriation and hybridization where transcultural forms circulate in more than one direction. This book builds upon and enhances that idea. When a transnational cultural form is appropriated and restyled, it might involve a creative process of engendering a novel form. Rather than merely being a substandard imitation of the 'original' global culture, this restyled form can be both creative and refined. Japanese adoption of European dress forms, then, can be much more complex than an allusion to uniform, global culture. In order to calibrate this idea effectively, I refer to the theory of 'format' and 'product' at various stages in this book.

The important point to consider in this argument is that the 'format', which becomes transnational, does not always originate from European and American cultures.[65] This becomes a persuasive idea when one thinks about 'Third World Music'. Different music genres, which have originated from the non-West, 'may become world city music, and then world music' as a consequence of being played by local musicians around the world with their own arrangements and interpretations.[66] Thus, theoretically, a transnational culture can originate from any culture. These intellectual concerns will be addressed through examining the cultural uses of fashion within Japanese cultural texts, namely films, publications, blogs and music videos. What is the relationship between reality and representation? Since this book concerns analysis of representations of gender and clothes in cultural texts, it is logical to pose this question.

Reflections and distortions: representations as a source for study

The accuracy and effectiveness of cultural forms as a source for research might be debatable. Art and dress historian Christopher Breward has noted that:

> until very recently, social and economic historians have retained a profound suspicion of fiction and artistic representation as a source, while dress historians have plundered the surfaces of novels and paintings too uncritically for depictions of historical appearances.[67]

Likewise, fashion and design historian Peter McNeil, in relation to dress in art, warns that art does not express straightforward truths, and thereby we should not seek in art depictions of historical appearances too uncritically.[68] Needless to say, neither fictional art objects such as films nor fashion merely mirror the actual world that first gave birth to them. According to the scholar of English literature Elisabeth Bronfen:

> One cannot speak of an 'essential' self preceding the social and cultural construction of the self through the agency of representations. Cultural

practices are defined as signifying systems, as sites for the production of representations which are not to be equated with beautiful things evoking beautiful feelings. The word *representation*, Griselda Pollock notes, 'stresses that images and texts are no mirrors of the world, merely reflecting their source. Representation stresses something refashioned, coded in rhetorical, textual or pictorial terms, quite distinct from its social existence'.[69]

It can be deduced from these authors that representations do not merely mirror the actual world that first gave birth to them; they also reflect refashioned images, intertwined with consciously constructed or manipulated ideals of the world. Moreover, mediated productions often provide a selective representation of a certain society and its multiple ideologies.[70] This means that the representations of a society in media and cultural texts could possibly be selected and distorted, mirroring both the reality and ideology of that certain society. This sentiment is also found in the scholarship of dress. For example, art historian and philosopher Ulrich Lehmann states that:

we cannot expect to ascertain historical facts merely from looking at clothes. This is not to say that no factual interpretation is possible; yet fashion will always remain too transient and ephemeral to simply explain historic causality—though its changes are very often anticipated. Obviously, a sartorial style at, for example, a certain point in the nineteenth century might be regarded as a reflection of contemporary society. But because of its transcendent autonomy it can never be seen as simply mirroring that society; instead, it projects forward.[71]

In this book, I concur with what sociologists Crane (1992) and Robert C. Bulman (2005) assert. Crane argues that what the media portray is not merely a reflection of real life in society or how people perceive it, but instead 'cultural producers in each medium shape content as a function of the ways in which they continually define and redefine their audiences'.[72] In other words, the intentions of the creators and producers to attract and capture the attention of their 'target' audiences, which Crane argues are the fundamental force of media representations, are (at least partially) reflective of a real life in society where their audiences dwell. Acknowledging these intellectual concerns that are suspicious of the adequacy of cultural forms as a source for research, Bulman also suggests that it is nevertheless worthwhile to examine representations of society, and hence reality through cultural productions, in his case films. He suggests that although films do not present a whole reality, they '[b]oth reflect and shape culture'.[73] Films, he argues, have 'the cultural power to influence how members of a society make sense of social life . . . Films *teach* us who we are as much as they *reflect* who we are'.[74] In this sense, the compound of the constructed ideals, biases or distortions demonstrated in cinema themselves are part of the society or culture that first produced them. If this sentiment can be read as reflecting cultural texts in general, then I assert that studying clothes and gender identity through such texts is legitimate.

The significance of clothes in literary texts is moreover endorsed by the idea that clothes themselves are nearly always animated and understood by a body. In other words, fashion and its aesthetic existence cannot be understood as an isolated product or cultural form unless it is actually being worn.[75] It might be extreme to argue that clothes have no significant aesthetic existence unless they are being worn. But since 'the clothes themselves are only complete when animated by a body', they are always animated and understood through other genres from literature to film, from music video to magazine, from classical ballet to museum-going.[76] For that reason I would argue that it is worthwhile to observe dress through cultural texts rather than, for instance, to study it through the garments themselves. In so doing, I attempt to bring cultural and media studies sensibility to a fashion studies tradition and to bring the rich empirical data of cultural texts into the realm of fashion history.

One of the limitations of this book is that it has focused on a very small portion of contemporary Japanese popular culture. There are a variety of styles present in contemporary Japan; some of them might suggest opposite arguments to the ones this book deduces. Furthermore, since this book focuses solely on representations of clothes in Japanese popular culture, I state that it is neither a work of ethnography nor a comprehensive study of lived experience. Rather, I choose certain texts that have resonance among a wide cross-section of Japanese youth. Therefore, I do not profess that the ways in which Japanese individuals or styles are represented in the given cultural forms might be representatives of other individuals in the culture. It is nonetheless worthwhile to study how these particular groups of individuals and art forms have been represented within the given narrative texts. This is because they are likely to represent a particular part of the whole reality.

One might also wonder why I use theories predominantly developed in the canons of European and American intellectual tradition, when this book's subjects are first and foremost Japanese. It is part of my aim to calibrate how these theories do or do not apply to the Japanese cultural context. As mentioned previously, the anthropological definition of culture is both sharable and learnable across cultures. Likewise, greater historical affinities between, for instance, Europe and Asia than Europe and North America are also noted.[77] Apparently Wilde was right by, quite ironically, saying: '[t]he actual people who live in Japan are not unlike the general run of English people.'[78] My aim to study contemporary Japanese clothing culture by using the theories of European, American and Japanese scholarship is thus justified. A brief guide to the journey of this book is as follows.

Tracing chapters

Chapter 2, 'Lost in a gaze: young men and fashion in contemporary Japan', focuses on a group of contemporary fashion magazines targeted at young men in Japan. It offers content analysis of three magazines, with particular attention to their prioritization of fashion over lifestyle contents and the specific age demographic of the readership. This chapter seeks to establish the idea that these magazines' emphasis on the necessity of taking care of one's appearance endorses, for the male readership, the importance of being subjected to other people's gaze.

Chapter 3, 'Boy's elegance: a liminality of boyish charm and old-world suavity', examines men's fashion publications further, with particular attention to the magazines' deployment of non-Asian models, alongside Japanese and Eurasian models. By using the theory of 'format' and 'product', this chapter focuses on the transcultural difference in the manners of conceiving modes of preferred male aesthetics, which these models highlight. With short case studies of the boyish reinvention of the 'Neo-Edwardian' dandy style in Japan, and renowned menswear label Milkboy, the chapter also seeks to establish the idea that stylishly elegant, youthful and sophisticated styles serve as an alternative to the established, 'hegemonic' mode of Japanese masculinity.

Chapter 4, 'Glacé wonderland: cuteness, sexuality and young women', explores a group of music videos in which female Japanese pop singers adapt and appropriate the imagery of Lewis Carroll's famous heroine, Alice. The emphasis in these videos is on the singers' girlish, cute, almost infantile appearances, mostly constructed through their choices of clothing. I argue that these performers offer an innovative representation of youthful femininity in terms of a negotiation between 'infantile' cuteness (*kawaii*) and forceful independence. This chapter also shows that these Japanese performers enact this innovation through an implicit parody of the sweet and innocent mode of girlish femininity once ascribed to Japanese female pop idols. Further, I explore how the 'cute' fashion displayed in these music videos possibly problematizes the established multiple binaries of sexualization, assertiveness and subservience in which women tend to be represented, particularly in (but not exclusive to) Euro-American cultural contexts.

Chapter 5, 'Ribbons and lace: girls, decorative femininity and androgyny', deals with Tetsuya Nakashima's film adaptation of Novala Takemoto's novel *Shimotsuma monogatari* (2004) and its representation of Japanese *Lolita* style, a lavishly flounced and self-conscious girlish fashion with references to European rococo and Romantic traditions. This chapter argues that *Shimotsuma monogatari*, via its predominantly positive representation of *Lolita* fashion, offers an alternative to the somewhat monolithic idea that amalgamates decorative girlish fashion and unfavourable passivity. This in turn reinforces one facet of the theory of gender performativity, that a young woman can 'perform' both 'masculine' and 'feminine' acts alternately, while being clad in the same dress adorned with flounces and ribbons. Indeed, this 'androgynous' representation renders the very idea of performative gender effectively and credibly.

In Chapter 6, 'An Ivy boy and a preppy girl: style import-export', through a short study of the 'Ivy style', I try to unite the two principal arguments made in this book: that transnational appropriation of culture reflects local characteristics and the presence of reverse flows of culture, and fashion acts on both men and women equally. It re-emphasizes the importance of recognizing the fluid nature of fashion, as well as its ability to affect individuals regardless of their gender and nationality.

'Concluding Japanese Fashion Cultures, Change and Continuity' summarizes and rounds up the main arguments.

2

LOST IN A GAZE: YOUNG MEN AND FASHION IN CONTEMPORARY JAPAN

'Do you understand muslins, sir?'

'Particularly well; I always buy my own cravats, and am allowed to be an excellent judge; and my sister has often trusted me in the choice of a gown. I bought one for her the other day, and it was pronounced to be a prodigious bargain by every lady who saw it. I gave but five shillings a yard for it, and a true Indian muslin.'

Mrs Allen was quite struck by his genius. 'Men commonly take so little notice of those things,' said she: 'I can never get Mr Allen to know one of my gowns from another. You must be a great comfort to your sister, sir.'

'I hope I am, madam.'

'How can you,' said Catherine, laughing, 'be so—' she had almost said, strange.

—JANE AUSTEN, *Northanger Abbey*, 1818.[1]

Written nearly two centuries ago, Jane Austen's delightful parody of gothic novels implies two important strands of the debates surrounding dress and gender, which are significantly current to this day. As the quoted dialogue that opened this chapter outlines, a young man of twenty-six, as embodied by Henry Tilney, could have a keen eye for fashion and clothes. Such an open demonstration of a man's fashion consciousness, however, might be perceived as rather unusual even in the Regency period where Austen's imagination operated. This is because, in the words of Mrs Allen, 'men commonly take so little notice of those things'. Have our conceptions of gender and clothes radically been revised after 200 years? The answer, I believe, is rather mixed. It is common knowledge that men can be as fashion-minded as women, and most scholarly examinations of dress and sociology have proved this. Histories of dress, including European and Japanese, suggest that in some periods, sartorial distinctions between men and women were rather subtle. In other periods, men could be adorned with ornaments as much as women were. Yet in modern times, men's fashionability comes with a sense of suspicion and ambivalence, particularly in mainstream popular culture. Not only that, there is a set of widely circulated preconceptions regarding ways in which men are assumed to engage with fashion. That is, men display less interest in fashion then women do, and they dress for functionality over aesthetics. The overflowing presence of Japanese men's magazines almost purely dedicated to concerns on fashion, we might think then, certainly gives a different picture of the relationship between men and fashion.

Readers unfamiliar with contemporary Japanese media might be puzzled by the appearance of men in fashion magazines. This is particularly the case for images of young men whose almost narcissistic concerns over their appearance and slender physicality are seemingly presented as requirements for romantic desirability and attractiveness.[2] Since Japanese men's fashion magazines offer significantly lavish sources for the study of images of contemporary Japanese masculinity, I dedicate two chapters to the subject. In this chapter I argue that a complex and overlapping series of aesthetic priorities and interests captivate young male consumers in contemporary Japan. A rich study of subjectivity and aesthetics might be made via these Japanese men's magazines, where male aesthetic sensitivities at a cultural level and 'the self' might be understood in different terms than they are in many Euro-American cultures. This is particularly evident in these magazines' acceptance of and even a pedagogy around men becoming the object of the appraising gaze, a status that has conventionally been assigned to women in Euro-American cultural contexts, regardless of their will.[3] On the contrary, in Japanese culture, not only women but men too have been regarded as the object of the gaze.[4] This chapter draws upon that hypothesis. I argue that these magazines illuminate a group of Japanese young men who are in the position to be the object of the gaze. Importantly, positive evaluations of their appearance can enhance these young men's self-assurance.

This chapter is divided into three sections. The first section gives a general overview of contemporary Japanese men's fashion magazines, with particular focus on three selected magazines, *Popeye, Men's non-no* and *Fineboys*. The second section offers a content analysis of three Japanese men's fashion magazines, with particular attention to their prioritization of fashion over lifestyle contents and the specific age demographic of their readerships. This section also looks at characteristics such as amateur models (*dokusha* models) and fictional narratives, which help maintain an extreme sensitivity to social change and trends as well as a social affinity between the readership and the contents that the magazines endorse. The final section seeks to establish the idea that these magazines' emphasis on the necessity of taking care of appearance, which is a requirement to render a fine impression, endorses for men the importance of looking pleasant to others and for themselves.

Reading men's fashion: a brief history of Japanese men's fashion magazines

A young man, about the age of eighteen, is sitting at the poolside, dipping his willowy right foot in the glistening emerald-green water. His delicate, boyish face with a faint smile is also slightly turned away, again with the gaze drifting far into the distance. He is attired in a short-sleeved, grey check shirt with white collar, buttoned up to the neck, and a pair of tight-fitting, knee-length black shorts. A black-and-white striped tie cascades gracefully down his beautifully pressed shirt. The genres of young women's fashion magazines or romantic Hollywood cinema are where we might assume these suave men dwell. Yet these images, just like the cover of this book, are what you encounter when looking at a group of Japanese fashion magazines targeted at young men, predominantly heterosexual.

As elsewhere, clothing and cosmetic regimes are recurrent interests in Japanese fashion magazines. A shade of uniqueness is added, though, to the 'gendered' distribution of the contents – that is, these interests are located in magazines targeting both women and men. Sociologist John Clammer, in his study of contemporary Japanese print media and representations of the female body, briefly refers to men's magazines as follows:

> Interestingly, men's magazines such as *Fine Boys* [sic] are the almost exact masculine counterpart of female fashion magazines, full of images of the young male body, advice on hair, clothes, skins, diet, and accessories. And all this, almost absent in the western media, is aimed at decidedly heterosexual men. The parallels in the print media for women and for men are remarkable.[5]

It should be noted that Clammer's comments are now more than fifteen years old, and the validity of his comparison between Japanese and Anglophone magazines may no longer apply. That being said, Clammer's quote illustrates the particularity of Japanese men's magazines. This is especially notable in relation to their approaches to men's fashion and beauty consumption, which, I contend, reflect the images of the highly fashion-conscious men widely circulated in contemporary Japan. Throughout this chapter, I argue that a group of Japanese men's fashion magazines offer a firm example that male fashionability can be interlaced with 'masculine' identity. The significance of analysing magazines targeting male readership lies in the possibility that representations of 'masculinity' found in magazines might both reflect and shape certain ideals and ideas of fashion and gender. Further research on the readership and their reception would surely be necessary in order to argue how these representations are actually consumed and interact with the male readership of the magazines. However, from this it can also be deduced that a collection of Japanese men's fashion magazines at least allow calibration of the ways in which Japanese conceptions of male fashionability are manifested.

Japanese men's fashion periodicals: past and present

Although there has been a decline in magazine sales recently,[6] the Japanese magazine market is known to be very dynamic.[7] A category of fashion magazines targeted at men, for instance, exemplifies this crowdedness; currently about 40 fashion magazines targeted primarily at men are sold monthly in Japan.[8] Since market categorization, by gender, interests, tastes and age, is very specific in Japan: 'the Japanese magazine market is overclassified'.[9] Accordingly, only a tiny selection of magazines has been selected for the primary subject of this chapter: *Popeye*, launched in 1976; *Men's non-no*, launched in 1986 first as a special, male edition of *non-no*, a fashion magazine for young women still popular now; and *Fineboys*, launched in 1986. These three monthly magazines are selected via four commonalities.

Firstly, they have an established, mainstream stature. *Popeye* has been on the market for more than thirty-five years, while *Fineboys* and *Men's non-no* maintain their popularity. As of 30 September 2013, the three magazines occupied seventh (*Men's non-no*), eighth (*Popeye*) and eleventh (*Fineboys*) place in the category of men's business magazines in Bunkyō-dō's online magazine ranking, competing with other men's fashion and non-fashion magazines alike.[10] The three magazines had average readerships of 173,334 (*Men's non-no*), 114,100 (*Fineboys*) and 49,084 (*Popeye*) respectively in 2011–12.[11]

Secondly, they target young men in their late teens to early twenties, particularly those who are in college. According to *Fineboys'* own survey conducted in 2007, 69 per cent of its male readers are aged between eighteen and twenty-one, 55 per cent are university students and 10 per cent are vocational college students.[12] It has also become an annual convention for *Men's non-no* and *Popeye* to include a feature about business suits in their April issues, clearly intended for those who are finishing school and about to enter the next stage of their career, assumedly as office workers.

Thirdly, they focus on similar neat and conservative styles of *kireime* (neat) or high-casual fashion; and fourthly, they have an almost complete absence of images of eroticized women, or sexually explicit materials.

I will return to look at all of these characteristics in more detail. My analysis of these magazines is primarily based on the issues released between May 2007 and June 2008. However, in order to keep abreast of the currency of these magazines, newer editions of the magazines have also been acquired and are analysed where possible.

The history of contemporary Japanese men's fashion magazine began with *Otokono fukushoku* (Men's Fashion, later renamed *Men's Club*, Figure 2.1).

The magazine was published in 1954 by Fujingahou-sha, as the first Japanese young men's magazine for prêt-à-porter clothes as opposed to *Danshi senka* (Men's Special Course, 1950–93), a magazine predominantly focused on bespoke clothing, which was targeted at tailors.[13] Still popular as a chic and sophisticated men's fashion magazine, *Men's Club* at its beginning was particularly well known for its close ties with the Japanese version of 'Ivy League' style, a fashion style inspired by students of American Ivy League universities in the 1950s and 1960s, and the Japanese brand VAN. The current form of Japanese fashion magazines targeted at young individuals is said to have begun with *an an*, a young women's lifestyle magazine published by Heibon-sha (now Magazinehouse). The magazine was launched in 1970, initially targeting Japan's first baby-boomers.[14] This young women's lifestyle magazine was born as a female equivalent of Japanese men's lifestyle magazine *Heibon Punch* (published from 1964 until the late 1980s) and as a Japanese edition of *Elle* magazine. *an an*, along with its follower and competitor *non-no* (launched in 1971 by Shūei-sha), marked a shift from young women's main roles as housewives and mothers 'towards a focus on women as consumers of fashion and luxury items'.[15] Its consumption and visual-oriented contents, with a significant emphasis on advertisements, have set various trends relevant not only to women's but also to men's magazines.[16]

Popeye, a magazine for 'city boys' with an emphasis on subcultural lifestyle with neat, sporty West Coast American fashions, was launched in 1976 by Magazinehouse. Popeye boys, who were believed to be influenced by the magazine and the styles it offered, came to symbolize the Japanized 'Ivy' style in the late 1970s and early 1980s, with a polo shirt and a pair of golf trousers as their signature look.[17] 1986 saw a boom in young men's fashion, which coincided with the launches of such men's fashion magazines as *Men's non-no* (Shūei-sha) and *Fineboys* (Hinode-shuppan).[18]

After the launch of these magazines, Japan witnessed the rise and fall of many men's fashion magazines: *Hot-Dog Press* (Kōdan-sha, 1979–2004), *Mr. High Fashion* (Bunka-shuppan, 1980–2003), *smart* (Takarajima-sha, 1995–), *BiDAN* (Index communications, 1996–2010, renamed B-St. in 2010), *Street Jack* (Bestsellers, 1997–), *men's egg* (Taiyou-tosho, 1999–2013), *Choki Choki* (Naigai-shuppan, 2000–), *Men's Joker* (KK bestsellers, 2004–), *Men's Knuckle* (Million-shuppan, 2004–) and so forth. These attest to Japanese men's high degree of interest in appearance and fashion consumption.

As we have seen, Clammer has noted that magazines targeted at heterosexual men that are filled with appearance-related images and other content are rare in

Figure 2.1 The cover of *Men's Club* no. 31, published in 1963 by Fujingahosha, currently Hearst Fujingaho Co., Ltd. Courtesy of Ishizu Office/Masakatsu Ide.

Western media. It might be a debatable statement today, but in Anglophone culture, there is still a sense of ambivalence shown when appreciating male beauty.[19] Actually, the emphasis of these Japanese publications is highlighted by the prevalent assumption in contemporary Anglo-Western culture that men prioritize functionality over aesthetics. In other words, men are assumed not to be affected by the 'frivolity' of fashion, but only dress for necessity. A considerable number of scholars such as Elizabeth Wilson, Joanne Entwistle, Sean Nixon and Christopher Breward have challenged this *idée fixe*, claiming that men have been affected by fashion as much as women. Arguably, the recurrence of such a debate implies the persistence of the idea that men's 'lack' of concern with clothes defines their 'masculine' identities.

Breward has proved that even during the time of 'the Great Masculine Renunciation' around the beginning of the nineteenth century, when men were supposed to have relinquished sartorial flamboyancy or ornamentation in favour of more 'austere' clothing, British men continued, albeit being largely ignored, to be loyal and active consumers of sartorial items.[20] For instance, the forms of men's dress associated with leisure pursuits such as weekend or holiday clothing in the late nineteenth century allowed more opportunities for the display of individual taste based on the choice of accessories, textures and colours.[21] Breward sees this 'concealment' of men's affairs with clothes, which was still sustained even in the 1990s, as deliberate. In accordance with the view of fashion as an entirely feminized phenomenon, male fashionability in late-nineteenth-century England was unjustly reduced to functional utility and to the role of distant observer of female fashion consumption.[22] Thus, the preconceptions that a fashion sensibility is a 'feminine' trait and that men primarily dress for practicability are seemingly crafted and sustained.[23] One only needs to think about a tie, of which maestro of men's fashion journalism G. Bruce Boyer writes, 'today serves no other purpose than pure decoration', to question the whole legitimacy of the above preconception.[24] In contemporary times, the increase in visibility of fashion-consciousness among men is also evident.[25] Men are increasingly viewed as consumers of fashion, especially in the cases of generation Y males (those born between 1977 and 1994) or younger.[26] However, even today it seems fashionable to claim that men are less concerned with clothes or fashion than their female counterparts. Many men's magazines with a notable amount of fashion contents, for one thing, are still called 'lifestyle' or 'style' rather than fashion magazines.

Is fashion truly 'feminine'? Indeed, some men are as fashion-minded as the most 'fashionable' women, while some women can be as careless about their appearance as some men are, and the motivations behind fashion can be complex. Entwistle convincingly argues that 'at different times we dress for different reasons and on some occasions women may dress for status and men to attract admirers' and vice versa.[27] In fashion and socio-cultural analysis, fashion is therefore not fundamentally 'feminine', but more likely labelled as such and 'othered' by a certain group of men (and women) in order to accentuate visually the distinction between the two gender categories.

It is important to refer to psychologist Sandra L. Bem, who argues that since 'conventional' masculinity is intertwined with power and privilege, the majority of men who are, quite inevitably, neither powerful nor privileged, would feel insufficiently masculine. Indeed, fully attaining conventionally defined 'masculine' qualities, which in their extremities are 'characterised by aggression, competitiveness, emotional ineptitude and coldness, and dependent upon an overriding and exclusive emphasis on penetrative sex', is next to impossible.[28] Hence '[t]raditional masculinity began to be regarded as a "neuro-muscular armour" that forced [men] to suppress tenderness, emotion and any signs of vulnerability'.[29]

In order to feel, at least marginally, a sense of belonging for 'real men', these men with neither power nor privileges are believed to exclude women from positions of public power and authority, and culturally marginalize male homosexuality.[30] In this sense, women and homosexual men are required for certain men as their 'others'. The significance of Bem's theory is further highlighted by the persistence of the misleading assumption that fashion or dress is 'feminine', and thus not 'masculine' even today.[31] In other words, man's lack of concern with the 'feminine' interest in dress would (deliberately or otherwise) define his 'masculine' identity. The cultural stereotype assuming that it might not be appropriately 'manly' for men to show a notable degree of interest in their own appearance is thus sustained.

Although some men dress in such a style simply for their stylistic preferences, strongly 'masculine' clothing is a simple way of achieving this sense of belonging. As a result, '[v]ery remarkable and fantastic male modes of dressing . . . are continuously adopted chiefly by the powerless, those not in the main stream of action'.[32] The suit is one such sartorial example closely identified with 'masculinity', both stylistically and symbolically. It not only emphasizes the male physical form (such as broad shoulders, chest and a phallic symbol in the form of ties) but the business suit has also been associated with 'masculine values of reserve, stature and efficiency'.[33] In a culture where pecuniary strength and status equals masculinity, the business suit is therefore a supremely potent source of male sexual appeal.[34] A sense of irony is created with this reading, for these men would 'other' fashion as a 'feminine' trait but attempt to maintain their 'masculine' identity through clothes nevertheless. If there is a sense of ambivalence attached to the relationship between clothes and the idea of masculine identity, how does Japanese men's fashion culture perceive such a relationship? Do Japanese men's fashion magazines offer representations of young men and their ways of engaging with clothes and fashion differently? One of the striking features of such men's magazines is the domination of fashion over lifestyle contents. I examine these points through three selected magazines: *Popeye, Men's non-no* and *Fineboys*.

Neat, fresh and smart: *Popeye*, *Men's non-no* and *Fineboys*

The three magazines that I have chosen enjoy a mainstream status in Japan, and, arguably, correspond to the widespread and accepted male fashionability, taken up by (ordinary/common) young men. Issues regarding fashion comprise more than 60 per cent of the total features in each of the three magazines.

This is especially true for *Popeye*, where more than 70 per cent of its contents are about clothes, bags, shoes and accessories. Most of these fashion photo pages provide details such as the name of the brand and its price, thus serving the dual functions of fashion catalogue and advertisement.

If we combine the numbers of fashion advertisements and fashion features, 78.80 per cent of *Popeye*, 68.50 per cent of *Men's non-no* and 65.56 per cent of

Table 2.1 Content analysis of the three men's magazines

		Popeye	Men's non-no	Fineboys
Advertising:	**Fashion**	**8.06**	**7.61**	**5.35**
	Technology	0.92	1.73	1.77
	Automobile	0.53	0.74	0.26
	Sexual Health, Cosmetic Surgery, etc	0.96	3.42	5.87
	Cigarettes	1.46	1.44	0.00
	Other	2.06	4.05	3.11
Total		13.99	18.99	16.36
Features:	**Fashion**	**70.74**	**60.89**	**60.21**
	Beauty	**0.71**	**1.66**	**5.40**
	Sport	0.07	0.35	0.26
	Automobile	0.82	0.35	0.95
	Technology	1.56	0.35	1.77
	General Articles	2.34	5.92	3.24
	Horoscope	0.43	1.02	0.52
	Stock Listing	0.25	0.35	0.52
	Girls	0.78	0.81	1.64
	Culture/Interviews	4.83	4.69	4.66
	Other	3.48	4.79	4.49
Total		86.01	81.18	83.66
Total number of pages		284.00	235.00	193.00

Note: Results based on the average of 12 issues between May 2007 and June 2008. All figures except the total page numbers are given in percentages.

Fineboys are comprised of fashion and appearance-related images. Only a few decades ago, British *Arena* and *GQ* magazines, with approximately 30 per cent of the editorial space dedicated to fashion, were considered to be significantly extensive.[35] Indeed, a ratio of fashion-related materials in these Japanese magazines is significantly higher than Euro-American men's 'lifestyle' magazines where fashion comprises about 35 per cent or less of their contents.[36] Calling these Japanese men's publications 'fashion magazines' is thus justified.

The price of *Fineboys* is the lowest of the three (520 yen in 2013, or approximately US $5) whereas both *Popeye* and *Men's non-no* are priced at 720 yen or $7. Perhaps corresponding to this, the fashion brands featured in *Fineboys* tend to be slightly more affordable, Japanese-oriented brands (although it also features foreign brands including Nike, Gap and Lacoste). In addition to featuring famous Japanese brands such as Milkboy, Journal Standard, Hysteric Glamour and Nano Universe, *Popeye* and *Men's non-no* are seemingly fond of such medium to high fashion European brand names as Louis Vuitton, Gucci, Giorgio Armani, Dolce & Gabbana, Paul Smith, Burberry, Christian Dior and Vivienne Westwood, among others. *Choki Choki* further supports this hypothesis about the relationship between the prices of the magazine and its endorsed items. The magazine predominantly features 'domestic' brand items and is lower priced than *Popeye* and *Men's non-no*.

In contrast to fashion, such 'traditionally men's interests' as sports, cars and alcohol are rarely featured in *Popeye, Men's non-no* and *Fineboys*. Each magazine devotes approximately one page each to technology and automobiles, but *Popeye* does not have a single regular feature page specifically dedicated to sports. As for representations of women, each magazine has one or two regular pages introducing a young female model, singer or actress (such as *Men's non-no Girlfriend*). However, as the titles indicate, these women tend to be presented as pseudo-girlfriends of the reader, and are interviewed in such a friendly manner that they might be objectified but are seldom eroticized. Their pictures accentuate their sweet and lovely qualities rather than their sensuality, thus reinforcing this idea.[37]

Occasionally these magazines run feature articles on sexuality and relationships. But they are concentrated within the black-and-white middle-section pages, which might indicate their less-important stature compared to clothes. These contents are, moreover, focused on the purpose of instructing how to become accepted by and hence popular with girls through adopting certain sets of manners and styles. Arguably, this defines the intended readership of *Popeye, Men's non-no* and *Fineboys* as educated middle-class and their intention to present themselves as 'fashion'-oriented publications. Again, these aspects illuminate the particularity of these Japanese men's fashion magazines, making a contrast to Anglophone men's lifestyle magazines, where the assumed and traditional 'men's interests' such as cars, alcohol and women still dominate.[38]

One notable characteristic shared by these Japanese magazines is the presence of advertisements for cosmetic surgery and sexual health clinics, attempting to bank on young men's anxieties about masculinity.[39] These advertisements are found towards the end of the magazine, and *Men's non-no* and *Fineboys* devote approximately ten or eleven pages to this kind of advertising. Importantly, male fear of negative female evaluation of their physicality is frequently exploited by such advertisements, suggesting the influence of women on male appearance consciousness.[40] I shall address this point in Chapter 3. Significantly, *Popeye* only includes one page of such an advertisement, just three or four pages before the back cover. This might imply the magazine's intention to present itself as slightly more 'sophisticated' and fashion-oriented. *Popeye*'s frequent deployment of international-based, professional models in contrast to the semi-professional or amateur models hired for other men's fashion magazines also corresponds with this quality. Another striking aspect of these Japanese magazines is the age of the target readership. They are significantly younger and more specifically defined than the estimated readership of Anglophone men's lifestyle magazines.

The age of sensibility: men's fashion magazines and defined age demographics

Sociologist Susan M Alexander's analysis of American *Men's Health* magazine revealed that the median age of the male readership is thirty-six, and men aged eighteen to forty-four comprise 71 per cent of its readership.[41] A wide age demographic of readership in Anglophone men's lifestyle magazines is reflected in magazine contents, where casually attired male models with youthful appearances (possibly in their twenties) feature in fashion spreads alongside sections about grooming, occupied by concerns to do with anti-aging and greying hair. By contrast, Japanese culture, including magazines, demarcates more specific age demographics.

It is estimated that those aged sixteen to twenty-four comprise 84.3 per cent of *Men's non-no* readership, 64.3 per cent of *Popeye* readership and 74 per cent of *Fineboys* readership.[42] High school, university and vocational college students consist of 61.6 per cent of *Men's non-no* readership, more than 41.7 per cent of *Popeye* readership, and 68.7 per cent of *Fineboys* readership. Further, the guidelines for *Men's non-no*'s annual model audition stipulates that only men under the age of twenty-three are eligible to apply, while *Fineboys* limits applicants to between the ages of fifteen and twenty-two. The median age of the former magazine's male models is twenty-three years old, but the age of twenty is highest (14.6 per cent), followed by twenty-two years old (12.5 per cent).[43] The presence of a group of fashion magazines targeted at older males further emphasizes the specificity of age demographic in Japanese publications.

Men's Joker (est. 2004) is seemingly targeted at men in their late twenties. *Men's Club* (est. 1955), and *Gainer* (est. 1990) might appeal to men in their thirties, while *Uomo* (est. 2005) is targeted at men in their forties who prefer neat and elegant styles. *Leon* (est. 2001) is a magazine for wealthy, middle-aged men who cultivate a wild, sensual look and a degree of 'bad boy' (*choiwaru*) attitude. Needless to say, the possibility of modest cross-readership between these magazines should not be disregarded. It is also noteworthy that men's fashion magazines targeted at older males tend to deploy older celebrities for their 'faces'.[44] Crucially, there is an obvious correlation between the three magazines' specific focus on young men between their late teens and early twenties as their main readership, and the age of the models they hire.

What does the specific age demographic of these magazines convey? It is widely believed that youths, particularly adolescents, manifest distinctive behaviours and consumption patterns.[45] Adolescence is not merely a chronological age; it is also a socially constructed category. Cultural anthropologist Merry White, for instance, points out that:

Teenagers in any modern society are a composite construction: they are the products of biological development, of institutions (educational and occupational) preparing them for economic and social participation as 'appropriate' adults, and of their own negotiations with their environment, themselves creating new cultural models and goals.[46]

White suggests that the concept of 'teenager' is defined by interactions between adolescents and the biological, economic, and social forces and expectations imposed upon them. Since half or more of the readership of these Japanese magazines are students, their assumed prolongation of financial dependency and leisure time might allow them to engage in lifestyle and consumption patterns more similar to teenagers than to adults. These are trends on which these magazines wish to capitalize. The well-defined demographic category these magazines articulate renders this objective more achievable. While contemporary Japanese culture has recognized and capitalized on the benefit of narrowing consumer segments for quite some time, it is a comparatively recent phenomenon in places like the United States.[47] Whether or not there will be a similar segmentation of the men's magazine market in Anglophone culture remains to be seen.

There is also a trend in Japanese fashion magazines to use readers and other amateur models. Amateur or *dokusha* models are most common in magazines intended for young women.[48] Nevertheless, they are also found in men's magazines such as *Choki Choki, Men's non-no* and *Fineboys*, among others.[49] Compared to the professional models, reader models tend to be more personalized, with their names and occupations or college names supplied. Also, these magazines regularly feature snapshots of apparently young men, found in the streets, who have a keen fashion sense. The significance of these Japanese magazines' attention to comparatively more 'ordinary' male images stands in contrast to the ideas of rather 'unordinary' male beauty prevalent in the Euro-American high-fashion culture. As theorized by Entwistle, '[t]he lack of correspondence between the male fashion model's "beauty" and ideas of male beauty outside' is often evident in Euro-American fashion scene.[50] This implies a distance, or a gap, between the images the fashion world offers and actual consumers. While these 'ordinary' Japanese male figures featured in magazines may reflect the interventions, selections and even manipulation of editors, they may well also reflect the magazines' intention to maintain extreme sensitivity to social changes and trends, and to create a social affinity between the target reader, the models, and the contents of the magazines.

The sense of social affinity crafted between the models and the readership of these Japanese magazines points to the precarious balance upon which fashion is motivated, namely integration and individuality. Sociologist Georg Simmel notably contended in the early twentieth century that fashion is motivated by the balance between two opposing forces: the desire to express both individuality and uniformity through the clothes we wear. For him:

> If one of the opposing forces is absent, or has been almost 'overcome' by its other . . . fashion will cease. If the desire for uniformity and imitation could reach fulfilment there would be no such thing as fashion, only mass similarity . . . an exacerbated individualism would also spell the end of fashion since 'the desire for integration' must be absent in a situation where self-assertion is so dominant.[51]

Thus, 'the fashioning of one's appearance in modernity has been a precarious balancing act between individuality and conformity'.[52] Simmel's theory of fashion is, quite straightforwardly, present in these Japanese magazines, and it is particularly evident in the fictional narratives these publications craft, which I discuss in the next section.

A boy's life

Creating fictional narratives to balance conformity and individuality

Because most readers are presumed to be young and lacking disposable income, these magazines frequently feature different ways to coordinate a few trendy items. To do so, they conventionally create a narrative about an ordinary but stylish young man with whom readers can identify. This type of feature is most notable in *Fineboys*, whose target readership includes fashion beginners. For instance, the April 2010 issue of the magazine ran an eight-page story on how to coordinate fifteen items, the total value of which is under 30,000 yen (approximately US $320 as of April 2010), to create outfits for ten days.[53] This story is synchronized with a narrative in which an actor and one of the magazine's exclusive models Tōri Matsuzaka appears as a college freshman recently arrived in Tokyo. The first ten days of his life in Tokyo correspond with the ten aspects of coordination of the nominated items.[54]

The February 2008 edition of *Men's non-no* offers a similar feature.[55] Models Jun Yamaguchi and Takeshi Mikawai play the roles of two fashionable eighteen-year-olds who have recently come to Tokyo for employment (Mikawai) and education (Yamaguchi). Thirty days of their lives in Tokyo correspond with thirty combinations of ten items each, with Mikawai dressed in the 'casual style' while Yamaguchi is identified with the 'European, chic-mode'. *Men's non-no* also runs a somewhat simplified version of this type of feature, following the fashion outfits over a short period of time of popular fashion brand publicists, stylists or actual college students.[56] As one would expect, this type of feature is intertwined with marketing, as often second-hand clothing shops or low budgeted clothing brands are introduced as the reader's saviours. Yet these instructions can also easily be applied to the reader's own already existing wardrobes. This concurs with what social anthropologist Brian Moeran argues about Japanese high-fashion publications. He notes that magazines that include high and renowned brands, such as the Japanese edition of *Vogue*, aim to appeal to and acquire international recognition. At the same time, they offer their readership advice on 'how to coordinate clothes and how to make a limited wardrobe go a long way'.[57] Rather than merely promoting consumption habits and desires, these Japanese men's magazines offer practical advice and encourage engagement with down-to-earth, everyday fashion.

The deployment of fictional narratives in these Japanese men's magazines can be interpreted in several ways. One of the most prominent ones, I argue, is that clothing is about both self-assertion and integration, reinforcing the applicability of Simmel's theory of fashion. Through the fictional narratives of young models and, less explicitly, of older stylists and publicists, these magazines instruct the readership about to dress stylistically and impressively, and hence to stand out among their peers. At the same time, the readership is integrated into society by conforming to 'acceptable' coordination of sartorial items on the market. The popular narrative themes these magazines use, such as young men newly arrived in a 'global' city, anxiety about graduation and the future ahead, friendship and romance, all involve a degree of integration. The assumed similarity of age between models and the readership further enforces the efficacy of the 'identification' process between models and the readership. In other words, these magazines enable the readership to assert themselves through being dressed immaculately, which also integrates them into society. And this is done in economically feasible ways.

In the next section, I proceed to look at the visual messages these magazines convey, with particular attention to their cover images. My intention is to examine how images of masculinity are represented in these periodicals, and to determine the modes of masculine images they are trying to convey to their readership. I would also argue that the variety of ways in which male figures are captured reflect the magazines' relatively flexible perception of masculine images.

The face of the magazines: first impressions of the encounter

What visual images do these magazines offer? One of the purposes that magazine covers accomplish is that 'they are themselves advertisements that increase the publisher's sales and, perhaps more important, the sale of products and services promoted inside'.[58] The roles that covers play may be particularly important for Japanese magazines. This is because, unlike Anglophone magazines which tend to rely heavily on subscriptions, in Japan 'a very large number of readers buy a magazine on the basis of what they read each month while standing in a bookshop or convenience store (called "stand-reading" or *tachiyomi*, in Japanese)'.[59] Magazine covers are thus essential in attracting the audience and in introducing what the magazine conveys. One of the most notable qualities of the covers of *Popeye*, before its editorial renewal or change in the June 2012 issue, is that it regularly features a non-Asian male model, approximately in his early twenties. Generally these cover models are photographed in a close to medium close shot, with a few exceptions in which the models are photographed in a medium-long shot from the knees, at a low angle.

According to the theory of visual analysis articulated by semioticians Gunther Kress and Theo Van Leeuwen, the direct gaze of the participant is often read as demanding something from the viewer, while the indirect gaze can indicate that the participant is the object of the viewer's gaze.[60] The direct gaze of a male model in a men's style magazine, for instance, can be read as persuading the reader of 'identification with the look of the male model', thus making them wish to purchase the products the model is endorsing.[61] A few models on the covers of *Popeye* wear a faint smile or gaze into space, sitting with chin in hand. The majority of them, in contrast, gaze straight at the reader, which arguably alludes to what feminist scholar Susan Bordo refers as 'face-off' masculinity, a pose displaying a 'martial rather than sensual', traditional masculinity.[62]

These 'armoured', sturdy masculine images are somewhat diminished by the neatly coordinated hair and dress, and particularly by the use of colour. In each issue, the title appears in different colours, including delicate, pastel colours such as light blue, yellow and (perhaps surprisingly) pink. The combination of the direct gaze of the models and the close-to-medium shot can be read as demanding that the reader look at the models, and thereby enter into a relationship of affinity with them. Reinforcing this reading is the size of frame, as close-to-medium shots signify intimate-to-close personal distance.[63] Yet as their 'face-off' posture suggests, the relation might not be entirely sensual.

For their covers, *Men's non-no* and *Fineboys* both feature young male celebrities. Many of them belong to Johnny's & Associates, a Japanese talent agency that specializes in male pop idols. But the covers also feature young actors such as Osamu Mukai, Masaki Okada and Junpei Mizobata. *Men's non-no* originally featured its own model on the cover when it was launched.[64] With few exceptions, celebrities are featured in medium shot, gazing directly at the viewer. The size of the frame indicates that the celebrities are familiar but not too personal. They are objects of appraisal, but their direct gaze prevents them from being too passive. Apart from a few recognizable settings such as the Eiffel Tower (*Fineboys*, December 2007), the background of the cover image is generally white, and undefined. This is one aspect of the magazines that parallels their female counterparts, for '[t]he lack of context means that the models are not doing anything other than posing for the viewers, a pattern typical of women's magazine images'.[65]

The use of celebrities has, I suggest, two possible interpretations. Firstly it might help attract readers because of familiarity, physical attractiveness and the cultured currency these celebrities carry. The presence of Japanese celebrities in such magazines as *Men's non-no* 'helps position them as representatives of contemporary Japanese popular culture'.[66] Secondly, the magazines also attract the fans of these celebrities, most of whom are (young) women, resulting in an increase of their circulation figures and revenue. As Merry White notes in *The Material Child: Coming of Age in Japan and America*, Japanese teenage girl fans are particularly keen for any information about their favourite stars, including magazine interviews.[67] Although monthly 'idol' magazines were in White's mind when she stated this, it could easily be extended to these young men's magazines, with their favourite stars either on the cover or inside the magazines. The magazines' careful avoidance of eroticized images of women also enhances this hypothesis. This idea holds in relation to *Popeye* and *Men's non-no*, where traditionally the female readership comprises 17.1 and 18 per cent respectively. *Fineboys*, on the other hand, enjoys predominantly male readership, as only 2 per cent of its readership is accounted for by females.[68] The presence of women is also evident in editorial sections of the magazines.[69] The high percentage of female readership might also point to the possibility that they get these men's magazines either for their boyfriends or for their own fashion interests.

The covers of these magazines, with the combination of 'face-off' masculinity and neat appearance, correspond to the images of young, appearance-conscious Japanese men who look comparatively 'feminine' yet retain some conventional 'masculine' attributes. In the fashion photo pages, young male models are presented in a myriad of poses. Apart from the 'face-off' position, there are at least two other main postures in which male figures are presented in magazines and advertisements; these are what Bordo describes as the lean position – 'reclining, leaning against, or propped up against something in the fashion typical of women's bodies',[70] or smiling boyishly, manifesting 'wholesome masculinity' as Alexander calls it.[71] The gaze of the male model in the latter position is 'neither defiant nor passive; rather, the model smiles at the viewer, sometimes broadly, sometimes shyly', thus revealing senses of intimacy and vulnerability.[72] Some significant findings regarding my analysis of male figures' postures in the fashion spreads of the three Japanese magazines are as follows: *Popeye* presents male figures in the lean position slightly more than the 'face-off' position, while more than a half of the male figures in *Men's non-no* display 'face-off' masculinity. *Fineboys*, on the other hand, predominantly prefers to feature its male models in the 'lean' position. Nearly 20 per cent of the male models in *Fineboys* are moreover smiling, in the position of intimate 'wholesome masculinity'. Such a representation is significantly rare in *Men's non-no*.

In her analysis of *Men's non-no* and its female equivalent, *non-no*, design and communication studies scholar Fabienne Darling-Wolf notes that *non-no* constructs a visual and verbal discourse focusing on female camaraderie and pleasure. In contrast, *Men's non-no* offers a visual discourse portraying models as physically disconnected from or smiling at one another, perhaps corresponding to the conventional idea of 'hard' masculinity.[73] With a few exceptions, my analysis of the magazines reveals that this is relatively still the case in *Men's non-no*. However, other magazines including *Fineboys* and *Popeye* feature models enjoying each other's company at a greater frequency. For example, the March 2010 issue of *Fineboys* has a spread titled 'With these layered techniques, a shirt is a million times as powerful'. In this feature, two male models are pictured as facing each other, playing cards or walking with a smile in what appears to be a college campus. One of the male models is also captured standing very close to

Table 2.2 Three postures of male models

	Face-off	Lean	Wholesome
Popeye	37.65	50.62	11.73
Men's non-no	50.18	48.77	1.05
Fineboys	14.38	67.81	17.81

Note: Results based on the October 2010 edition of the three magazines. All figures are given in percentages.

a young female model, smiling. Another male model is walking arm in arm with another female model, although they are not gazing at each other.[74] Arguably, these elucidate the magazines' relatively elastic perception of masculine images.

What significances does the fluid image of masculinity in Popeye, Men's non-no and Fineboys have? Bordo articulates that boys and very young men in Anglophone advertisements tend to be portrayed in 'lean' positions, suggesting the social acceptability of them as the 'object' of the observing and desiring gaze. Conversely, older men are almost forbidden to appear passive. Thus, 'somewhat different rules for boys and men' are still present.[75] The models who appear in such magazines as Men's Health are estimated to fall within the twenty-five to thirty-five age groups.[76] They are slightly older than the models who appear in the Japanese magazines I have been analysing in this chapter. Do the male models in Anglophone and European magazines, then, elucidate to the unfavourableness of men becoming objects of the gaze, whether the gaze belongs to men or women? Sociologist Federico Boni writes of Men's Health that although the magazine promote the image of nurturing and appearance-conscious 'new man' masculinity, a young, androgynous model of masculinity would be rejected as unfavourable. The magazine, after all, aims to allow the reader to (re)discover 'the pleasure of being a man'.[77] Nixon argues that the interplay between the male readership's identification with and acquisition of visual pleasure in the male models takes place when he engages with men's 'lifestyle' magazines.[78] Yet even when these male models are presented as the object of a desiring gaze, overly 'masculine' qualities such as the model's muscular physique, rugged or hard visual qualities of either the model or the context, or the presence of female figures, would pre-empt him from becoming a sole object of such gaze. This sentiment is articulated by Negrin, who writes that despite the 'feminine' gaze and posture displayed by male models:

> signs of traditional masculinity are still present to reassure us of their masculinity. Thus, the models are typically well muscled, projecting an air of strength and solidity, despite their apparent passivity. They are also well endowed, as the body hugging underwear makes clear, and their hair is often slightly dishevelled, indicating a rugged masculinity that is not overly narcissistic.[79]

These can be read as reflecting the ambivalent feelings men in Europe, Australia and North America feel, or at least are expected to feel, about becoming an object of the gaze, whether it has a trace of heterosexuality or homosexuality. In this sense, conventional ideas of 'masculinity' and the restrictions they carry are still influencing the ways in which men and fashionability are represented. The Japanese magazines' elastic approach to the representations of men, on the contrary, cultivates a possibility that Japanese men are, at least to a certain extent, less preoccupied with conventional gender roles and restrictions they carry. Particularly through their notable applications of the 'lean' and 'wholesome' positions, the ways these magazines represent men problematize the established notion that men are the bearer, not the object, of the gaze.

The pleasurable gaze: looking and being looked at

The widespread yet largely unproven belief that men do not take serious interest in gazing at male figures, whether their own mirror-reflection or other men, amplifies the stereotyped assumption that it is woman, not man who occupies the position of the one to be gazed at. Germaine Greer is by any means not the only one who articulates the hostility still present in Anglo-Western culture to appreciating male beauty in her book *The Beautiful Boy*.[80] Feminist theorist Laura Mulvey in her famous essay on cinema and the gaze has also argued that traditional narrative films are structured around masculine pleasure. This pleasure system is constructed on the pattern of the male/viewer and the female/object of the gaze. Consequently, unlike women who are displayed as erotic objects for both the male characters in the screen and the spectator, male characters are unlikely to be gazed upon as erotic objects, precisely because men are reluctant to gaze at their more perfect ego.[81]

E. Ann Kaplan contends that the gaze in cinema is not necessarily male, but is often based on the dominance-submission pattern, and to own and activate it is to be in the 'masculine' position.[82] According to her, the dominance of the male gaze lies in its possession of power and action, whereas women, while receiving and returning the gaze, are unable to act upon it like men.[83] Bordo argues that this conception of men as the bearer of the 'gaze' and women as the objects of such a male gaze is reproduced and distributed through the media and advertisements, which instruct us to follow certain gendered behaviours.[84] Thus, the assumption of men as indifferent to the 'gaze' is likely constructed through mediated images, among others. This assumption is also closely tied to the expected roles of men as viewing subjects and women as the objects of their 'gaze'. This does not mean that men have never occupied the position of the gazed-upon. Art historian and film theorist Kaja Silverman, for instance, has argued that the position such as the object of the gaze, can indeed be more powerful and pleasurable than the bearer of the gaze in cinema. This is because the narrative is centred around the object of the gaze, and male characters in such films as Liliana Cavani's controversial *Il Portiere di notte* (1974), Silverman argues, occupy the 'passive' position.[85]

The reverse of such roles is, however, considered to be inappropriate, unfavourable or even interdicted. As design historian Peter McNeil and fashion theorist Vicki Karaminas write, for many conservative straight men, being 'gazed at' would be so distressing that they might even try to stop it with violence.[86] We can deduce from these authors that becoming an object of the gaze predominantly carries a negative attribute, and this is particularly strong for some men. Questions I wish to raise here are: must becoming an object of the gaze automatically involve negativity? Do men ever actively or willingly seek to be in the 'passive' position? I attest to the view that the gaze can be owned by both men and women. This means that men do not necessarily have to be controlling subjects, nor do women always have to be passive objects, and this is particularly applicable to Japanese culture. Laura Miller's suggestion that Japanese women have also occupied the position of the 'viewer' might be usefully deployed here. This interpretation has largely been ignored, possibly due to established assumptions that disregard the presence of a female 'gaze', as it is men who objectify women, and not the other way around. However, as far as Japanese visual media is concerned, not only men's but women's gaze has been recognized and incorporated. Miller writes that '[i]n pre-Meiji prints, for example, men are often depicted as objects for the female viewer, particularly in erotic prints or *shunga*'.[87] Miller's contention is firmly supported by scholar of Japanese literature and *shōjo* culture Tomoko Aoyama, who, in relation to Greer's work *The Beautiful Boy*, notes that it is unnecessary for Japanese women to advocate for 'reclaiming their capacity for and right to visual pleasure'.[88] This is because individuals, regardless of gender, did and still do admire and appreciate beauty in both young men and women in Japan.[89] Also, as we shall see, Japanese magazines such as *Fineboys* can be read as reflecting the presumed necessity of men to appear pleasing to women, thus reinforcing Miller's view.[90] I contend, then, that Japan is a significant cultural site in which to examine the presence of a different kind of relationship between men and the gaze. This is visually evident in the men's fashion magazines analysed here.

The April 2010 edition of *Men's non-no* offers a fashion spread under the title of 'Chiaopanic's Culture Mix' (*Chiaopanic no karuchā mikkusu*), in which one of the oldest *Men's non-no* models Remi (b. 1979) is attired in Japanese clothing brand Chiaopanic. In the three pages, he is presented in a slightly leaning yet still face-off position, in profile with an indirect gaze in medium-long shot, and in a wholesome position in a long shot alongside another model. Remi's colourful clothes such as a pair of knee-length shorts and a cap, as well as the context of the images such as a beach, connote a seaside resort, and the casualness and leisureliness associated with it. Although all of these are situated outside conventional, hard and mature 'masculinity', his abundant beard and dishevelled hair clearly accentuate his mature and rugged masculinity. Likewise, the model's passive gaze and smile signify his acceptance to serve the viewer's gaze, although perhaps not in an overtly sensual or intimate fashion. The images' sizes of frame – medium-long to long shots – semiotically indicate a low level of intimacy shared by the viewer and the pictured model.[91]

Two significances can be deduced by reading this series of images. Firstly, the magazine's portrayal of the model in various positions (i.e., face-off/defiant, lean/passive and wholesome/vulnerable) illustrates its elastic approach to the representations of men. Secondly, and more importantly, representing a man with a rugged, masculine look in passive positions suggests that becoming an object of the viewer's glance does not automatically invoke the unfavourable (and sexualized) passivity and submissiveness of the 'gazed at'. Does this hint at the possibility that, unlike the tendency found in Anglophone popular culture as articulated by Bordo, not only younger men but older men could also be the 'passive' object of the gaze? Here it is also useful to pay attention to the Japanese magazines targeted at older males.

Magazines targeted at maturer men such as *Leon* and *Men's Club* tend to deploy younger-looking models in their fashion spreads, as Anglophone men's lifestyle magazines do. For instance, a May 2010 fashion spread of *Men's Club* titled 'Burberry Black Label: Seductive Monotones' features an Austrian model, Gerhard Freidl, who was twenty-six years old at the time of shooting.[92] But these magazines are also full of images of middle-aged men. This is particularly notable in *Leon* where European-looking men who are clearly older than those featured in the three young men's magazines that I focus on are featured extensively. Many of these men are presented in a similar way to the 'street snapshot' features in young men's magazines; that is, they are pictured in the streets.

What is noteworthy about these images is that these men are often captured showing the indirect gaze.[93] Many of them are facing away from the camera or looking into the distance, as if unaware of being pictured. Yet these men are also seemingly engaged in action, such as walking, talking on the phone or smoking a cigarette. As we have seen earlier in this chapter, semiotically having an indirect gaze points to the passive status of the viewing subject, where the reader is in a position of power, initiating the gaze. In most of the cases where women are depicted with an indirect gaze, they tend to be in the 'lean position', reclining, seated or leaning against something but not in obvious action, in contrast to the men featured in *Leon*. Instead of being presented in the 'lean position', these men are depicted in motion and therefore their senses of agency are emphasized.

It is arguable that these male images in *Leon* are considerably older and, as their abundant beards and rather sturdy physiques indicate, conventionally more 'masculine' than the younger, more slender male images dominating the magazines like *Fineboys*. In addition, most of these men are fully clothed, and hence there is no explicit sexual undertone. Combined with the strong heterosexual context of the magazine, the active stance and the masculinity and virility of the male images in *Leon* might prevent them from fully being in a 'passive' position.[94] A converse reading, however, suggests that magazines like *Leon* tell us that even with certain conditions and limitations, older men can also appear in less than 'controlling' positions, serving someone's objectified gaze in

Japanese culture. This points to the possibility that these Japanese men's fashion magazines might encourage their male readership to at least acknowledge the pleasures of being gazed at and appreciated, particularly but not exclusively by women. This in turn raises the issue of vanity, another concept that has been deemed 'unmasculine' in our contemporary society.

Through the magic looking-glass: men and vanity

The image of a young man looking at his own reflection in a looking glass is not uncommon in Japanese men's fashion magazines like *Popeye*. Indeed, the March 2008 issue of *Popeye* ran a fashion story titled 'Magic Mirror', in which TV personalities and actors Keita and Shōta Saito (twins) are presented as a young man and his mirror reflection, wearing identical brand clothes but in different colours. In a similar fashion, the May 2008 edition of *Popeye* featured an image of the pop star Takuya Kimura with his mirror reflection. What do these images tell us about contemporary Japanese men and their relationship to appearance? Gazing into a mirror traditionally symbolizes vanity. The practice has predominantly been associated with beautiful women, particularly in modern European art history where '[t]he vanity mirror, in particular, conjures up the traditionally feminine trait of narcissism, or the act of contemplating one's self as a work of art'.[95] Paradigms of such operas as George Frideric Handel's opera *Semele* (1744) and Charles Gounod's operatic adaptation of Johann Wolfgang von Goethe's *Faust* (1859) give memorable examples that connect a beautiful woman, a mirror and vanity.

In Euro-American culture, the idea of men gazing into mirrors is usually thought to be decidedly 'unmanly'.[96] This is largely because mirror-imagery is considered a positive danger to mainstream heterosexual masculinity by way of being connected to homosexual 'self-love'. Narcissus, a beautiful male figure in Greek mythology who loved his own reflection, represents perhaps the strongest link between homoeroticism and narcissism. Such a link between men, mirrors and homo-narcissism often relates to a sense of fatality, as exemplified in such films as Jean Cocteau's *Orphée* (1950), René Clément's celebrated film *Plein Soleil* (1960) – a cinematic visualization of Patricia Highsmith's classic *The Talented Mr. Ripley* (1955) – and Martin Scorsese's film *Taxi Driver* (1976). According to Sigmund Freud's psychoanalysis, homo-narcissism occurs when an individual locates the ego ideal and object of desire in a single sex, as in *Plein Soleil*'s portrayal of the mirror sequence.[97] According to this reading, then, appreciating one's own mirror-image can be interpreted as connoting homoeroticism and homosexuality.

Indeed, male narcissism and homosexuality are closely connected in psychoanalytic theory. This is based on the assumption that heterosexuality is about distinguishing self and other (his or her object of desire). For the male subject, women are their 'others' while other men are the 'same' as themselves. Consequently, both homosexuality and narcissism 'are seen as essentially an interest in self rather than in the other'.[98] According to this Freudian reading, the homosexual is not attracted to another individual of the same sex, but to 'himself' in another's disguise.[99] Unlike the 'primary narcissism' where 'a child cathects itself in a vanity with its parent, without differentiation, without a developed ego', homosexual narcissism comes about in the later stage.[100] This occurs when:

> the individual seeks in another some ideal excellence missing from his own ego. And this is the type of narcissistic choice made by the homosexual, by which Freud generally means the male homosexual: the choice of what he himself would like to be.[101]

French psychoanalyst Jacques Lacan's famous work *The Mirror-phase as Formative of the Function of the I* (1966) is also important when considering the relationship between man and his visual identity conceived in the mirror. Although his work is too complex to include properly here, it is appropriate to mention that Lacan contended that humans acquire the sense of 'I' first through identifying themselves with their mirror-reflections. The visual identity obtained from the mirror, for Lacan, can be a metaphor of the other humans:

> We have only to understand the mirror-phase as an identification in the full sense which analysis gives to the term: namely, the transformation which takes place in the subject when he assumes an image – whose predestination to this phase-effect is sufficiently indicated by the use, in analytical theory, of the old term *imago*.[102]

In this sense, the mirror-reflection of the self bestows on them a sense of visionary 'wholeness' to their 'fragmented' identity. The gloominess surrounding these psychoanalytic readings of the mirror-image and narcissism is the negative connotations they offer. For Lacan, the mirror-phase connotes immaturity. The child's process of identification through the mirror image, he argues, starts at sixteen months and lasts up to the age of eighteen months. Leaning towards the mirror is also symbolic of infancy, connoting the child's motor incapacity and nurseling dependency.[103] Moreover, for Freud, homosexuality, with which narcissism is deeply intermingled, is regressive. He 'concludes that homosexual desire *reduces* to narcissism without significant remainder and hence is a developmental misdirection'.[104] Lacan, too, describes 'homosexuality as a perversion, not because of the contingency of morals, nor because of the supposed needs of biology, but because of the narcissistic structure of homosexual desire'.[105] Social theorist and scholar of English literature Michael

Warner articulates limitations found in these theoretical perspectives, saying that '[e]veryone undergoes – and indeed requires – the kind of narcissism Freud describes', and hence '[h]omosexuality may indeed be a way of loving one's own ego, but so is heterosexual romance'.[106]

'Vanity has traditionally (although not theoretically) been seen as primarily a feminine trait', says Steele.[107] This does not seem to be so different in the history of Japanese culture. Art works such as Utamaro Kitagawa's 'Seven Women Applying Make-up in the Mirror' (1790s) and Jun'ichi Nakahara's 'A Young Woman through 12 Months' (1940) are but two examples to illustrate the association between women and mirrors, whereas examples of the same relationship between men and mirrors are fairly sparse. Rather than perceiving it as a magnifying glass that reflects and grotesquely inflates vanity, however, the pictorial images of men with mirrors in Japanese men's fashion magazines allude to the positive quality of mirror. Namely, the mirror can function as a device essential for achieving the fashionable 'look', or perhaps even as an essential tool in the creation of certain kinds of masculinity. 'We assume that the mirror reflects our real selves', Hollander has said, 'while using it to create a better look – dress, make-up, etc'.[108] Accordingly, in order to be successfully fashionable, and in order to maintain that look, a considerable length of consultation with a mirror is necessary.

This idea seems particularly true when men in younger generations who tend to demonstrate significantly high interests in beauty consumption and grooming practices are concerned. Marketing writer Megumi Ushikubo, in her book on the recent increase in the visibility of young men with significantly more candid attitudes towards such concerns as fashion and beauty consumption than more stereotypical males, illustrates this case.[109] For instance, she observes that people often complain of long queues in men's rooms, created by young men who are spending hours in front of the mirror, restyling their hair.[110] Here, it is fair to conclude this section by saying that the mirror is necessary for men to craft and maintain fashionable looks. In the next section, I look at the ways in which Japanese men's fashion magazines conceive male appearance as an object of the gaze. With a short case study of Grooming/Beauty sections in GQ Australia and Men's non-no, I pose a question: do the two magazines manifest a transcultural similarity or difference in their attitudes toward the relationship between men and appearances?

Science versus the art of taking care of appearance

Perhaps it is no coincidence that in the 'Grooming' section of the April/May 2010 issue of GQ Australia, anti-aging cosmetic products are presented in a fashion redolent of scientific laboratory. The section features robot-like hands gripping well-known brand cosmetics like Chanel and Lancôme alongside a beaker, and a burnt and melted product dripping onto Lab Series age-less face cream. Against a backdrop of such images, one of the magazine's contributing editors Alexandra Spring writes: 'A beginner's guide to the acids, peptides, oils and anti-oxidants you're slathering all over your skin.'[111] Words such as beauty, cosmetic, radiant or shimmering are carefully avoided in this feature. This echoes contentions made by Bordo and Negrin that different discourses are applied to the promotion of men's and women's beauty products in English.[112] As Bordo has noted, advertisements of men's products often adopt a discourse that obscures the fact that their function is to enhance appearance. Instead, they imply that such products are 'for utilitarian or instrumental purposes'.[113]

The extensive use of dark, metallic colours, as well as a scientific ambience, strongly suggests that the practice of gazing into the mirror and taking care of one's appearance is supposed to be done for or in search of scientific reason, without much emotional involvement. It is presented as an inevitable routine rather than a practice in which a man might find delight. This may be a visual endorsement of the fact that men have frequently been portrayed as machine-like: virile, hard-bodied yet apathetic.[114] This is a representation also, quite commonly, found in contemporary Anglophone men's lifestyle magazines. The connotation derived from such an instrumentalization of the male body is in line with 'an insistence on sexual difference and a refusal of male eroticization evident throughout the modern period'.[115] This 'hypermasculine' visual discourse presumably reassures its male readers of their 'masculinity' while aligning with or endorsing the conventional assumption that cosmetics and taking an interest in one's appearance are 'feminine' concerns. Hence, it mirrors the ambivalence towards appearance-consciousness that Anglo-Western men are (imagined) to feel.

The April 2010 issue of *Men's non-no* offers a much more 'organic' visual approach to men's skin care. 'A Beginner's Skin Care Lesson that Improves Your First Impression' (*daiichi inshou UP no 'debyu' sukin kea kouza*) is aimed particularly at freshmen who make a new start in April, either as new students or as working members of society. The feature tells us that unlike women, men cannot rely on make-up to conceal dry, defective skin, and uneven skin tones. The aim of this feature is to help men obtain spotless, smooth naked skin by following a series of simple and easy lessons, which are divided into three basic segments: facial cleansing, toning and moisturising. Earlier in this chapter, I referred to the characteristic strategy of these Japanese men's magazines of creating narratives, which help the reader to form closer identification and engagement with the magazines' models and the products they are endorsing. Following this tradition, the abovementioned feature proceeds with one of the magazine's exclusive models Hiroto Higa (b. 1987), who the text tells us was concerned with the increasing dullness of his complexion, and has gone through all the lessons it introduces.

The sophisticated layout in which the products are promoted is contrasted to the previous page in the magazine that has a series of cartoons, comically telling why Higa is concerned with his skin and seeking advice. The colourful cosmetic products are, according to the magazine, created specifically for the age demographic of *Men's non-no* male readership and their skin. Some of these products are significantly less expensive than those promoted in the *GQ* grooming section, and are presented in a rather simple and clean fashion. The dominance of whiteness in the pages arguably signifies the importance of the spotless, clean and clear complexion that the feature emphasizes. In a stark contrast to the stylishly scientific, almost mechanical image of *GQ*, *Men's non-no* adds green vines including ivy, and thin layers of white sandstone, on which the products lean against each other. The description of one item, a bottle of toning water, even says 'floating inside are the flower petals of Calendula, whose scent flows every time you splash it'.

The combination of organic plants and substances, and slightly irregular placement of the cosmetic products connote nature. Arguably, these suggest that the magazine sees and promotes the practice of skin care as a 'natural' rather than a systematic requirement of masculinity. Remarks from Higa in speech bubbles like 'infiltrative, smooth toner. Feels awesome!' and 'The balance between moistness and refreshment is v. good', reflect the emotive approach the feature takes, further underlining its contrast to the scientific, descriptive and mechanical approaches of *GQ Australia*. Needless to say, *Men's non-no*, too, linguistically underlines the practice of skincare as 'masculine', and hence does not undermine the masculine identity of the readership. By using such gendered discourse as 'the scent preferred by men' and '3 basic steps for men's skincare', male interest in skincare is justified for the reason that men, unlike women, are unable to conceal their complexions with make-up. Yet the feature's reference to the model's positively emotive remarks on how he felt when applying these products, combined with the pleasingly neat and simple visual discourse, also teach the reader that skincare can be pleasurable.

Possessing an aesthetically pleasing appearance and a clear, beautiful complexion as the foundation of such a look, is a requirement not only for women but also for men who wish to create a good impression. That is what the feature in *Men's non-no* tells us, and this in turn endorses for men the importance of being subjected to the gaze. Thus, the roles that equate men as viewing subjects and women as the objects of the gaze are differently and perhaps less rigidly defined in Japanese culture. This problematizes and possibly subverts the often assumed 'complete dominance of the so-called male gaze'.[116] Conversely, as my analysis of the magazines reinforces, men could also be positioned as the objects of the gaze in the Japanese cultural context. This approach is used, at least partially, by these Japanese men's fashion magazines in order to motivate fashion interests and consumption among the group of young men at whom these publications are aimed.

Conclusion

Through the analysis of three Japanese men's fashion magazines, this chapter highlighted three important points. These magazines prioritize fashion over lifestyle contents, and they cater to a specific age demographic, which helps them to maintain sensitivity to cultural change and trends. Their deployment of non-professional models, particularly in *Fineboys*, moreover seems to help create a social affinity between the readership and the contents of the magazines. In these ways, the magazines emphasize the importance of appearance, fashion and scent. They tell the readership that not only women but men can be the object of the gaze, and, moreover, that this may be delightful if done successfully. The next chapter offers further insight into young men's fashion cultures analysed in this chapter. In particular, I try to make sense of the presence of Japanese as well as non-Asian male fashion models, and a suave, boyish and slender male aesthetic that these models as well as fashion brands like the famous Milkboy display. Does such a mode of aesthetic sensitivity impose a challenge on more established, older and conservative masculinity?

3

BOY'S ELEGANCE: A LIMINALITY OF BOYISH CHARM AND OLD-WORLD SUAVITY

T-shirts with voluminous scarves are now in store . . . the big scarf looks lovely!

The T-shirt itself is made of fabrics with faint luster and its slightly shortened sleeves make it a perfect item for this coming spring.

We recommend a chic coordinate, wearing it under a cardigan or a jacket!

—*Milkboy Staff's Blog* entry, 28 January 2013.[1]

In a photograph of a medium-close shot, a young man is facing off the camera, showing a fleeting smile. He is wearing a loose and 'flowing' crew neck T-shirt of vanilla colour. A big black scarf, which is attached at the neck of the T-shirt, is tied in such a cute fashion that it is more rightly described as a big ribbon, matching the boy's unthreatening, almost androgynously lovely countenance. This is an image of teenage amateur model Musashi Rhodes wearing Milkboy's scarf tee, which made its appearance in the brand's blog in early 2013 (Figure 3.1a).

We might be surprised by the fashion brand's inclusion of conventionally 'feminine' attributes such as 'cute' and 'lovely' when describing fashion items. Equally striking is that such terms are, to a certain extent, not imposing a threat to the 'masculine' identity of the consumer. In the previous chapter, I demonstrated that a group of Japanese men's fashion magazines encourage their male readership to recognize the importance of being subjected to the gaze. This chapter continues exploration of the Japanese young men's publications I put forward in Chapter 2, with particular focus on *Popeye, Men's non-no* and

(a)

Figure 3.1 High school student Musashi Rhodes wearing (a) Milkboy's scarf tee and (b) a shirt with studs.

Styled by KENJI and photographed by SHINGO. Image reproduced with kind permission of KENJI/ Milkboy.

(b)

Fineboys, and introduce renowned men's street-casual fashion brand Milkboy as a paragon of fashion aesthetics that these magazines illustrate.

Psychoanalyst J. C. Flügel famously contended in the 1930s that '[i]f heterosexual men were "to dress a little more to please women," rather than striving for respectability from their fellow males, some very concrete pleasures would result'.[2] For him, recognizing and valuing the gaze of women would render men's fashion more progressive, more attractive. Are Japanese men's fashion cultures a visual testament of Flügel's contentions? Or are they instead a demonstration of what Michel Foucault contended in 'The Concern for Truth'? In this interview conducted one month before his death, Foucault said in relation to morality in Greek and Roman antiquity:

> It was a matter of knowing how to govern one's own life in order to give it the most beautiful form possible (in the eyes of others, of oneself, and of the future generations for whom one could serve as an example). That's what I tried to reconstitute: the formation and development of a practice of self whose objective was to constitute oneself as the worker of the beauty of one's own life.[3]

Foucault's idea of 'the worker of the beauty of one's own life' is thus not motivated only for the eyes of others, but also for oneself. I argue that these two desires are what Japanese men's fashion culture negotiates in order to motivate fashion interests in men. One of the significant strands that this chapter focuses on is the strong presence of a mode of slender, elegant male aesthetic sensitivities, which both Japanese and non-Japanese models in the aforementioned men's fashion magazines embody. I contend that this is a manifestation of masculinity different from either an emphatically muscular mode as favoured in mainstream European and particularly American culture, or 'salaryman' masculinity which many find dowdy and confining. In short, this chapter aims to substantiate that Japanese young men's almost 'narcissistic' concerns about appearance and fashion, as represented in men's fashion cultures, might offer a different and more 'relaxed' approach to understanding men's relationship with fashion.[4]

The first section of this chapter attempts to make sense of the magazines' deployment of non-Asian along with Japanese and Eurasian models. I identify both practical and aesthetic reasons to explicate this point. Transcultural differences in male aesthetics, highlighted by the magazines' models, are the focus of the second section. By using the theory of 'format' and 'product', which I will explain, this section pays attention to the male slenderness so predominant in the contemporary Japanese fashion scene. With short case studies of the boyish reinvention of the 'Neo-Edwardian' dandy style in Japan, and menswear label Milkboy, the final section seeks to establish the idea that slender, boyish and sophisticated images of contemporary Japanese men serve as an alternative to the established yet unfavourable image of Japanese masculinity as epitomized by worn-out, middle-aged men. I also explore two factors that contemporary Japanese men's fashion culture deploys and negotiates in order to motivate and increase fashion interests in males, namely a desire to attract admirers and a desire to dress for their own pleasures. The images of masculinity these examples offer, while not entirely subverting the expected gendered looks, elucidate the aesthetic importance of dress. Instead of merely making and sustaining a clear gender distinction, sartorial styles can be appreciated and incorporated, even if they disagree with the socially or culturally expected masculine identity of the wearer.

Fusion of European and Japanese aesthetic senses

The first European sartorial style that Japanese culture adopted and appropriated from outside was a male dress form. European style clothing was officially and actively adopted by Japanese culture towards the end of the Tokugawa and the early Meiji (1868–1912) periods 'as part of the drive for modernization of the country'.[5] It was not solely a practice of random, sudden or forced adoption. There were cultural affinities between European and Japanese sartorial aesthetics, to which I shall refer later in this chapter. Since contemporary Japanese men's fashion has its basis in European dress forms, whether or not the country's contemporary fashion culture signifies or endorses the 'Westernization' of Japanese youth is a question I pose here. Indeed, the presence of non-Asian-looking male models in these men's fashion magazines is highly suggestive of this contention. Many of the models appearing in *Popeye*, for example, are non-Asian, including those who are Caucasian and black. This ratio is slightly changed in *Men's non-no*, where, among non-Asian models, some Japanese or Eurasian models are visible. In *Fineboys* the presence of Japanese models is increased and Japanese models Shunsuke Daitō and Atsushi Harada were exclusive to the magazine in around 2010. In addition, *Fineboys* tends to feature amateur models (*dokusha-moderu*) more frequently than the other two magazines.[6]

We might ask whether the presence of non-Asian-looking models in these magazines recreates a long-existing debate in which 'many critics and scholars interpret the new physical aesthetics as emanating from an imported racist beauty ideology that denigrates Asian physical appearance'.[7] Indeed, Laura Miller points out that new beauty ideals among Japanese young men, such as dyed brown hair, have been presumed by some foreigners and older Japanese individuals as these men's desires to imitate their Euro-American counterparts, and hence signalling the 'Westernization' of Japanese youth.[8] Echoing this criticism, Japanese women's attempts to obtain a look that does not evoke conventionally 'Asian' qualities, whether or not it might be (unintentionally) associated with the physical characteristics of black, Caucasian or 'imagined-Japanese' have been criticized as 'unnatural' and extreme.[9] Does the presence of non-Asian-looking models in these Japanese men's fashion magazines, then, allude to their Westernized nature? It might be so, since *Popeye* was launched as Japan's first lifestyle magazine to introduce many trendy American youth lifestyles and sports, such as skateboarding in the 1970s.[10] We might also consider other interpretations. It is simplistic, and perhaps shallow, to assume that the deployment of non-Japanese-looking models solely represents the range of Japanese desires to emulate and identify with Westerners. The presence of Japanese men in all of these magazines, for instance, needs to be recognized.

The nationality of fashionable men

As we have seen in Chapter 2, many of Johnny's stars and young actors as well as employees of well-known Japanese brand clothing shops appear in every issue of these magazines, often with interviews and photo shoots.[11] As for *Men's non-no* and *Fineboys*, the celebrity who appears on the cover would also be featured in three or four pages of fashion and interview. Photographic images of selected, ordinary, young men found in the streets or university campuses across Japan are moreover presented in such regular two-paged features as 'Fashion Snap' (Fashion Snapshots, *Men's non-no*) and 'Campus Snap' (Campus Snapshots, *Fineboys*). This type of feature is periodically developed at an international level. 'Snap the World' (Snapshots of the World, *Men's non-no*) and 'World Snap' (World Snapshots, *Popeye*) sometimes include young men (and, to a lesser extent, young women) in such internationally recognized fashion capitals as New York, London and Paris. This type of feature lends itself to a number of readings. Perhaps the obvious one is that these magazines present the reader with the idea that their country is part of the larger fashion world.

Yet if we look at the images more closely, we can see some sartorial differences between photographs taken in the Euro-American and Japanese cities. For instance, these features show the tendency of dressing Euro-American young men more trimly and conservatively. The Japanese men selected for this type of feature, by contrast, appear to be dressed more elaborately, even flamboyantly, with layers of sartorial items and accessories like scarves in vivid colours.[12] Whether it reflects a transnational fashion sense or the editors' intention to distinguish between men of different nationalities, these subtle differences arguably remind the Japanese readership that their fashion culture is not entirely standardized with their Euro-American counterparts.

The presence of Japanese men in these magazines suggests that even though Japanese readers consume fashion that is largely associated with Europe and America, their lives are not likely to be utterly standardized or 'Westernized'. This amplifies social-cultural anthropologist Arjun Appadurai's argument; in relation to the widespread popularity of renditions of American popular songs in the Philippines, he states that even if individuals adopt a transnational cultural form, this does not necessarily mean that their lives are completely infiltrated and standardized by the culture where the transnational cultural form originated.[13] The presence of Japanese men in these magazines indicates that the readership is constantly reminded that these magazines are Japanese fashion magazines targeted at Japanese men. Therefore, their lives are inseparable from their 'local' cultures. There is also a more practical reason to explain the co-presence of Japanese and non-Japanese men in fashion publications.

Advertising scholar Mariko Morimoto and independent researcher Susan Chang point out that foreign advertisers tend to prefer foreign-titled publications in Japan, where 'these advertisements are likely to be standardized to convey the Western images to Japanese consumers'.[14] In contrast, Japanese advertisers tend to prefer Japanese magazines, often emphasizing 'Japaneseness'. One method 'for international advertisers to maintain congruency between their culture and images', they argue, 'is to use models from their home culture. Western models can convey Western values and images that are preferred by Japanese consumers'.[15] This idea, at least partially, explains why magazines with a considerable amounts of European luxurious designer wear, such as *Popeye*, prefer to feature non-Asian-looking models while Japanese models are more prevalent in *Fineboys* or *Choki Choki*, where Japanese designer clothes are more frequently featured.[16]

Miller convincingly argues that the new male physical aesthetics in Japan, including a large eye shape and brighter hair colour, represents Japanese young males' rejection of older modes of male identity rather than a rejection of their own ethnicity. She argues:

> When American ravers or cyberpunks appropriate non-Western forms of body modification, such as nose piercing or tattooing, we do not hear anyone accuse them of trying to turn themselves into Dani warriors or Maori islanders . . . if looking Euroamerican includes having a hairy body, I doubt that very many young Japanese men would be interested. It seems to me that this is an aesthetic that combines many features and is not merely 'failed Western' or 'faux-American.' It pulls in ideas from outside Japan for inspiration in certain of its traits, but it also draws on local concepts and proclivities.[17]

This sentiment is shared by media and cultural studies scholar Meredith Jones, who puts it beautifully that fair complexion, which Japanese women endeavour to obtain, might be 'influenced by global (Western) notions of beauty but have a distinct Japanese flavour'.[18] Respecting the contentions of the above authors, I argue that images of the Euro-American culture presented in these Japanese men's magazines, including the non-Asian-looking models, are more precisely described as being about an imagined Europe or America. Indeed, both non-Asian and Japanese models deployed in the Japanese magazines outline a preferred mode of masculinity in contemporary Japan. This differs from the modes generally favoured in European and particularly in American cultures; namely, it values ideals of extreme slenderness and youthfulness.

In praise of youthful slenderness: preferred modes of male aesthetics in Japan

The presence of different models of masculinity preferred in Japan, particularly the slender and 'androgynous' model, is compelling (Figure 3.2). Slenderness among Japanese young men has been prominent in recent times, but this does not mean they are dramatically losing weight. For example, annual surveys conducted by the Ministry of Health, Labour and Welfare point to the steadiness of the percentage of Japanese men between the ages of twenty and twenty-nine who are considered to be too thin according to Body Mass Index (BMI, Table 3.1). The statistics show that most men in this age group are in the 'average' range.

According to writer Megumi Fukumitsu, these images allude to an increase in the preference for a slender 'look' and fashion among young men rather than thinness for nutritional or medical reasons. This has led to a blurring of the boundaries between women's and men's dress sizes. Some young men increasingly seek slighter silhouettes and they wear items of clothing, like trousers

Table 3.1 BMI of Japanese young men between the ages of twenty and twenty-nine

	1986	1996	2006	2007	2008	2010	2011
Too Thin	9.4	9.9	9.5	10.6	9.6	12.3	8.4
Average	77.5	76.6	70.9	68.1	75.8	69.2	70.4
Obese	13.1	13.5	19.6	21.3	14.6	18.5	21.2

Based on *Kokumin kenkō/eiyō chōsa no gaikō (The Survey Results of Health and Nutrition of the Nation)*, Ministry of Health, Labour and Welfare, 2006: 7; 2007: 174; 2008: 186; 2010: 15; 2011: 110.

and T-shirts, that are designed for women.[19] Not only that, but Milkboy, a men's fashion brand to which I shall return later in this chapter, has designed men's clothes in small sizes, which is part of what appeals to female consumers. We should keep in mind some variations in male physicality in addition to race are evident in *Men's non-no* and other similar titles.[20] Nevertheless, the models gracing these Japanese men's fashion magazines, it is fair to say, possess slender physiques, which are considered to be barely normal or slightly underweight. The average height and weight of *Men's non-no* models is, for example, 182.64 cm and 63.26 kg (6 ft and 139 lbs).[21] These magazines promote attractively healthy bodies, as the magazines concurrently feature instructions on how to exercise and body build.[22] However, as the feature in April 2008 issue of *Fineboys* noted, it is 'the adequately muscled, beautiful' (*tekido ni hikishimatta utsukushii*) body that the magazine promotes, not the Greek god-like, 'Adonis-complex-obsessed' body so often found in Euro-American men's publications such as *Men's Health* and even *GQ*.[23]

It has been noted that the increase in more androgynous male images is also visible in many Euro-American countries, particularly in women's magazines or fashion advertising and runways.[24] Indeed, such young male models as Clément Chabernaud, Baptiste Radufe and Ben Allen have notably more slender physiques than other popular models like Sean O'Pry, Matthew Terry and Marlon Teixeira, all of whom are ranked in top ten of Models.com's 'Top 50 Male Models' as of 5 September 2013.[25] Susan M. Alexander also argues that despite the fact that all the models in *Men's Health* magazine she examined have well-developed muscles, they clearly are not as muscular as those 'supermales' featured on the covers of magazines devoted to bodybuilding. For her, '[t]he cover images present the image of masculinity, at least for white males, as a well-toned but not overly muscled body'.[26] Yet the muscularity of male models still tends to be emphasized in many Euro-American men's lifestyle magazines, let alone *Men's Health*. Llewellyn Negrin has moreover pointed out that these male models tend to accentuate rugged, 'manly' characteristics even when they are presented in the 'feminine' way, such as through their postures.[27] This leads us to wonder if the word 'slender' is connoted differently in Japanese, European, North American and Australian contexts.

Joanne Entwistle offers a standard body size of male fashion models in contemporary New York and London. She states, 'the required height for most agencies is between 180 and 191 cm (5 ft 11 in. to 6 ft 3 in.) and the standard measurements are, usually: chest, 96–107 cm (38–42 in.), and waist, 76–81 cm (30–32 in.)'.[28] Male models in *Men's non-no* demonstrate some significant differences in body size: 170–92 cm (5 ft 7 in. to 6 ft 4 in.) in height, with the measurements of chest being 73–95 cm (28.7–37.4 in.) and waist 63–81 cm (24.8–31.9 in.). They have significantly smaller or less developed chests than models in the USA/UK. Also, *Men's non-no* models vary in body size and shape significantly more than their British and American counterparts, where '[t]he male fashion model's body is a very standard one in terms of size and shape'.[29] This is particularly evident in the waist size of male models in *Men's non-no*; few models have a waist as thin as 63 or 65 cm (25 in.). This all indicates that models in Japanese men's fashion magazines like *Men's non-no* tend to have much less muscled bodies than standard male models in the United States and United Kingdom, who are themselves very thin by Euro-American standards.[30] The difference outlined by the comparison between models in Anglophone and Japanese magazines are further highlighted by fashion magazines like *Choki Choki*, where many of the models hired are amateur or semi-professional.

As shown in Table 3.2, the Japanese amateur models of *Choki Choki* generally have daintier body frames than the models of *Men's non-no*, many of whom are professional models of non-Asian or Eurasian races. Since the average height and weight of Japanese men aged twenty to twenty-nine are 172 cm and 66. 63 kg, as far as their height is concerned, the amateur models of *Choki Choki* correspond even more to the size of average Japanese men than the *Men's non-no* models.[31] Needless to say, these 'ordinary' Japanese male figures could reflect the interventions, selections and even manipulation of editors, as observed in Chapter 2. But, as also noted in Chapter 2, they may well reflect the magazines' intention to maintain extreme sensitivity to social changes and trends, and to create a social affinity between the target reader and the preferred mode of masculinity in contemporary Japanese youth culture.

The presence of less conventionally 'manly' models also outlines senses of ambivalence and negation found in Euro-American popular culture towards slender male physiques.[32] The idealized male body image in the United States, as circulated widely in the media, has continued to be the muscular ideal originated in ancient Greece. This mode of ideal male image comes 'with a consistent focus on taller frame, broad shoulders, slim hips and waist, and well-defined (but subtle) musculature in the chest, legs, and arms'.[33] Actors Bradley Cooper or Channing Tatum are the *beau idéals* of such masculine ideal while Robert Pattinson, self-described as 'literally the only actor in LA

Table 3.2 Body size of male models in Men's non-no *and* Choki Choki

	Tallest	Shortest	Heaviest	Lightest	Average height	Average weight
MEN'S NON-NO	192	170	75	52	182.64	63.26
CHOKI CHOKI	183	164	65	44	174.72	53.8

Reproduced with the kind permission of *Berg Encyclopaedia of World Dress and Fashion*.

who doesn't have a six pack', is allegedly 'ashamed' of his body and has determined to 'get in shape' after having missed out on some roles because of his 'less' muscular body shape.[34] To put it simply, these male figures, particularly with a boyish-looking face, need to have a body that resembles a Greek god in order to be recognized widely as the male 'ideal'.[35] Thus, we can infer that a muscled physique is still part of preferred male aesthetics especially in mainstream Anglo-European cultures. This male body is moreover displayed frequently without clothes, adding further significance to its physical muscularity.

With a 26-inch waist: slenderness as the flower of Japanese male beauty

Male models are frequently (partially) unclothed when they are used to advertise clothes and fragrances. One only needs to glance at such advertising campaigns as Calvin Klein Jeans with the Northern Irish model, singer and actor Jamie Dornan (2010), and that of Armani with Portuguese soccer superstar Christiano Ronaldo (2010), to see the legitimacy of this contention. What are the significant meanings derived from this emphasis on the nude male body? Such images are capable of several readings, including the intention to capture and serve the desiring gaze of gay men, who are often conceived, even if stereotypically, as the primary consumers of male fashion. These male figures are moreover pictured in the lean position with medium to medium-close shot frames, which accentuate their well-articulated, upper-body muscles, further suggesting their statures as the object of the viewer's gaze. It is noteworthy that heterosexual men tend to display either strong forms of rejection or strongly stated lack of interest in looking at such images of male nudes. According to sociologist Beth Eck, this kind of reaction mirrors these men's strong urge to reactively construct and accentuate their 'hypermasculine' heterosexuality.[36]

Or could it be simply that the virile physicality of a male and its aesthetic qualities diminishes as it is clothed? And conversely, would clothing not appear attractive on such physicality? Anne Hollander articulates the idea that European civilizations have long been fascinated by human nakedness, and modish fashion of each era has left traces on how nudity was (artistically) conceived.[37] In other words, the favoured visualization of the human nude has always been influenced by contemporary fashion. The naked body did not, however, always enjoy the stature of fascination and eroticism in Japanese culture. Actually, nudity and the shape of the body have not been important in Japanese aesthetics.[38] In the Heian period of Japan, for instance, the nobility wore elaborate layers of silk robes carefully selected through the art of matching colours.[39] The clothes and how they were coordinated had much more importance than the actual physicality of the wearer in this era. Consequently, general lack of interest in the body was noted. Japanese studies scholar Ivan Morris had stated:

> The humanist idea that the naked body can be a thing of aesthetic joy and significance is alien to the Japanese tradition . . . Murasaki [the author of *The Tale of Genji*] comments, 'Unforgettably horrible is the naked body. It really does not have the slightest charm.'[40]

The dissociation between fashionability and emphasis on the male nude body in Japanese culture is also evident in an October 2010 feature story of *Fineboys*, titled 'No-no Styles that Would Turn Girls Off'. Four 'stylish' young women are invited to discuss what girls like and dislike about young men's fashion styles in this story. Importantly, one of the women, nineteen-year-old Rei Handa, does not like men wearing their shirts open too much, for when they bend down, their chests are shown. She says, 'I don't like that odd sexiness'. Her comment is followed by another participant, twenty-year-old Mayuko Iguchi, who claims: 'I would think, what do they want to do by showing that much. Basically, girls don't want to look at boys who reveal their body too much!'[41] Needless to say, nudity, particularly female nudes, are conceived as erotically charged in contemporary Japanese culture, too. However, if we invert the point made by Hollander that modish fashion influences the portrayal of the nude in European culture, the emphasis on the male nude and his muscularity might have its reflections in the currency of men's fashion. Although any generalization should be avoided, contemporary American and European men may be encouraged to have a muscular body frame and to dress in a very simple fashion, so a trace of their (well-built) physicality is visible on his clothed body. Hence, the emphatically muscled male physique is still seen as a 'requirement' for these men to be considered attractive.

The context in which such unclothed male images is presented – that is, in men's lifestyle magazines such as *GQ, Loaded* or *Men's Health* – would allow the heterosexual male readership to assume that the primary purpose of these images is to sell the product, not to sensually allure the bearer of the gaze. This implicit message might offer the male reader another way to engage with the image of an unclothed male other than displaying strong forms of rejection or stated lack of interest. Sartorial styles proposed in these Japanese magazines, on the other hand, often involve layering of a number of items. This is particularly so in magazines like *Fineboys* and *Choki Choki*, whose models are even more slender than the models in magazines like *Men's non-no*, as we have seen. In order to present layered styles effectively and attractively, thus, a slender physique, like a hanger or a mannequin, is more desirable. What adds further significance to this slender male physique is that this male image is perceived as aesthetically pleasing if not sensually alluring by Japanese women, and importantly, it is not the only mode of male aesthetics existent in the culture.

Hidetoshi Nakata (b. 1977), a Japanese former soccer player known to be a 'fashionista', is one of the four celebrities who endorsed the 2010 Calvin Klein underwear advertising campaign with American actors Mehcad Brooks and Kellan Lutz, and Spanish tennis player Fernando Verdasco. He appeared to be slightly less muscular than the other three but still displayed a visibly muscled, athletic physique. His body utterly corresponded with a preferred mode of male physicality in the Euro-American tradition. Presumably, this image was targeted primarily at male viewers who would actually wear the product he was endorsing. His direct, piercing gaze and slightly leaning, but otherwise hard, 'face-off' posture, and the context of the model as a star soccer player, all connoted his nude body as athletic rather than sensual. Significant divergence is illuminated by the images of nude males that are ostensibly targeted at heterosexual Japanese women.

Japanese singer and actor Teppei Koike (b. 1986) appeared unclothed in his photo book (2006). In a similar fashion, in 2010, Sho Sakurai (b. 1982), singer, actor and member of Johnny's boy band Arashi, appeared nude in well-established women's lifestyle magazine *an an* (January 2010).[42] The medium shot and the lean position of the young men suggest their statures as personal and familiar objects of the desiring gaze. Koike and Sakurai clearly have unthreateningly slender and undeveloped, almost androgynous physiques, making a stark contrast to the more muscular bodies of Nakata, Jamie Dornan or Cristiano Ronaldo in the aforementioned advertisements. Although the images of Koike and Sakurai may take on different connotations for gay or heterosexual male consumers, they officially target the heterosexual female market. This reinforces Miller's contention that such a slender, 'androgynous' male can be aesthetically, and perhaps sensually, alluring to Japanese women.[43] The firmly established presence of two different types of male physicality in Japanese popular culture (one muscular and the other slender) also signals a degree of ambivalence involved in male slenderness in Euro-American mainstream culture where one body image of muscular male still tends to be preferred. The images exuding these different aesthetic sensitivities are also present in the three Japanese magazines. The next section will examine this transcultural difference through a D&G advertisement campaign for the summer 2010 collection.[44]

Elegant cowboys: D&G garments and stylistic transformations

Such internationally distributed advertisements as Dolce & Gabbana, Chanel (e.g. Allure Homme Sport) and Diesel are also featured in these three Japanese magazines. Although all of them have a non-Asian-appearance, the male figures appearing in these advertisements differ visually from the actual models adorning the fashion photo pages. Undoubtedly, well-developed, muscled bodies are shared by the models appearing in these advertisements.

One such example was a series of D&G's advertisements for their summer 2010 collection. At first glance, the male models in the D&G advertisements appear more boyish, or at least less 'hypermasculine' than their counterparts in other advertising campaigns. Except for one model in the far right, the indirect gaze of the models connotes a degree of passivity, which might diminish their 'hypermasculinity'.[45] Yet their very short hairstyles and postures, particularly those of the model in the middle, who has his left foot on the sofa and his right hand in his trouser pocket, connote a more conventional and confident masculinity. Inclusion of women in the background, although vaguely visible, also alludes to the intention of accentuating a normative heterosexuality of an otherwise homosocial image. On closer observation we see the well-developed, muscled bodies of the models, with strong facial features and broad shoulders. This is reminiscent of the male models who appeared in Euro-American men's magazines like Men's Health,[46] and thus reflecting the European and American 'ideal' masculine physical image. Arguably, these almost contradicting qualities reflect the negotiation process between hypermasculine and the more androgynous kind of male images.

In contrast, the April 2010 issue of Popeye and Men's non-no offer an illustrated story with the same D&G collection. The fashion spread of Popeye is of great significance for my argument. In the story, the same D&G sartorial items that appeared in the advertisement campaign are worn by Australian model Benjamin Wenke, but are styled and photographed by Japanese artists, and targeted at the Japanese readers.[47] In comparison with the D&G advertisement campaign, Wenke in Popeye appears significantly younger, more boyish, slender and elegantly dressed than the models in this campaign. The photographic aesthetics of these images, notably a type of dreamy, melancholic and soft-focused effect, also highlight the credibility of my reading. Wenke's youthful, androgynous appearance corresponds with his 'lean' posture, presented in a medium to medium-long shot, all of which connote his stature as an 'object' to be looked at and appreciated. The title of the fashion spread, 'The Cowboy Way', adds further significance. As fashion scholar Shaun Cole theorizes, such sartorial styles as the cowboy traditionally connoted a virile masculinity and the qualities of toughness, aggression and strength associated with it.[48] However, the cowboy is reinvented as a youthful, slender and elegant male fashion model in Popeye, a male aesthetic largely echoed in Milkboy's blog picture, which I referred to at the beginning of this chapter.

In order to make sense of these differences, it is useful to refer to the theory of 'format' and 'product' as articulated by Keiko Okamura. This theory allows a cultural form to be seen as a 'format' when becoming transculturally accepted. This standardized 'format' becomes a carrier of a local culture, making its characteristics visible, and comparable with those of other cultures.[49] In line with this theory, a Caucasian male model in the D&G clothes (the 'formats') becomes transnational, and then 'localized' in Japanese culture (as in the form of *Popeye*). When the 'format' is then combined with local aesthetic ideals, it engenders a male image largely favoured in Japan. The 'product' of this transcultural flow reflects an emphasis on the fusion of a youthful and slender male image, a quality yet to be fully favoured in European and American mainstream fashion scenes. These differences perceived in modes of male aesthetic sensitivities allude to the ideas of cultural hybridization and 'glocalization', informing us that local aesthetics projected upon models gracing Japanese men's magazines, regardless of their nationality or race, should not be disregarded.[50] At the same time, such a view also rings an alarm bell and reminds us that we should not fall into simple cultural essentialism.

In Chapter 2, I demonstrated that the target readerships of these Japanese men's publications are in their late teens to early twenties. Therefore, the male images that appear within these Japanese magazines tend to be situated between boyhood and manhood. Except for youth subculture styles, European and American scholarship on fashion still tend to treat males in their teens and twenties, as well as those in their thirties or older, as a 'collective entity' when referring to the issue of men and fashion, and thus it has yet to offer full analysis of young male styles in specific age segments. Contrary to this tendency, the concept of young men in terms of stricter age segments have been important to some scholars who focus on Japanese men and appearance. Such youthful masculine aesthetics might, for example, imply Japanese young men's attempts to reject an older mode of masculinity. According to Miller, '[t]he model of maleness being opposed [to the youthful, suave one] is age-graded, associated with an older generation of *oyaji* (old men) with different values and aspirations.'[51] The images of males embellishing these Japanese men's fashion magazines, including the 'ordinary' young men pictured on the streets of Japan, make a vivid contrast to the widely circulated images of uniformly worn-out, older men in Japan. Here the mode of masculinity associated with older males most likely points to that of the 'salaryman'. In a derogatory sense, a certain kind of older salaryman is typified as a symbol of unpleasant masculinity, with frumpy clothes and crude mannerisms.[52]

The 'salaryman' masculinity is said to have embodied the dominant discourse around masculinity in modern Japan, particularly since World War Two with such qualities as 'loyalty, diligence, dedication, self-sacrifice, [and] hard work'.[53] Idealized portrayals of the 'salaryman' as masculine, austere and sexually virile, are prevalent in Japanese popular culture, particularly the ones targeted at middle-aged men.[54] According to Romit Dasgupta in his study of 'salaryman', such representations are more likely the mirror-image of the ridiculed and caricatured images of tired, weak and shabby middle-aged man.[55] Typically, a 'salaryman' devotes his time to his company, and thus would have little time to spend with his family, let alone on his appearance.[56]

Importantly, some argue that younger generations of Japanese men believe this lifestyle to be inadequate.[57] The burst of the bubble economy in 1991 and subsequent recession in the early 1990s, along with changes in the status and rights of women, are often given as direct causes of the decline in the legitimacy of this once hegemonic, 'salaryman' masculinity.[58] One way Japanese young men show their opposition to this older mode of masculinity is through fashion. Although there are stylistic variations in *Popeye, Men's non-no* and *Fineboys*, the concept of elegance inscribed to the 'Neo-Edwardian Dandyism' is one style associated with this 'rebellion'.

Boyish reinvention of the 'Neo-Edwardian' dandy style

Exemplified by such figures as Cecil Beaton, 'Edwardian Dandyism' appreciated elegance, grace and sophistication with a handful of mannerisms retrieved from the past, particularly from the Regency period. Although it is not completely a unified style, the orthodoxy of the style, as Sean Nixon describes of the 1980s revival of 'Edwardian male style' in the UK fashion scene, consists of 'taupe, cream and beige jackets and trousers set off with coloured silk ties, cravats and waistcoats. Courduroy [sic] and brogues compliment [sic] the soft edges of a cream raincoat and a straw hat'.[59] The importance of this suave style in contemporary Japanese fashion culture is that the 'Edwardian Dandy styles', once ascribed to certain social classes in England, have been claimed in contemporary Japan as neat yet youthful and rather casual men's fashion.

The adoption of elegant fashion as a form of revolt against other notions of masculinity has also been exemplified by Takuya Kimura, singer, dancer, actor and member of the longtime Japanese boy band SMAP. Kimura is captured in a distinct fashion in the May 2008 issue of *Popeye*.[60] He is dressed in a loud Gucci check suit, shirt, tie, knit sweater and shoes, completed with a straw hat. In the black-and-white photo, Kimura is sitting cross-legged on a modern chair, holding a walking stick. More 'relaxed' appropriation of this 'Edwardian Dandy' style with a modern nuance is also found in the April 2010 issue of *Men's non-no*.[61] In a fashion spread titled 'United Arrows White Label: Wearing the Suits Freely! Daily!', one of the models is pictured wearing a black jacket with a *gilet*, a blue shirt and a pair of indigo corduroy trousers, completed with a check bow tie and a hat. The elegant aesthetics conveyed in these images are reminiscent of famous *fin de siècle* dandies who imposed a direct influence on their Edwardian descendants, notably Oscar Wilde and Aubrey Beardsley in the case of Kimura, and the young Lord Alfred Bruce Douglas in that of the *Men's non-no* model.

According to Ellen Moers, author of *The Dandy: Brummell to Beerbohm*, Oscar Wilde made sartorial transitions in the 1880s as 'Professor of Aesthetics' with a costume of 'knee breeches, drooping lily, flowering green tie, velvet coat and wide, turned-down collar which first made him famous'.[62] In the 1890s, with fame and notoriety achieved, his dress 'became coldly and formally correct. He was content to express individuality (aside from his enormous and oddly proportioned bulk) with a single detail: a green boutonnière, a bright red waistcoat or a turquoise and diamond stud'.[63] In either case, the *fin de siècle* dandyism appreciated elegance, grace and sophistication with a handful of mannerisms retrieved from the past. The concept of elegance and sophistication becomes particularly important in relation to the negative stereotypes of middle-aged Japanese men. Jan Bardsley, in her study of middle-aged Japanese men and their demeanours, points out that negative traits commonly associated with the (middle-aged) 'salaryman' are often due to the lack of elegance and sophistication both in his appearance and in his manners.[64] What, then, is the relevance of European dandyism to Japanese contemporary men's fashion? There is in fact a significant link between dandyism and contemporary Japanese men's fashion. Indeed, the formal introduction of the European sartorial style to Japan, which was initially a male phenomenon, coincided with the eve of the revival of dandyism in the UK in the late nineteenth century.[65]

Art and dress historian Toby Slade suggests that there existed an equivalent to European dandyism in the Japanese context, which allowed Japanese men to adopt and appreciate the aesthetics of the suit.[66] And what is in his mind when Slade is making this statement is *iki*: a traditional aesthetic ideal, believed to have emerged from the worldly and urbane merchant classes in the 1800s, late-Edo period in Japan. Often roughly translated in English as chic or stylish, *iki* is usually used to describe a simple, nonchalantly refined and stylish thing, behaviour or appearance. Upon *iki* as articulated by philosopher Shūzō Kuki, Slade argues that:

> While some reservations can be placed on its exact equivalence, it can be concluded that some of the aesthetic factors that shaped the suit's development in Europe were at work in the Japanese experience as well.[67]

The concept of *iki*, then, 'bears an unmistakable resemblance to Baudelairean dandyism'.[68] This cross-cultural affinity of dandyism reinforces the claim made by Nederveen Pieterse that cultural hybridization expresses cultural affinities rather than 'exoticism' or difference.[69] Rather than blindly following the modes of the past in their untouched form, the elegant styles offered by contemporary Japanese youth fashion culture shows a degree of innovation. I argue that the significance of its elegant aesthetics is twofold: it has modified and restyled *fin-de-siècle* and 'Edwardian' dandy aesthetics as slightly more casual by combining them with other, more nonchalant styles. This has rendered the 'elegant' styles both more youthful and accessible. Likewise, young men's embrace of these neat yet youthful, classic yet attainable styles contributes to the crafting of an image of masculinity that imposes, however indirect, a repudiation of the worn-out, dowdy and 'mature' image of masculinity predominantly ascribed to Japanese men.

A marriage of the casual and elegant: popularization of elegance in contemporary Japanese men's styles

The elegant style considered by these magazines also includes 'European Traditional', 'Mod', 'Ivy' and 'preppy'. These styles correspond well with the *kireime* (neat) and high-casual styles preferred by the three Japanese magazines. Compatibility of the Japanese concept of male elegance with other styles, such as 'Military', 'Rock' or even 'Working Clothes' styles, is another significant quality. These magazines show commingled styles, which add elegance and neatness to rather rough, dishevelled and real styles. The March 2008 issue of *Men's non-no* illustrates this point by offering examples of elegant or chic coordination for the flannel shirt. The feature suggests that wearing it with a tie achieves a chic look; with a matching jacket and trousers comes an elegant look; and layering it with a pastel-coloured pinstripe shirt completes an innocent look.[70] Almost all these magazines include the styles coming with the coordination of a shirt and tie, jacket or pea coat, and thus resembling men's suit styles. According to Hollander, the suit has undergone only slight stylistic modifications since 1820, the time when it was virtually established.[71] Thus, the dominance of the elegant male aesthetics presented in these magazines privileges an allusion to turn of twentieth-century Europe and *fin-de-siècle* dandyism, which were closely tied with the original dandy movement that occurred in late eighteenth-century to early nineteenth-century England. What is significant is that such a privileged, suave male aesthetic has been recreated as everyday elegance in Japan. Whether it is an Edwardian-dandy elegance or the insignia of elite Ivy Leaguers, Japanese fashion culture has incorporated it into everyday style, making it available for virtually everyone who can afford it.

Although stylistically different, such elegant styles offered by these magazines correspond conceptually to the mid-1880s British Wildean costume, 'open to the influence of taste, which dictated a return to the Regency ideals of grace, youthfulness, and elegance'.[72] Rather than affirming the relationship between

Figure 3.2 Teenage actor Ryutaro Akimoto looking cute in Milkboy's bow-tie shirt and a pair of sarouel trousers.

Styled by KENJI and photographed by SHINGO. Image reproduced with kind permission of KENJI/ Milkboy.

fatigued, unattractive masculinity and the suit, these magazines show their male readership that they can look youthful, elegant and sophisticated even when dressed in the sober suit. These Japanese men's fashion magazines, then, are able to encourage their male readership to acknowledge the pleasures of looking pleasant. Do these suave males, then, suggest the formation and development of Foucault's theory of a practice of self? If so, can their acquisition of 'the beautiful form in the eyes of others and of themselves' through governing their lives with a set of fashion principles indicate their repudiation of the preconception that men dress for utility rather than aesthetics?[73] If such a preconception reflects conventional sex role ascriptions, do appearance-conscious men who are notable in Japanese fashion culture point to images of masculinity that are less preoccupied with conventional gender roles?

The presence of cute (kawaii) aesthetics, which is increasingly becoming applicable to male fashion styles, has also contributed to the crafting of a context where this image of boyish yet suave, edgy yet classical masculinity is nurtured. This importance is not only visible in fashion magazines, but also is notable in actual fashion houses. A prime example is menswear label Milkboy, the precursor of the modern Japanese street style. What is striking about Milkboy is that it is a paragon of the qualities I have hitherto described in relation to a 'newer' image of male fashionability in contemporary Japan—edgy, boyish, slender, suave and kawaii.

Boyish playfulness and old-world elegance: an aesthetic continuity and transformation of Milkboy

Milkboy was established in 1974, four years after Hitomi Okawa, described by Tiffany Godoy as the 'Muse of Harajuku', opened her shop for ladieswear Milk in Harajuku, Japan.[74] While Japanese mainstream fashion culture was predominantly looking at American casual styles for its inspiration after the hippy movement, Milkboy preferred European, and particularly British, fashion culture as its inspiration. The exceptional and cutting-edge style of Milkboy is evident in its first shop interior designed by influential designer Shirō Kuramata, and visits paid by numerous international designers and artists, including John Lennon and David Bowie in the 1970s and Stephen Jones, Jean Paul Gaultier and Public Enemy in the 1980s. Milkboy has also been known for initiating new trends and movements. While the original Milk brand has been frequented by Vivienne Westwood and was the first shop in Japan to sell Comme des Garçons, Milkboy is the driving force behind Japan's punk boom in the 1990s with its popularization of bondage trousers as 'everyday wear', the 'urahara' boom in the early 2000s, and made famous such fashion labels as Jun Takahashi's undercover/undercoverism.[75]

One notable characteristic of Milkboy is its encompassment of various styles. According to the owner and designer Hitomi, the brand aims to design clothes for the *youth* of each period.[76] The brand's fashion philosophy is to continue designing and creating clothes that a seventeen-year-old boy can understand and thinks cool. Accordingly, the muses of the brand, while they could be celebrities and models, include more 'ordinary' young men such as the label's shop assistants and students.[77] This also alludes to a social affinity between the clothes of Milkboy and the consumer, and so does the sensitivity that bridges Milkboy's brand image and the real lives of its wearers. A degree of change in Japanese young men and their fashion can therefore be observed in Milkboy items over time. This 'elasticity' makes vain the attempt to generalize the label's styles, and there are at least four main stylistic essences that are quite indelible to Milkboy's fashion aesthetics; punk/rock, hip-hop/street, military and the British schoolboy/dandy. Here, what seems particularly noteworthy is these aspects of clothing are, like *Men's non-no*'s commingling of an elegant look and 'work clothing', shaped by a few key words: *kawaii* (cute), boyish, elegant and slender.

The flexibility of Milkboy and its fairly versatile adaptability to given ambiences can mirror the trend of time while retaining its more fundamental aesthetics. A fashion spread dedicated to Milkboy in the December 2006 issue of *Popeye*, styled and directed by Hitomi herself, for example suggests a tougher, 'man-kid', 'hip-hop' style with set-ups of loose fitted sweaters and sweatpants, big accessories and caps, along with more punkish items of plaid trousers and black boots.[78] The models who appear in the spreads, including the brand's shop assistant, fellow designers, a stylist, teenage models, and musicians, are predominantly pictured in the 'face-off' position, most of whom stare at rather than smile to the camera, further upholding the tough, rough, 'man-kid' kind of masculine image. While the designer later recalls that this rather edgy, hard, and masculine style was more like a blend of the magazine's request and her impressions drawn from the models used in the actual photo shoot, the concept of 'man-kidness' and, by implication, a kind of boyishness is significant.[79]

A fashion spread appears in the August 2013 issue of fashion and culture magazine *spoon.*, styled by Kenji and photographed by Shingo (leaders of the Milkboy design and art direction team), that illustrates the brand's preference to a cuter, gentler and more boyish image of masculinity.[80] In the eight-page photo shoot that accompanies a soft-focused, dreamy and highly romantic fashion spread of Milk with popular fashion icon Amo, teenage amateur model Musashi Rhodes, smiling, puts up an umbrella while wearing a three-piece grey regimental jacket, vest and a pair of trousers, and a shirt with a polka dot tie of pale blue. Rhodes is also captured standing straight on an avenuea boulevard, wearing a neat coordination of a white shirt with large black letters spelling 'AMAZING', a pair

Figure 3.3 Musashi Rhodes and Yota Tsurimoto wearing clothes from Milkboy's 2013–14 collection.

Styled by KENJI, photographed by SHINGO, and hair and make-up by Kyouichi Hirota. Image reproduced with the kind permission of KENJI/Milkboy.

of skinny black trousers and loafers; in a medium shot, he shows a faint smile to the camera, wearing a white T-shirt with a print of a cute teddy bear, a pair of beige, floral pattern-like camouflage bondage trousers, a black top hat and a number of accessories. The clean-cut, boyish and rather sweet image of this shoot conceptualizes Hitomi's perception of the brand that Milkboy garments are designed in part for the 'prince' of the girl who dresses in Milk.

The cute but edgy image of boyishness remains unchanged in another fashion spread of Milkboy in the December 2013 issue of *spoon.*, again styled by Kenji and photographed by Shingo under the theme of 'Team Boys' or 'buddy-ness'.[81] Presenting Rhodes and the brand's shop assistant Yota Tsurimoto, both seventeen, as 'buddies' in the setting of an amusement park, the sixteen-page feature story is a commingling of playful teenager and cute, unthreatening and wholesome boyishness. The young men are wearing sartorial items of Milkboy's 2013–14 collection, from a relaxed coordinate of hoodies and a pair of tartan check trousers, to a more sophisticated, schoolboy-like suit with a white shirt, a matching plaid jacket and trousers, and a pair of golden penny loafers (Tsurimoto), and a black, red, blue and white regimental vest and a pair of matching shorts, accompanied by a black pair of penny loafers (Rhodes). The photo shoot captures the young men enjoying activities like playing at a game arcade, eating ice creams and driving go-karts, and in the stunningly cute image of blowing bubbles together (Figure 3.3).

This unique amalgam of light, boyish delinquency and cute, wholesome and youthful suavity is evidence of the brand's aesthetic continuity and transformation. Seeing these recent Milkboy photo shoots, we might be surprised by the fashion brand's translation of the concept of 'cute (*kawaii*)', a typically considered as a 'feminine' attribute, onto men's wear.

Edgy, cute and suave: Milkboy as a candy-box of boys' fashion aesthetics

As already mentioned, a blurring of sartorial boundaries between men and women is an aspect increasingly becoming visible in contemporary Japanese youth fashion culture. And the concept of *kawaii*, which we shall see in detail in the next chapter, can be applied to both men's and women's fashion in Japan. Yet how the brand assimilates the concept into men's wear designs is quite mesmerizing. This aspect is well observed in Milkboy's blog, managed and updated regularly by the brand's staff, and appropriately named *Milkboy Staff's Blog*.[82] In the blog, Milkboy items are described as *kawaii* or cute quite frequently, whether it is a pair of colourful striped socks (28 February 2013), a pair of saxon blue trainers with large white polka dots and pink lining (20 April 2013), a short-sleeved shirt with a big ribbon tie (30 April 2013) or a polka-dotted blouson jacket with fur collar (9 November 2013). The blog, for example, describes the polka-dot pattern of the blouson jacket as 'cute', and it looks *kawaii* when worn with the collar standing up. In addition to these sartorial items, which might be considered rather 'feminine', or even girlish in the conventional sense, Milkboy has also translated the concept of *kawaii* onto more 'masculine' items.

Milkboy has been known for its association with a punk style, particularly famous for bondage trousers, and more recently, hip-hop fashion styles with hoodies and overalls, both of which are generally known as 'masculinist' subcultures. Its bondage skinny trousers, released in 2013, however, come with a number of different patterns, including a floral pattern with shades of blue, and of grey (the latter of which had already sold out when introduced in the blog on 10 July 2013), and a black jersey hoodie is scattered with a vivid pattern of golden bananas and adorable teddy bears (18 March 2013). In this sense, Milkboy has reinvented ostensibly 'masculinist' styles as more cute and pop fashion items. This reinvention indicates that a concept of kawaii has been integrated as one type of 'cool', stylish aesthetics in Japanese men's fashion scene. In other words, Milkboy items can be seen as creatively and effectively using and merging the antithetical poles of 'girlish' and 'masculine' sartorial concepts.

While the label has brought aspects of 'feminine' fashion to men's style, it also signifies the blurring of men's and women's fashion in another way; namely, its cool and cute designs have attracted female customers. Milkboy is the male line of Milk, a women's fashion brand known for its romantic, girlish styles with a 'twist', but Milkboy is also worn by women, including famous icons like pop star Kyary Pamyu Pamyu and fashion model Amo in recent times.[83] According to Kenji of Milkboy's design team and press, women currently occupy approximately 20 per cent of Milkboy consumers.[84] For women customers who wear Milkboy, Hitomi says that Milk is worn by girls who want to be princesses, and Milkboy is taken up by girls who want to dress just like their princes.[85] By the 'prince' she means a beau of that moment, and he can look different depending on the ideal male vision each woman holds. Nonetheless, judging from the photo shoots of the brand, currently the cute and rather androgynous type seems to best express the image of 'Milkboy prince'. Corresponding to this point is a slender silhouette that the label assimilates.

Milkboy stocks loose-fitting items, including sarouel trousers, overalls and large-size hoodies. Yet many of the trousers come in one or two sizes; Slim bondage trousers (27 August 2013), for example, are 98 per cent cotton with 2 per cent elastic fabrics, and come in five different colours and patterns but have two sizes – small with the waist size of 78 cm (31 in.) and medium with an 80 cm waist (31.5 in.). Check pocket trousers that match the dolman Jacket, again, come in two sizes; small with a 76 cm waist (30 in.) and medium that fits a waist size of 80 cm (31.5 in., 31 October 2013). Zip-lined slim trousers (28 September 2013) and Ceremonial trousers (23 December 2013) come in one size with 78 cm and 82 cm (32 in.) waists respectively. This tendency mirrors actuality of the physicality of contemporary Japanese young men. According to surveys conducted by Japan's Ministry of Health, Labour and Welfare, nearly 60 per cent of Japanese men between the ages of twenty and twenty-nine have a waist size of 80 cm or smaller. The highest group, falling between 75 and 80 cm, accounts for 24 per cent, followed by 70–5 cm (22.75 per cent) and 80–5 cm (17.6 per cent).[86] This indicates that Japanese men in this age group predominantly, but not exceptionally, have smaller waists, and Milkboy both reflects and is instrumental in this trend. This confirms the aforementioned point that dress sizes for men and women are increasingly blurring in contemporary Japanese fashion culture. Not only that, the brand's embrace of slender silhouette further reinforces the idea that an androgynous and boyish image is important for Milkboy. This is because a conventional and perhaps widely held view of the androgynous look makes allusion to, as Hollander has pointed out, a kind of beauty belonging to the adolescent male, which is often typified by an exceptionally slender physicality.[87] I believe this can be more complex than that, and I explore a different mode of androgynous look in Chapter 5, but the slender male silhouette gives a definite boyish flavour, and that is what Milkboy espouses.

The length of the forenamed Ceremonial trousers can be adjusted with button tabs on both sides of the trousers, to make them three-quarter length. Especially with the neat and tight silhouette of the matching jacket, this crafts a boyish look. Indeed, Milkboy's suits, such as a plaid Crest jacket and Crest slim trousers, and the aforementioned dolman jacket and check pocket trousers, render the wearer's look significantly boyish, as if alluding to the look of elegant Edwardian schoolboys. This is especially so when coordinated with a pair of penny loafers and a top hat, the latter of which was a bestselling item in late 2013 (Figure 3.4).

Alternatively, more on the elegant side, the coordinate of a regimental jacket, regimental vest and regimental trousers, worn with a pale blue shirt with a matching polka dot tie, as the cover image of this book bespeaks, creates a suave look reminiscent of the 'Neo-Edwardian' dandy. Since the brand philosophy emphasizes the concept of male youthfulness, this cute, slender and boyish 'schoolboy' look is an important one for Milkboy.

As previously mentioned, Hitomi describes her brand philosophy as designing and offering clothes that seventeen-year-old boys can love and understand. The significant meaning of this philosophy is that established fashion brands tend to transform themselves into more high-end fashion identities as both designers and consumers age, which could result in their items gradually 'speaking' less to younger consumers.[88] Kenji states that Milkboy is actually purchased by real seventeen-year-olds as well as older individuals, but the age of seventeen can also be symbolic of youth in a more general sense.[89] In the Japanese social system, seventeen-year-olds are situated in a space one step before going into society. The imagery of boys for whom the brand primarily designs their items is thus situated in a liminal space between boyhood and manhood. The boyish cuteness that is unconstrained of many social trammels accords well with the

Figure 3.4 Musashi Rhodes with a 'Neo-Edwardian' schoolboy look, wearing a dolman jacket, check pocket trousers and a top hat.

Styled by KENJI, photographed by SHINGO, hair and make-up by Kyouichi Hirota. Image reproduced with kind permission of KENJI/Milkboy.

edgy coolness of playful street fashion. Combined with this is a sense of suavity, which is added by items of old-world chic such as a plaid suit and especially a top hat, a wardrobe that G. Bruce Boyer calls a reminder of 'the days of empire and studied elegance' and 'the social ideal of gentility'.[90] Such a stylistic amalgam of diametric opposition – perky, boyish cuteness and manly elegance – epitomizes a distinctive and largely untapped image of youthful Japanese men. The brand's frequent collaborations with such figures as Rhodes, Tsurimoto, boyish-looking actor and former amateur model Yudai Chiba, and teenage actor Ryutaro Akimoto (Figure 3.2) as its preferred models further reinforce this image. A subtle balance between street style coolness and schoolboy cuteness, coated with Edwardian dandy elegance, is an image of masculinity that offers a striking alternative to the images of dowdy and largely unflattering middle-aged 'salaryman' and impuissant, 'passive' young men, both of which tend to have typified the images of modern Japanese males, especially in non-Japanese contexts.

The Milkboy blog almost never mentions romantic desires as a primary motivation to acquire or dress in Milkboy clothes. Obviously, it does not disregard or even refuse such desires. Since Milk and Milkboy stores in Harajuku are located in the same building, and as already mentioned, Milkboy clothes are also purchased by women, the store is frequented by college-age couples, creating a lovely sight of boys shopping together with their girlfriends.[91] That being said, what the brand considers most important is its principle that the wearer enjoys and looks pleasant by wearing nice clothes for themselves, and this should not be achieved by sacrificing functionality for aesthetics. In this sense the brand focuses on the Foucauldian notion of beauty as a practice for one's self, to look good for oneself regardless of what motivations lie behind this desire. By refusing to conform to a set of clichéd assumptions for men and fashion, Milkboy makes men's fashionability significantly more complex. Respecting this point, I argue that the fashionability of Japanese young men conveys and even uplifts both romantic desirability and self-confidence.

Dressing for time and occasion: negotiating romantic desires and narcissistic impulses

Contemporary Japanese men's fashion culture points to at least two possible factors contributing to the rise of fashion-consciousness among young men. Miller argues that '[a]n emphasis on male appearance counters the salaryman reification of men as workers, while women appreciate these new styles because they are aesthetically pleasing and erotically charged'.[92] In similar fashion, Megumi Ushikubo notes that Japanese women in their twenties and thirties are likely to find overtly fashion-minded men, whom they take to be unassertive, calm and willing to share domestic work, to be more attractive romantic partners than older men who tend to be framed within rigidly defined gender roles.[93] Having said that, Ushikubo suggests that the appearance-consciousness among these young men reflects their attempt to gain self-confidence rather than to attract the attention of women.[94] That being so, I suggest that two factors are the keys to understanding this rise of fashion consciousness: a desire to attract admirers and an attempt to gain self-confidence or pleasure.

Importantly, male fears that women will criticize their appearance are one of the primary factors concerning men's beauty consumption in contemporary Japan.[95] These concerns are frequently the subjects of magazine features, such as the aforementioned 'No-no Styles that Turn Off Ggirls'.[96] In this feature, the reader is instructed how to avoid coordinating pieces in unflattering looks. For example, it tells the reader that wearing a loose-fitted top and trousers together would make an unattractive silhouette. Instead, the reader is advised to wear a tight-fitted top and loose-fitted trousers, or vice versa. This story also features a group of young women and their spicy, scrutinizing comments on each outfit. These magazines, particularly *Fineboys*, are predominantly concerned with the looks and styles that presumably attract young women. At the same time, a fashion feature in the April 2010 issue of *Men's non-no* introduces styles and coordinates that are designed to make pleasant impressions on both men and women.[97]

In similar fashion, a feature story about bodybuilding, which these magazines offer sporadically, particularly in the summer, is often framed within the discourse of the heterosexual, and young women's evaluations are frequently used as motivations.[98] But the April 2008 issue of *Popeye* offers a kickboxing feature that instructs the readership to build a slender body that fits tight-silhouetted clothes.[99] In other words, this *Popeye* feature tells us that Japanese young men dress not only to attract admirers but also for their own desire and pleasure. This view corresponds with Milkboy's, which emphasizes a sense of pleasure gaining from wearing clothes one likes as an important motivation for the male customer. This not only indicates that Japanese young men's fashion culture persuades their participants to dress to make themselves feel attractive, along with presenting a good impression on other individuals, and that taking pleasure in clothes enhances their self-assurance. Its pedagogy around crafting a fashionable self for both the eyes of the other and for themselves by following a set of principles and regulations, and hence governing one's life, also endorses Foucault's idea of a practice of self.[100]

Valerie Steele emphasizes, in relation to Victorian women's fashion, that 'attractive dress gave its wearer considerable self-confidence, which contributed to an improved appearance'.[101] This is what Japanese men's fashion attempts to convey. These two possible driving forces of male fashion-consciousness are also in the process of negotiation. A prime example is a 2007 *Fineboys* article on fragrances that offers a number of the latest colognes for specific situations, including those to be worn at school and on dates.[102] In this sense, these men's fashion magazines revolve around the negotiation process between the two forces of romantic desire and narcissistic impulses.

Japanese men's fashion magazines do not entirely disregard 'hegemonic' masculine tones (as, for example, *Men's non-no* often accentuates, by saying 'if you are a man . . .' in its feature stories). Unlike the Milkboy blog, magazines like *Fineboys* and *Choki Choki* also instruct their male readers not to be too fashion conscious. This is particularly notable in 'what girls like/dislike about boys' styles' feature stories. These features repeatedly cite young women as saying that although they like men who take care of their appearances, they do not like men who are exceedingly and explicitly appearance-conscious, or who wear items that explicitly connote 'femininity' or 'girlishness'. For instance, the 'No-no Styles for Girls' feature story in *Fineboys* tells the reader that college-aged women have voted for a frilled shirt and a skirt as the items they want men to wear the least. According to the magazine, young women find the frilled shirt too 'girlish' (*onnanoko-ppoi*), and they think the skirt does not look good on men unless worn by those with an exceptional sense of fashion.[103]

While the skirt is rarely featured as a men's outfit in men's fashion magazines like *Fineboys* and *Men's non-no*, the frilled shirt is sometimes depicted as an 'elegant' item.[104] What is striking is that Milkboy's beautiful Frill shirts are described in the blog as airy, elegant, gorgeous and unisex (25 January 2012), and apparently do not pose any threat to the wearer's masculine identity. Hence, fashion houses like Milkboy have even more relaxed attitudes towards the relationship between men and fashion. Importantly, '[h]istorically, attention to male beauty [has] not [been] unusual in Japan'.[105] As for the relative lack of emphasies on 'hypermasculine' traits and activities in contemporary Japanese men's fashion culture, there may 'be less stigma attached to men looking feminine in Japan'.[106] Thus, within a broader historical context, fashion has not necessarily been treated as a 'female-only' trait in Japan. This indicates that the boundaries between 'masculine' and 'feminine' are placed differently in Japanese youth culture. The significance of these representations is further emphasized by a fundamental role of clothes to demarcate and manifest gender distinctions as an imaginative necessity.

The established hetero-romantic influence on (young) men and their fashion consumption might explain the significantly different attitudes Japanese men display towards fashion compared to their Euro-American equivalents, where the strong ties between fashion practices and a gay subculture are assumed.[107] If we recall the idea put forward by Sandra L. Bem that a group of men customarily marginalize homosexual men, let alone women, in order to affirm and strengthen their 'male' identities, it can be deduced that these men tend to have ambivalent feelings for fashion consumption.[108] This is because fashion consumption in Anglophone culture is stereotypically deemed as being associated with women and homosexuals, the 'others' of these heterosexual men, and hence consuming it might impose a threat to their 'masculine' identities. This also offers an explanation for the allegedly ironic yet strong emphasis on 'conventional' masculinity and on heterosexuality, notably predatory attitudes towards women, still found in Anglophone men's lifestyle magazines.[109]

As we have seen in Chapter 1, the desire of men and women to express a clear sartorial distinction between the two gender categories, which has occurred periodically in the European history of dress, would usually emerge when the visual differences between men's and women's clothes are blurred.[110] Slade, moreover, argues that one of the appeals the European three-piece-suit had to Japanese men in the late nineteenth century was its ability to offer clear sartorial distinctions between male and female. This would appeal to Japanese men, since the Japanese kimono was perceived as relatively vague about gender distinctions.[111] In other words, the existing notion that assumes male indifference to fashion, and ambivalence in male interests in fashion or appearance, possibly reflects the instable nature of 'masculinity' or, more precisely, of gender. 'Masculinity' might be so flimsy that it needs visual (and hence explicit) divides from 'femininity' in order to sustain it, and vice versa.

Since the requirements of sartorial distinction point to the instability of gender – in this case 'masculinity' – 'feminine' sartorial elements, when excessively adopted or incorporated in men's fashion, might be perceived as inflicting a threat to men's heterosexual 'masculine' identity. As the editor of now discontinued British men's magazine *Loaded Fashion* Adrian Clark said in 2005:

> Experimenting with colour is one of the few opportunities men have today to freely express themselves without ridicule. It is, therefore, a pity that many choose to limit their palettes to stereotypical masculine hues, such as black, grey, indigo and natural shades.[112]

Arguably, both the Japanese men's fashion magazines and Milkboy's perceptions of the young male and what he likes to wear offer an alternative to this tendency.

To what extent does this change in Japanese male aesthetic sensitivities reflect the actual conception of gender relations among Japanese youth? Miller suggests that although Japanese young men have changed in their appearances and their aesthetic sensibility, 'it has done little to alter the structure of basic gender relations'.[113] A young man 'will still expect the women in his life to fulfil traditional and subservient gender roles'.[114] More optimistically, Ushikubo suggests that both Japanese men and women of younger generations are considerably less concerned with traditional gender roles.[115] There is, however, one thing that is clear through studying the aspects of contemporary Japanese young men's fashion culture: a stylish outfit gives its wearer pleasure and confidence, and men too, wish to be aesthetically appreciated. Dress is, to recall what Elizabeth Wilson has said, the cultural metaphor for the body through which we manifest our identity into our cultural context, and it constantly demarcates our conceptions of gender and its boundaries.[116] The influences of the suave male aesthetics flourishing in contemporary Japanese culture on the structure of actual gender relations thus remains to be seen.

Conclusion

At the beginning of this chapter, I referred to Flügel, who contends that recognizing and valuing the gaze of women would make heterosexual men's fashion more progressive and attractive. As we have seen, the male aesthetics flourishing among young Japanese men, as evident in Japanese men's fashion publications and menswear labels like Milkboy, are highly favoured by Japanese women. Yet fashion is not only based on young men's wish to attract the female gaze, but also their desire to look good and to increase their self-confidence through their enhanced physical appearance.[117] For example, the popularity of elegant, 'Neo-Edwardian' dandy aesthetics reinforces the view that a group of young men hope to identify themselves with a mode of masculinity other than the more established 'salaryman' masculinity. At least for younger generations, chic, fashionable, elegant and even feminine outward appearance, to a certain degree, does not necessarily threaten 'masculine' identities. Instead it recasts notions of masculinity for a new age. Their incorporation of some 'feminine' sartorial items into their styles suggests that the boundaries between the two gender categories are placed differently in Japanese youth culture.

Since male heterosexuality does not necessarily conflict with beauty consumption in contemporary Japanese society, young men do not need to justify their engagement with fashion. At the same time, through the negotiating process between young men's desire to attract admirers and their own hedonistic pleasures, Japanese men's fashion culture presents fashion interests and consumption as both enjoyable and a strategy to enhance self-esteem. In this sense, adoring oneself in nice clothes, with stylish hairstyles and delightful perfumes, at least for a certain group of young men, provides confidence and a sense of pleasure. Importantly, this repudiates the anachronistic yet persisting preconception that men are less concerned with clothes than women, and prioritize functionality over aesthetics. It is noteworthy that slender body types are also gaining popularity despite the prolonged preference of the 'hypermasculine' muscularity of male physique in Anglophone cultures. Whether or not this type of male image, as embodied by such male models as Clément Chabernaud (b. 1989) and Andrej Pejic (b. 1991), will become mainstream remains to be seen.

My analysis of aspects of Japanese men's fashion cultures underscores that Japanese adoption of Euro-American male models and clothing styles does not manifest a simple, cultural imperialism in which one cultural aspect infiltrates the other. Rather they unearth the different modes of male aesthetic sensitivities present in Japan. This offers a potential for different approaches to men's fashion and the possibility to create a new, more practical aesthetic. The next chapter will address the Japanese aesthetic concepts of *kawaii* (cute) and *shōjo* (girls). With a case study of Japanese female performers' appropriations of Lewis Carroll's *Alice's Adventures in Wonderland* in their music videos, it will examine the given aesthetic concepts' potential to affirm 'infantile' cute fashion while sustaining senses of agency and autonomy.

4

GLACÉ WONDERLAND: CUTENESS, SEXUALITY AND YOUNG WOMEN*

Kawaii is like love of humanity, you need a certain mental capacity, strength and experiences to appreciate the fragile.
—HITOMI of Milk and Milkboy, 2013.[1]

In a song named 'Bloomin'!', the sugary voice of Tomoko Kawase flavours this slightly kitsch, overly sweet candy-box of lyrics.[2] She sings:

> Bloomin' flowers dance with me; So darling, you're my fantasy; Shower of jelly beans pouring heavily; My lips are here to stay; Tonight. . . if the stars flow; Fate forbids us to part Ah Ah.

Whether she sings it on stage, or in the famed music video where she takes up the image of Lewis Carroll's immortalized heroine Alice, she wears an air of cuteness, or *kawaii* as it is called in Japan.[3] What renders her performance puzzling for the eyes of those unfamiliar with Japanese culture is perhaps the almost complete absence of sexuality or assertiveness. The 27-year-old Kawase, in the guise of one of her alter egos Tommy February, crafts a look that unites the girlishness of the school girl and the infantile cuteness of the preadolescent. Significantly, whether wearing a flowing, baby pink knee-length tunic or a lace-trimmed, tight-silhouetted pastel grey pinafore dress, Kawase's girlish style is not about overt sexual allure. The significance of such a cute representation is dramatically different to the 'kinder-whore' look of the 1990s, and more recent

*Parts of this chapter first appeared as 'Being Alice in Japan: performing a cute, "glrlish" revolt' in *Japan Forum* (26, Issue 2 [2014], pp. 265–85).
DOI: http://www.tandfonline.com/doi/full/10.1080/09555803.2014.900511). I thank Taylor & Francis for their permission to include it here.

vogue of 'porno-chic' style in Euro-American culture, where women, presumably young, are represented in scantily clad ways, with explicit references to pornography and pole dancing.[4] The concept of cuteness, particularly when it is mingled with sweet, girlish and 'infantile' qualities, is deemed as unfavourable, demeaning or even pathological in Euro-American culture. In this chapter, I argue the opposite, namely that a certain kind of the Japanese concept of *kawaii* can be interpreted as a 'delicate revolt' that softly and implicitly opposes and subverts stereotyped preconceptions connected to sexuality and gender.

I explore the particularly Japanese concepts of *kawaii* and *shōjo* (girls), which allow Japanese women to retain a girlish, almost 'infantile' cuteness without emphasizing mature female sexuality. A group of Japanese mainstream female performers have taken up the performative nature of these concepts, crafting and parodying the cute 'look', which consequently enables them to operate in a position that moves between sweet, non-sexual and autonomous conditions. In short, I argue that the sweet and largely asexual representations of young women as demonstrated by the performers might offer a representation of youthful femininity that is not too sexualized, too demurely 'feminine' or too 'masculine', but comfortably situated somewhere between these three positions.

This chapter begins with a general overview of the concept of *kawaii*, explaining how this concept is a manifestation of interactions between Japanese and Euro-American cultures. The first section also looks at another Japanese aesthetic concept of *shōjo* (girls), which might refer to the subtle state between 'child' and 'adult', 'male' and 'female', and is comparatively detached from heterosexual economy. The significance of *shōjo*, which I will argue, lies in the possibility that it allows Japanese women to appear girlish and cute while being segregated from obvious sexualization. Through an analysis of three Japanese music videos, the second section develops these ideas further. In particular, by examining how these three female performers adopt and appropriate the imagery of Alice, this section argues that 'infantile' cute and girlish appearances do not automatically invoke passivity, vulnerability or sexualized objectification. The final section aims to explore the idea of the *kawaii* aesthetic as a 'soft revolt'. It seeks to establish the idea that the amalgamation of 'asexual' cuteness and girlish reinvention of 'authenticity' can serve as an alternative to the established multiple binaries of aggression, sexualization and modesty in which women tend to be represented.

In the name of *kawaii*

For many both in and outside Japan, the character of Hello Kitty (1974) embodies the concept of *kawaii*, which has come to represent, at least partially, the quintessence of Japanese popular culture.[5] Fashion magazine *Numéro Tokyo* has stated that Hello Kitty embodies a particular concept of cuteness that is loved and appreciated by adults and children both in and outside Japan.[6] The application of the Japanese word *kawaii* is, however, contested, contentious and above all amorphous. As Laura Miller points out, 'although literally the word kawaii means "cute" it has a much broader semantic meaning than does the English term "cute"'.[7] This sentiment is shared by scholar of Asian studies, popular culture and psychology, Brian J. McVeigh. In *Wearing Ideology: State, Schooling and Self-presentation in Japan*, he precisely summarizes Japanese cuteness as:

> baby cuteness; very young cuteness; young cuteness; maternal cuteness; teen cuteness; adult cuteness; sexy cuteness; pornography cuteness; child pornography cuteness; authority cuteness; and corporate cuteness.[8]

Kawaii is not only used to describe straightforwardly hyperbolic cute but can also combine the elements of cute and grotesque or erotic qualities (e.g. *guro-awaii/kimo-kawaii* and *ero-kawaii*).[9] The diversity of *kawaii* aesthetics can also be illustrated by young women's fashion in which different kinds of *kawaii* exist for different purposes. For example, the concept of *kawaii* can display different connotations depending on the styles endorsed by different fashion magazines.[10] In the magazines known for 'conservative' styles, *kawaii* signifies an aesthetic quality that is precisely woven together with the concept of *mote-kei*, a 'conservative' style that, without displaying obvious sexual allure or individuality, is designed to attract men. In magazines associated with less conservative styles, the concept is used to describe a more mainstream-individual style. To put it simply, the aesthetics of *kawaii* in the former case signify the 'uniform' qualities that are believed to attract desirable men, whereas *kawaii* becomes more individualistic in the latter case. But in simple definitional terms, *kawaii* refers to an aesthetic that celebrates sweet, adorable, simple, infantile, delicate and pretty visual, physical or behavioural qualities.[11]

One of the core elements of the *kawaii* aesthetic is to appreciate 'youthfulness', and one archetype of *kawaii* fashion is that it is 'deliberately designed to make the wearer appear childlike and demure'.[12] This includes bright-coloured clothes for boys and pastel shades with lace for girls.[13] Not unexpectedly, the concept of *kawaii* is applicable to men as much as to women, and this is increasingly obvious, as Chapter 3 indicates. The unisex qualities of *kawaii* aesthetics are also evident in styles favoured by *Olive*, a now- discontinued subcultural magazine for 'cosmopolitan' girl culture, which, in fashion scholar Reiko Koga's opinion, marks the beginning of *kawaii* as a mode of fashion in the 1980s.[14] Two of the three main styles subscribed to by *Olive* were frill and lace-adorned, 'romantic' girlish dresses and a cute 'boyish' style with very short hair, the latter of which was said to be influenced by such popular icons in the 1980s as The Checkers, an all-male rock/pop band who were frequently costumed by Milkboy, and the pop idol Kyoko Koizumi.

Fashion styles with notable *kawaii* essences have been present in Japanese culture for a long time, at least from the 1970s, as evident in the popularity of the clothing brands such as Hitomi's Milk (1970), Isao Kaneko's Pink House (1972) and Rei Yanagikawa's Shirley Temple (1974). Milk in particular has set a modern example of 'glocalizing' European fashion forms and adding 'Japanese' style to them.[15] Fashion editor and consultant Tiffany Godoy articulates this point as follows:

> Milk took in all of fashion's disparate parts and made its own combination on looks, creating something entirely new. Before Milk, no one would ever say that punk is cute. But in Okawa's hands, it really was. She took tracksuits from the States and punk fashions from the U.K., redesigned them to fit smaller Japanese bodies and revised them into something entirely new and of the moment.[16]

The name Milk conceptualizes Hitomi's principle that things that look fragile but vigorous inside are *kawaii* while things that look strong both in and outside are uncool.[17] Her interpretation of *kawaii* is worth including here: the concept is like a modern-day *wabi-sabi*, which is easy for individuals born and raised in Japan to grasp, but problematic for those without such backgrounds. For Hitomi, *kawaii* can be something infantile, fragile and perhaps imperfect, and particularly those whose culture praises maturity over infantile fragility and imperfection would require a certain mental capacity and experiences in order to be tolerant of, comprehend and adore such qualities. In this sense, for Hitomi, *kawaii* and appreciating that concept is almost equal to the etymological definition of philanthropy – that is, 'love of humanity'. Equally strikingly, Milk integrated *kawaii* fashion aesthetics with their emphasis on sweetness, without overly hinting at sexual allure. 'Milk clothes were – and continue to be – girly, romantic, and feminine but not sexual. All these elements are the base for what would later become *kawaii* culture', notes Godoy.[18]

The mid-1970s saw the vogue of romantic folklore style among young women. A 'Japanized' hippy style, this fashion embraced a simple, dreamy aesthetic resembling the worlds of Lucy Montgomery's *Anne of Green Gables* (1908) and Johanna Spyri's *Heidi* (1880).[19] The subculture of *Olive* in the 1980s and 1990s, and the revival of romantic, floating folkloric dresses of pastel shades around 2010, followed.[20] Similarly, in Japanese popular music culture, female 'pop idols' in the early 1980s were closely associated with *kawaii* aesthetics. Pastel-coloured, frilly and lace dresses were their unofficial uniform, connoting innocent, girlish femininity as well as artificiality.[21] Although the concept of *kawaii* is most prominently ascribed to Japanese culture, these fashion styles often combine some European elements, be they romanticized or realistic. In this chapter, I focus largely on this type of *kawaii* aesthetics, perhaps with a faint 'twist', which can softly challenge and even subvert the common ways in which young women are perceived, understood and represented.

What is noteworthy is that Euro-American cultural influences are perceived as important ingredients of *kawaii* aesthetics.[22] Alessandro Gomarasca, for example, implies that 'Kawaii appears in the moment in which the shōjo bunka (culture of teenage girls) encounters the Euro-American culture of cute, the playful, childish aesthetic imported to Japan from the West'.[23] Although Gomarasca was referring to the post-war period when making this statement, the case of the illustrator, doll maker, fashion designer and stylist Jun'ichi Nakahara indicates that Euro-American influences and subsequent Japanese appropriation shaped the modern concept of kawaii even before the 1940s.[24]

Nakahara (1913–83), particularly celebrated for his illustrations and fashion designs in girls' magazines, continuously promulgated the European-inspired visual images of elegantly dressed, ladylike young women. As the lavish image of Figure 4.1 illustrates, his ideal girls are exquisitely dressed, upper-class European with delicately coiffed hair, tiny ribbons, thin waists and long limbs.[25]

Nakahara has also imposed a notable degree of influence upon Japanese fashion designers. Such fashion figures as Hanae Mori, Kenzo Takada, Keita Maruyama and Isao Kaneko have declared their admiration of, if not influenced by, Nakahara.[26] The girlish art of Nakahara points to the Japanese adoption and interpretation of European cute culture even before the post-war period. There is also a possibility that an aesthetic concept similar to kawaii, one that admires anything young, small, fragile and cute, was present in Japanese culture as far back as the Heian period (AD 794 to 1185).[27]

Indeed, Japanese culture has long placed aesthetic importance on the state of youthfulness. Japanologist and scholar Donald Keene has noted that one of the four characteristics in Japanese culture that he thinks have special importance is 'suggestion', which grants immense importance to beginnings and ends, such as the crescent and waning moon, or buds and strewn flowers.[28] This is because 'the full moon or the cherry blossoms at their peak do not suggest the crescent or the buds (or the waning moon and the strewn flowers), but the crescent and the buds do suggest full flowering'.[29] While it might be too extreme to assume a direct link between the Heian aesthetic and contemporary cute, this nonetheless alludes to the possibility that kawaii, which predominantly appreciates something small, fragile and young, could be deep-rooted in Japanese culture rather than a more recent phenomenon.

The concept of kawaii and its Euro-American influences are most visible in the medium of comics (manga), which as Jaqueline Berndt, an art and media studies scholar specializing in manga aesthetics, rightly puts it, 'is . . . the result of intercultural exchange' between 'Chinese ink-painting, European tableau with its central perspective, European caricature, and American superhero comics'.[30] Museum curator Mizuki Takahashi argues that it was illustrator Macoto Takahashi who, through the influences of Nakahara's art, shaped the aesthetic style of shōjo manga including the introduction of glamour, fashion and visual conventions such as starry eyes, which can be described as the intersection between early 1900s shōjo culture and more modern kawaii aesthetic.[31] As a matter of fact, this

Figure 4.1 Jun'ichi Nakahara's illustration of a chic and lovely *shōjo*.

kind of girlish, *kawaii* aesthetic might be seen as closely related to the concept of *shōjo* (girls) and its slightly anachronistic sister *otome* (maiden).

A liminal space of dreaming: Japanese concept of *shōjo*

The term *shōjo* frequently points to a culturally constructed concept.[32] While literally *shōjo* means 'girl or maiden', it is laden with values and history.[33] Masuko Honda, pioneering figure in Japanese girl studies, perceives the state of *shōjo* as the period between girlhood and womanhood, which the girl's imagination turns into a romantic space of liminality where the 'girl' can indulge in a momental reverie unconstrained from social trammels attached to 'womanhood'.[34] It is a culturally constructed space that starts after one's adolescence, which differentiates girls from boys who used to be in the 'same category'.[35] Honda's idea of *shōjo* assigns a degree of independence to the category of adolescent girls and hence separates them from both older and younger women under the name of *shōjo*.

The concept of *shōjo* had originally an ideological purpose, constructed by the Meiji government in the late nineteenth century in order to educate girls to embody *ryōsai kenbo* (good wife, wise mother), an ideology inspired by 'Victorian notions of "true womanhood"' – that is, nineteenth-century European ideas.[36] According to the government, the *shōjo* demonstrated three virtues – 'affection' (*aijō*), 'chastity' (*junketsu*) and 'aesthetics' (*biteki*) – in order to discipline female students between the ages of twelve and seventeen who, until the modernization of the state, would have been either married off or put to domestic work.[37] Regardless of the effectiveness of the concept as a regulatory principle, *shōjo* can refer to 'a hyper-feminine ideal' in the early 1900s.[38] A common image of the *shōjo* 'was often defined in literature and art by qualities associated with femininity at the time – sentimentality, interest in flowers, clothing, dolls, and dreamy thoughts of the moon and stars'.[39] These imageries are both well captured and distributed via the genre of *shōjo* novels and the works of *jojo-ga* (lyrical illustrations) artists such as Yumeji Takehisa (1884–1934) and Kashō Takabatake (1888–1966). Takabatake's modern and sophisticated works, which were partly inspired by Pre-Raphaelite artists, included beautiful male and female, young and mature, but was particularly popular among young women in pre-war Japan (Figure 4.2).[40]

Notably, many of these qualities are amicably parodied by Kawase in her songs. This is the case in the quote that opens this chapter. The core ingredients of the *shōjo* aesthetics are valid even in the present day. A common form of the *shōjo*, for instance, involves ribbons, frills and flowers.[41] It can be deduced from these cultural representations that a clothing form that is adorned with frills and lace has occupied a special place in Japanese girl cultures for many decades.

What is striking about this girlish concept is its presumed 'asexual' qualities. One of the three virtues of *shōjo* that the Japanese government imposed in the late nineteenth century, as sociologist Shūko Watanabe points out, was chastity.[42] Over a hundred years, this has seemingly been modified to connote a kind of innocence and 'asexuality'. For instance, John Whittier Treat, in his seminal essay on Banana Yoshimoto's early novels, claims:

In English, gender is binary – at every stage one is either 'male' or 'female'. But in Japan, one might well argue that *shōjo* constitute their own gender, neither male nor female but rather something importantly detached from the productive economy of heterosexual reproduction.[43]

As gender and cultural studies scholar and specialist of girl studies Catherine Driscoll says, caution with such a claim is required.[44] But it is no coincidence that ambiguity in gender has been a strong theme in *shōjo manga* since the 1950s, including Osamu Tezuka's *Princess Knight* (Ribon no kishi, 1953–6; revised version, 1963–6), whose protagonist is born with both a boy's and girl's hearts,

Figure 4.2 Kashō Takabatake's beautiful girl with flowers.

© The Yayoi Museum. With thanks to Asako Takabatake (The Kasho Museum).

as a famous but not the only example. Elaborating upon Treat's idea, the anthropologist Karen Nakamura and the journalist Hisako Matsuo further contend that '[p]erforming *shōjo* [can be] one active and dynamic way that Japanese women can control their sexuality'.[45]

When the concept of *shōjo* was initially implemented, girls from certain class backgrounds, for whom this concept of *shōjo* were most likely created, took advantages of this 'good wife, wise mother' ideology and secured their opportunity to be educated. This is because they could argue strongly that education was a requirement for becoming a 'wise mother'.[46] Melanie Czarnecki and Alisa Freedman have noted that the position of schoolgirls in the era allowed for latitude and self-establishment for some girls, and drew both fierce criticism and racy curiosity from the public.[47] But Czarnecki argues upon the common accusations of schoolgirl prostitution at the time, which should be read as 'the desire for an education was such that some girls would willingly prostitute themselves [only] to obtain one'.[48] The concept of *shōjo*, therefore, can be read as having two faces – one being an idealized construction imposed by older males, and the other being embraced and possibly manipulated by girls themselves. With the latter explanation, crafting and performing *shōjo* through gestures, and particularly clothes, allows Japanese women to present themselves as being segregated from obvious sexualization. The concept of *kawaii* shares this conceptual duplicity of *shōjo*. Miller contends that there is a difference between 'cute' as a cultural aesthetic circulating in Japanese girl culture, and 'cute' as an aesthetic appropriated or manufactured by companies such as Sanrio.[49] Within Japanese girl culture, 'cuteness often gets modified, parodied, or deliberately inflated in diverse ways', thus implying autonomous controls of girls.[50]

A certain degree of risk is, however, involved when one is perceived as acting or appearing too innocently cute or girlish. The term *burikko* (or its predecessor *kamatoto*) is a Japanese label used to describe women who exhibit feigned and sugary innocence and cuteness, particularly via manipulation of vocal pitches and gestures.[51] Although sometimes considered an obsolete word, the concept has nevertheless survived to the present day, and this label can be derogatory. Miller's insights into *burikko* indicate three significances: that it is a performance of exaggerated girlish femininity, that this 'downplays or masks the adult sexuality of the woman doing it', and that it is a double-edged sword.[52] Performing *burikko* might allow a woman to assert her position in an appropriate situation. It could also stigmatize her for being cunningly pretentious and immature, if done inappropriately.

It might be tempting to consider *shōjo* as a clearly established, 'organic' category – the third gender perhaps, as authors like Treat are inclined to do. However, we must acknowledge that the term *shōjo* is a very ambiguous one, as the term is often used for its literal meaning of a 'maiden/girl' as well. Nevertheless, as these authors argue, *shōjo*/'girls' are often considered as asexually 'pure', comparatively autonomous beings, though it does not necessarily mean *shōjo* are immune from either eroticization or the objectifying male gaze. But as Sharon Kinsella indicates, often it is the contrary that is suggested.[53] Lewis Carroll's Alice in his two famous novels might be described as an embodiment of an idealized *shōjo*. Although she was a creation of Victorian England, Alice has enjoyed a long-lasting popularity in Japanese culture. In the next sections I shall look at Alice and analyse her as an embodiment of the Japanese concept of *shōjo*. I ask, what has made Alice popular in Japanese culture, as an icon of *shōjo*? I shall then proceed to examine contemporary Japanese performers' appropriations of the character Alice in their music videos. Particular attention will be paid to how they demonstrate ground-breaking representations of cute yet 'asexual' femininity through their performances of Alice.

Alice's voyage to the empire of the sun

Lewis Carroll's two books featuring Alice have had a strong presence in Japan since the first Japanese translation of *Through the Looking-Glass* appeared as a sequential novel of eight episodes published in *Youth's World* (*Shōnen sekai*), a magazine for boys throughout 1899.[54] Maruyama Eikan's *Fantastic Tales of Ai* (*Ai-chan no yume monogatari*), published in 1910 by Naigai shuppan kyōkai, is said to have been the first complete translation of *Alice*. This 209-page book with Tenniel's illustrations where the heroine is called Ai instead of Alice indicates the difficulty of fully translating Carroll's word play and puns into Japanese.[55] Nonetheless, the Japanese literary world's fascination with *Alice* has continued, and nearly 200 editions of Japanese *Alice* and *Looking-Glass* (including reissues) have been published between 1908 and 2004.[56] The current popularity of Alice is largely thanks to Sir John Tenniel's celebrated illustrations (1865 and 1872) and Walt Disney's now classic film *Alice in Wonderland* (1951), which was first released in Japan in 1952.

One of the arenas where the imagery of Alice has been a colourful and enduring inspiration is in the world of fashion. Most notably, Japanese *Lolita* fashion, which I shall examine in Chapter 5, has displayed the compatibility of the elaborate version of historic 'little girl' dress and the style's sartorial philosophy. In a less 'decorative' example, the October 2007 edition of *Sō-en*, one of the oldest Japanese high fashion magazines, offered twenty-two pages of fashion spreads and feature articles on the theme of *Alice*. With particular regard to Czech filmmaker Jan Švankmajer and his surreal cinematic visualization of *Alice* (*Něco z Alenky*, 1988), this feature story tells how Japanese fashion brands such as Jane Marple (est. 1985) derive inspirations from Carroll's character.[57] The feature story in *Sō-en* moreover endorsed the idea of Alice embodying the idealized image of *shōjo*, saying 'even after 142 years since its publication, Alice exists as the ideal of *shōjo*'.[58] Another Japanese fashion brand known for its girlish styles, Emily Temple Cute, affirms the link between Alice and sweet sartorial aesthetics.[59] In 2009, the brand published *Wonderland*, an eighteen-page catalogue/book in which its 2009–10 winter collection was photographed according to the images of *Alice*.[60]

Filled with layers of tight yet flowing knee-length dresses, long-sleeved polo necks with delicate lace trims, knit cardigans with patterns of ribbons and flowers, striped high socks and a lace headdress, fragments of the girlish sartorial aesthetics envisaged in Emily Temple Cute's *Wonderland* are also captured in the music videos of a number of Japanese young female singers, particularly since the early 1990s. Before proceeding to the analysis of these performances, it is useful to look at the imagery of Alice and the possible factors that have contributed to her popularity in Japan. The popularity of Alice among Japanese culture, especially as an icon of the idealized *shōjo*, is undoubtedly due to the heroine's intricate combination of aloofness, autonomy and girlish appearance.

A Victorian girl with independence: Alice and a sense of autonomy

Although she is a child of seven (and seven and a half in *Through the Looking-Glass*) in Carroll's books, Alice tends to be represented, particularly in illustrations, as a girl in her early adolescence.[61] One of the reasons for this visual 'misrepresentation', apart from the absence of depictions of the heroine's appearance in the original books, can be found in the fairly independent personality of Alice. If we consider the typical concept of *shōjo* as sweet and innocent on the outside, and considerably autonomous on the inside, the imagery of Alice displays similar characteristics. Despite her appearance of being a demure, Victorian child, Alice is depicted as a rather emotionally flat, yet autonomous character. As television and film studies scholar Will Brooker points out:

> the heroine never seems troubled by them [the grotesque inhabitants]. There is no sign that she is terrified, that she fears she won't escape Wonderland alive, that she is ever praying to get out of this place and go back home to the river bank. . . she remains calm, and so the adventure never sinks fully into the 'darkness' that some contemporary critics see in the text.[62]

Driscoll interprets the complexity of Alice, saying she 'is as self-interested as she is generous and is not unambiguously a good girl (i.e., loving, courteous, or trustful). . . the little girl in Carroll is marked by curiosity and delight'.[63] Author, poet and translator Sumiko Yagawa, in the afterword to her Japanese translation of *Alice*, offered her interpretation of Alice as a symbol of loneliness attached to autonomy, indicating that this reading is also shared in Japanese culture.[64] Carroll's Alice is thus neither assertive nor passive, but is rather positioned comfortably in between these two.

Alice's sense of agency is further conveyed by her dress. With regards to Tenniel's illustrations, Elizabeth Ewing, an author of numerous books on fashion history, elucidates this point as follows: 'Alice is a spirited, uninhibited, outspoken little girl, though always a polite one, and her clothes too are unrestricting.'[65] Tenniel's Alice is particularly important since the imagery of Alice as cultural icon was largely fixed by his illustrations. Indeed, the visual qualities that shape our imagination of Alice are not solely the creation of Carroll. This is because the contextual analysis of Carroll's books indicates that they are 'surprisingly vague about the appearance of [their] characters and settings, and [were] designed from the outset to rely on illustrations rather than written description'.[66] In other words, Alice's visual descriptions, let alone the clothes she wears, are rarely delineated in Carroll's original work, and are mostly a creation of John Tenniel whose illustrations accompanied the first edition of *Alice*. Together with the animation of Disney, Tenniel's Alice has become a kind of template for *Alice* illustrators.[67]

The immortalized vision of Alice was not what Carroll imagined. Illustrations of Alice by Carroll's own hands in his original *Under Ground* instead showed her wearing 'a soft, clinging tunic' and he allegedly 'begged Tenniel, "Don't give Alice so much crinoline"'.[68] This illustrates the author's desire to distinguish his Alice clearly from the fashionable young lady of his time. If our images of Alice have been fixed by the illustrations of Tenniel, how exactly did his Alice dress? His Alice is apparently dressed in a fashion current to the time of the book, with a faint hint of the practical future.[69]

Tenniel's Alice and her dress thus convey Victorian girlhood or feminine adolescence.[70] How do we, then, make sense of the popularity of *Alice* in Japan, since the story does not evoke any immediate cultural or periodical similarities to contemporary Japanese culture? I contend that the imagery of Alice as an independent girl with 'infantile' cuteness is a highly appropriate vehicle for women in Japan, let alone artists, to perform and negotiate a compromise between female autonomy and the concept of *kawaii*. Subtly nuanced, sweet aesthetics with no overt hint of female sexual allure is what we notice when viewing the music videos of three Japanese female performers in their homage to Alice.

Being Alice in Japan: music videos of Alisa Mizuki, Tomoko Kawase and Kaela Kimura

Although since the 1970s, several Japanese singers have performed songs with the theme of *Alice* this chapter focuses on three singers who appeared in their own music videos dressed in the fashion redolent of Alice.[71] Alisa Mizuki (b. 1976), Tomoko Kawase (b. 1975, as Tommy February) and Kaela Kimura (b. 1985) offer similar yet distinctive portrayals of Carroll's heroine. One of the earliest examples of *Alice* adaptation in a Japanese music video is found in Alisa Mizuki's *Town of Eden* (Eden no machi, 1991). Mizuki, child actor and fashion model since the age of five, made her successful singing debut in 1991 with the CD titled *Legendary Girl* (Densetsu no shōjo).[72] Her second single, *Town of Eden* was released in Japan in August same year. At the time of release, she was fourteen. The lyrics tell a story of innocent, fleetingly romantic memories that are seemingly lost, and the melody is rather cheerful and poppy.

Ten years later, the imagery of Alice made another appearance, this time with Tommy February in her song 'Bloomin'!'. Tommy is an alter ego persona of Tomoko Kawase, vocalist for Japanese pop rock band The Brilliant Green. Known for its sweet synthetic-pop sound and hyperbolic romantic lyrics inspired by and playfully parodying American teen films and 1980s American and British pop music, Tommy is a part of Kawase's solo project.[73] Preppy-looking February is contrasted by her other alter ego, Tommy Heavenly, who is characterized as darker, slightly more aggressive, and has a Goth sound and demeanour.[74] Five years after Tommy, in 2007 Japanese pop rock singer and model Kaela Kimura released her third album *Scratch*, which topped the charts in February of that year. One of the songs on the album, 'Snowdome', whose music video was initially included in the limited edition of the album, offers Kimura's visual rendition of Alice.[75]

The imagery of *Alice* adopted in these music videos comes with variations. Apart from the obvious image of falling down into darkness, which is present in all the three clips, these videos do not straightforwardly visualize the narrative of *Alice*. This reflects the nature of music videos, which lack narrative structures like those found in classic Hollywood films.[76] Thus other aspects such as clothes becomes of greater significance in music videos, to 'quickly [show] a character's role and its relation with others'.[77] These musicians perform Alice through the repertoires of clothing, which also have variations. Anne Hollander has pointed out that the absence of sartorial descriptions in literature might cause a 'mis-visualization' when recreated in different media, 'as in the case of the Hollywood visualization of *Pride and Prejudice* (1940) – the novel was set in 1796–97 but cinematic visualization took place in around 1835'.[78] According to this logic, the three music videos do not present the singers dressed exactly like either Tenniel's or Disney's Alice. Mizuki is attired in a black, knee-length, puff-sleeved flared pinafore dress with a white collar and white gauzy apron (Figure 4.3).

As can be seen in Figure 4.3, the layers of what appear to be a white lace petticoat are shown under the dress, with white stockings and a pair of black

Figure 4.3 Alisa Mizuki in *Town of Eden* (1991).

Director/Producer unknown. Reproduced from the DVD *History: Alisa Mizuki Single Clip Collection* (2005). Avex Track, Japan.

ankle boots. A black ribbon adorning her long hair brings to mind the ears of a rabbit. Apart from the colour of the dress and the boots, Mizuki's outfit displays the influence of Tenniel's and Disney's Alice.

Kawase's version of Alice, as Figure 4.4 indicates, involves a short-sleeved, tight-silhouetted silky grey apron dress, worn over a layer of white lace petticoats, with two lace trims running vertically from the top to the bottom of the dress. Under the dress, she wears a long-sleeved black polo neck, and a pair of high-heeled, black boots. Her blondish, rolled and permed hair is adorned with a red velvety ribbon. The vertical, tight-silhouette of Kawase's dress might suggest the influence of young girls' princess dresses in 1880s Europe, but a sash is worn knotted at the waist, with no sign of the bustle. Undoubtedly, it has modern nuances, as wearing a pinafore over a blouse is a style that became common after the 1930s with the introduction of gymslips, and a black polo neck was a sign of intellectuals in the 1940s and 1950s.[79] This makes a subtle contrast to the outfit of the white rabbit, who is dressed in a beige tweed 'University' jacket and knickerbockers, Argyle-pattern grey socks, and a pair of large brown shoes, a clear reference to those worn by social reformers and members of the Aesthetic Movement in late-Victorian England (Figure 4.4).

Figure 4.4 Tomoko Kawase/Tommy February in 'Bloomin'!' (2002). Directed by AT, produced by Ryuji Seki. Sony Music Entertainment, Japan.

As Figure 4.5 shows, Kimura is attired in a flared blue dress with red floral patterns, the collar of the dress and the chemise worn underneath are trimmed with white lace, and a pair of long, thin red ribbons cascade from the collar. She wears a black cardigan over the dress, with black and red striped stockings, and a pair of black high-heeled boots (Figure 4.5).

Since the cardigan commenced its life as military wear, allegedly invented by James Brudenell, 7th Earl of Cardigan during the Crimean War, it was a part of male attire in Victorian England until interest in European folk art introduced a 'Tyrolean' cardigan to girls' fashion in the late 1930s.[80] Hence the cardigan adds a modern nuance to Kimura's otherwise mid-Victorian girl look. In short, the summary of the differences from Tenniel's and Disney's Alice is as follows: Mizuki is dressed in black instead of blue, Kimura wears a cardigan instead of an apron dress and Kawase's apron dress is grey and tight-silhouetted. In addition to the dress, all three wear a pair of black boots instead of Alice's traditional Mary Janes. These sartorial variations indicate the performers' or stylists' artistic

Figure 4.5 Kaela Kimura in 'Snowdome' (2007). Directed by Daisuke Shimada, produced by Kaela Kimura. Columbia Music Entertainment, Japan.

interventions, showing that they have created their own Alice. We can deduce that the aesthetic of historical European girls' clothing forms is what unites these performers' perceptions of Alice.

These dresses, modestly trimmed with frills, ribbons and lace as worn by the Japanese performers, clearly show that they are crafting a *kawaii* 'look' that resembles the beautiful designs and images of a girl Jun'ichi Nakahara has limned in his art, which has been and still is an embodiment of *shōjo*.[81] By contemporary Euro-American standards, however, these would only be worn by young girls. In other words, seen through a Euro-American lens, they are dressed in rather 'infantile' fashion, and their clothes refer to children's dress of upper-class, mid-to-late-Victorian England. This is particularly evident with the calf length of the skirt. Up until the 1920s, an age hierarchy of female dress style in upper-class of Europe was largely maintained through the length of skirts. Young girls would wear short skirts whereas the length of skirts increased with the age of the wearer, and the skirts of teenage girls would approach ankle length.[82] Therefore, the 'infantile' qualities of these Japanese performers, which are one kind of the *kawaii* fashion aesthetics as already noted, are emphasized by their short, 'little girl' dresses.[83]

French philosopher and semiotician Roland Barthes argued in *The Diseases of Costume* (1972) that good costume 'had a powerful semantic value; it was not there only to be seen, it was also there to be read, it communicated ideas, information, or sentiments'.[84] It is not my intention here to judge whether or not the dresses that these Japanese performers wear are good costumes in the Barthesian sense. Rather, I pay attention to his idea that (good) costumes convey signs. If the Alice costumes carry signs, what are the meanings they convey? It is my belief that the *kawaii* appearances of these Japanese performers in the music videos have two symbolic significances. Firstly, they signify the possibility of detachment of eroticism from both the representation of cute femininity as well as from 'infantile' sartorial style. Secondly, they show a degree of creative authority being exercised. I assert that the 'infantile' cuteness enacted by the Japanese performers is largely detached from the heterosexual economy. This is evident in the embrace of predominantly young girls' period dress, the absence of male figures and the obvious girlish qualities such as the dreamy, fairy-tale narratives and sugary voices in these videos.

A fairy tale without a prince: Japanese music videos and narrative themes

In the music videos we are analysing, their almost saccharine cuteness does not primarily operate in order to accentuate a normative heterosexuality in their music videos. Whether because of the tendency in which stars' sexual or romantic relationships are kept low profile, or because '"giving off the scent" of sexuality is publicly frowned upon' in Japanese culture (hetero)sexual narratives are generally less visible in Japanese music videos than in their American counterparts.[85] These three Japanese performers' videos are no exception. Of Mizuki's twenty clips created between 1991 and 2003, there is only one that opaquely refers to the narrative of an innocent romance with a male lead (her debut single in 1991).

This becomes even more significant for Kimura and Kawase, as none of their music video clips, of which sixteen (between 2004 and 2008) and twenty-one (both as February and Heavenly, between 2001 and 2009) have been created respectively, display overt romantic narratives. Despite their lyrics narrating innocent and romantic love, these Japanese performers' renditions of Alice are not entirely framed within heterosexual romance, either. For example, in *Town of Eden*, Mizuki travels briefly through the narratives of *Snow White and The Seven Dwarfs, Romeo and Juliet* and *Cinderella*, all of which are known for their romantic narratives. But significantly, the singer is impersonating Alice, not the love-struck princesses, and hence deliberately eschews being a romantic object of the male figures in the video. Hence, these performers are, at least in these videos, not defined in relation to male figures. This absence of romantic narrative marries well with a degree of infantile qualities manifested through the demeanours of the singers.

Toby Slade articulates that the sexualization of female clothing is about accentuating the nuances of the female form, whereas its desexualization is to remove its element of seduction, its mystery.[86] The Japanese versions of Alice do connote sexualization as well as desexualization of dress. The Alice dresses, especially the ones worn by Mizuki and Kimura, with their knee-length full skirts, connote a 'female' quality meaning that limbs and waist are accentuated. Yet their 'demure' forms do not emphasize or reveal other parts, notably, bust and shoulders. Despite the emphasis on girlishness – or perhaps because of it – the representations of these Japanese singers do not evoke sexual qualities strongly. In this sense, their 'little girl' dresses affirm Honda's notion of the decorative, girlish (hirahira) aesthetic that allows 'simultaneous denial of womanhood and emphasis of femininity', just the part of 'femininity' being replaced by 'girlishness'.[87] In the music videos, they do not moreover engage in gestures or dance movements with pronounced erotic overtones. Kawase's 'Bloomin'!' frequently cuts back to a segment where she sings and dances, wearing a pale pink mini tennis dress, blue socks and a pair of high-heeled platform shoes. However, Kawase, not seemingly trained as a dancer, dances in a rather half-hearted fashion, and two chubby Caucasian cheerleaders who dance with her add a comical rather than erotic touch. Her slender physique as accentuated by her tight mini tennis dress moreover suggests a type of androgyny most famously identified with Twiggy. The 1960s British fashion icon was accredited with querying 'several parameters of female sexuality and attractiveness of the time through blurring the distinction between child and adult, male and female, as well as emaciated and skinny'.[88] Like Twiggy, these three Japanese performers do not invoke either strongly 'feminine' or 'masculine' visual qualities.[89]

The striking nature of such 'asexual' representations of young women is highlighted by the 'sexualized' culture of American music videos. It might be contested that significant differences in the representation of youthful feminine identities have been manifested within Japanese and American music video cultures. Central to this difference is the degree to which young women are visually sexualized, particularly through clothes.

Alice vs Barbie: sexualization of femininity in American music videos

In contrast to mainstream Japanese culture where the concept of (infantile) cuteness is supported, societies like the United States have been known to have a tendency to encourage even small girls in elementary school to dress in mature clothes.[90] Although music videos can vary in themes and scenes,[91] and 'individuals may interpret [them] differently based on a variety of factors, including social class, ethnicity, gender, interests, and experiences', American music video culture is one of the arenas where this tendency is highly visible.[92] One predominant argument regarding the music video culture, particularly the American one, is that it is a cultural arena where images of powerful and dominant men and of sexually objectified women are prevalent. For 'love and sex predominate as themes'[93] in music videos, and such programmes 'tend to depict women as thin and beautiful, scantily clad, and involved in implicitly sexual and subservient behaviour'.[94] In this sense, American music is conceived as reflecting 'real world' gender stereotypes in that male singers are assumed to be aggressive while female singers are assumed to be coquettish and fragile.[95] The sexually alluring 'mature' female look is, however, another subject of controversy.

Styles such as 'porno-chic', which is strongly identified with 'Barbie doll' musicians who represent an ideal, sexualized female type and are dominant in contemporary American popular music,[96] are perceived either negatively, as endorsing female eroticization or positively, as articulating 'women's sexuality with individual autonomy'.[97] For example, this sort of sexualization of young women might not need to be read as wholly negative. Feona Attwood, whose research focuses on sexuality in contemporary popular culture, implies that if seen through a positive lens, this kind of fashion can be symbolic of feminine pride and confidence, emphasizing a positive and empowering version of female sexuality.[98] American pop musician Katy Perry's music video to *California Gurls* (2010) offers a good example of an amalgamation of cute aesthetics and highly sexual overtones in order to connect young femininity and empowerment. The negativity surrounding styles emphasizing the sexualized female body, however, is that they tend to be 'mandatory' rather than matters of individual choice in Euro-American culture.[99]

The aim to challenge 'normative', 'passive' 'femininity' through clothes can be seen in 'porno-chic', in subcultures such as contemporary Goth subculture, and in contemporary Punk. 'Punk girls' attempt to resist mainstream adolescent femininity and normative feminine beauty through the adoption of punk style, which is stereotypically and historically characterized by an aggressive, rebellious and dominantly masculinist aesthetic.[100] What these styles elucidate is a cultural construction of young women's fashion through a set of extreme binaries. Social scientists Linda Duits and Liesbet van Zoonen articulate this point in relation to the Dutch public debate about Muslim headscarves and 'porno-chic' fashion. They argue that the permeation of the virgin-whore dichotomy reflects the conflicting approaches of Euro-American popular culture to young women: ideals of virginity and innocence in girls, and obsession with overt female sexuality.[101] This dichotomy has contributed to the difficulty of achieving the concept of the 'nice girl', an idealistic social standard girls often feel the need to live up to. Such standards could be achievable by managing to 'balance her sexuality on the decency continuum; neither showing too much of it (G-string) nor denying it (headscarf)'.[102] But this balance is nearly impossible because girls in particular are most often represented as being defined by either extremity, with nothing in between.[103]

For the three Japanese Alices, the predominant lack of typical sexual qualities, combined with the absence of heterosexual narrative, enables a manifestation of an 'infantile' kind of cuteness without being subject to overt eroticization. The comparison with mainstream representation of young women in American popular music culture demonstrates that this kind of representation of youthful femininity can offer 'a place somewhere in the middle of this decency continuum'. Such a *kawaii* look can enable women to appear cutely and sweetly but not sexually suggestive.[104] But it is not without controversy. Their impersonation of preadolescent girl Alice via the clothes of little girls brings forth the issue of negative female 'infantilization'.

Too cute to be good: some criticism of *kawaii*

The concept of *kawaii* has attracted its fair share of criticism. For some, the concept endorses asymmetrical gender relations as women are evaluated and judged within it, and are sexually commodified by being reduced to vulnerability, submissiveness, and immaturity.[105] Furthermore, Japanese female idols' emphasized youthfulness and *kawaii* aesthetics have been dismissed as only covering their lack of talent while serving Japanese men's paedophilic gaze.[106] This is rather a monolithic, simplistic view of *kawaii* aesthetics as well as of Japanese singers and actors. As noted previously, the concept of *kawaii* is multiple and diverse. This view also claims that even a lack of overt sexual allure in young women is perceived as serving the objectifying male gaze, while this kind of view should instead point out that almost no individual, regardless of their age, gender, race and physicality are thoroughly immune from the eroticization of the gaze. Nevertheless, Japanese female performers, particularly those who are young and considered physically attractive, have frequently been deprived of serious attention due to their apparently marginal amount of creative contribution and emphasis on their appearance. Thus, being 'a performing tool, as they were seen to be, is a feminized, devalued, and inauthentic role in rock and pop'.[107] Likewise, these three Japanese performers, with their Alice dresses and *shōjo* mannerisms, might be subjected to the criticism of favouring unhealthy 'infantilization' of young women. As influential feminist Andrea Dworkin had been cited as saying:

Infantilizing women is society's way of keeping women inferior, weaker, smaller and dumber . . . It would be a lie to think that this is about adult women. It's about children, about having a sexual interest and obsession with children. Women are choosing to do something that's very detrimental by letting this preoccupation continue.[108]

Scholar of communication studies Deborah Merskin endorses Dworkin's point. She warns that the sexualization of teen and preteen girls as well as the 'infantilization' of young women, particularly in American fashion advertising, is primarily for an objectifying male gaze. Consequently, such representations signify the objectification and infantilization of women, and furthermore, the willingness, passivity and availability suggested by these images have the potential to fuel paedophilic desires.[109] Such concerns and criticism point to the tendency prevailing in Euro-American cultures that perceives 'infantile' cuteness as highly unfavourable and demeaning, even when applied to very young women. Performing Alice carries a significant risk in this regard, as the character is sometimes seen as a 'Lolita', a preadolescent girl perceived by a middle-aged man as a sexual nymphet. This ambivalence is evident in North American performers' appropriation of Alice in their music videos. At this point it is useful to look at how non-Japanese (in this case predominantly North American) performers perceive, adopt and interpret Alice in their music videos. As noted in the previous chapter, the theory of 'content' and 'format' can demarcate both differences and similarities through the shared 'format' (Alice and music video in the present setting) when it becomes transculturally understood and accepted.

Gloomy wonderland: darker sides of the Victorian girl

There is a certain curiosity ascribed to the character of Alice. For example, Brooker refers to the 'duality' associated with Carroll's books. He has pointed out that *Alice* can be understood on the basis of two schools of thought:

those who choose to enjoy them merely as a pretty nonsense (broadly speaking, the nineteenth-century approach) and those who insist the text has hidden meanings that they want to shake out (to generalise, the twentieth-century method).[110]

This tendency in Western culture to inspect the 'dark side' of *Alice* has increased in recent times. 'Rather than offbeat speculation', Brooker notes, 'the idea that Alice has adult overtones and a dark heart seems to have become key to the way the story resonates in the broader public imagination'.[111] This duality is largely due to the 'enigmatic' sexuality of the author. The tendency to perceive Carroll in dualistic terms as 'a national treasure and a vaguely suspect enigma' includes the speculation on his paedophilic attachment to children, which is largely unproven.[112] Like her creator, Alice herself has been perceived and interpreted with variations from 'a child of her time and class', to a brashly sexualized Lolita, for example.[113] The idea of Alice as being steeped in sexual overtones is arguably endorsed by the fact that Vladimir Nabokov, (in)famous for his creation of *Lolita* (1955), translated *Alice* into Russian in 1923.[114] The influences of *Alice* on *Lolita* is further assumed, for Nabokov allegedly said, 'I always call him Lewis Carroll Carroll because he was the first Humbert Humbert.'[115] Accordingly, 'whether intentionally or not, Humbert's style has distinct Carrollian echoes in *Lolita*'.[116] Thus, the contemporary perception to parallel Alice and Lolita, and Carroll and Humbert Humbert, was born. Such an eroticized reading of Alice is also present in Japanese culture, as Mary A. Knighton (2011) discusses in her analysis of Mieko Kanai's novella *Rabbits* (*Usagi*, 1973), about a young girl implicated in sadomasochistic eroticism and an incestuous relationship.[117] Nonetheless, while Japanese performers perceive Alice as an incarnation of the *kawaii* aesthetics, North American performers tend to prefer the adult overtones projected on the character and her world.

Although the mainstream illustrations of *Alice* after Tenniel are not overtly sexualized, embroidering the 'darker' sides of Alice is a practice recognizable in the arenas of Euro-American popular culture. American psychedelic rock band Jefferson Airplane's song *White Rabbit* (1967) includes comparisons of the hallucinatory effects of illicit drugs with the imagery of *Alice*. When the imagery of *Alice* is adopted by male performers, the helplessness and passivity of the heroine tend to be emphasized. Whether or not the woman who plays the role of Alice is young, they tend to be dressed in the fashion of Victorian girls, obviously referring to Tenniel's pictures while male vocalists are often dressed as the hatter.[118] In contrast to the passivity of their Alice, these male performers are much older and in authoritarian positions. Perhaps, these treatments of Alice, deliberately or otherwise, reflect the asymmetrical gender relations that allocate the position of 'power' to the male and that of 'submission' to the (young) female.

So, what if Anglophone female musicians perform the role of Alice in their music videos? American singer-songwriter Gwen Stefani's famous video for *What You Waiting For?* (2004) offers visual references to *Alice*. In comparison to the visual aesthetics of the Japanese music videos analysed in this chapter, the dominant sexual overtone of Stefani's references to *Alice* is illuminated. Arguably, Stefani offers a dominantly kitsch yet more mature visualization of *Alice*. She both appears as the heroine and Red and White Queens in dresses allegedly designed by John Galliano, for example. One of her Japanese/ Japanese-American 'Harajuku Girls' backup dancers is dressed as a white rabbit in a somewhat 'Playboy Bunny-style' and her dancing movements invoke obvious sexual overtones.

Darker and less kitsch, Canadian singer-songwriter Avril Lavigne sings the soundtrack to Tim Burton's film *Alice in Wonderland* (2010). In the music video of her song *Alice* (2010), Lavigne traces the narrative of Carroll's *Alice* – following the white rabbit, falling into the hole and appearing at the tea party. The video cuts back to segments of the film frequently. What is noteworthy is that, like Stefani, Lavigne is dressed in a casual style at the beginning; T-shirt, mini skirt on skinny jeans, and a pair of black Dr Martens boots. After the fall, however, she is dressed in a black, late-Victorian full dress and white stockings imprinted with patterns of playing cards. Trimmed with a frill of keyboard patterns, the front of the skirt is shortened to look like the dress of Tenniel's Alice, while from the side, Lavigne appears to be dressed like a mature late-Victorian lady in the fashion of Madame X, the Parisian socialite Virginie Amélie Avegno Gautreau immortalized in a portrait by John Singer Sargent (1884). Lavigne, as signified by her 'normal' clothes, follows the rabbit and transforms into Alice. Here the sartorial transformation signifies an identity transformation. A brief comparison between Japanese and North American female performers' visualizations of Alice suggests two strands of significance. On the one hand, almost complete absence of male characters is a shared characteristic by both Japanese and North American female performers' interpretations of Alice. Perhaps this reflects Alice's independent and autonomous character, which made her distinctive from other girlish heroines in the late nineteenth century.[119] The 'infantile' cuteness that the Japanese performers so visibly embraced is, on the other hand, absent in North American appropriations.

Indeed, neither Stefani nor Lavigne wear 'little girl' dresses. Lavigne's visual rendition of Alice is obviously less 'sexualized' than Stefani's, as she is fully clothed throughout the video and rarely engages in explicit, sexually alluring movements or gestures. But her dress might signify an ambivalence towards maturity and infantility, perhaps echoing the film, whose Alice is nineteen years old with an emphasized sense of agency. Crucially, Lavigne's interpretation of Alice manages a balancing act – it both respects the image of the original books' Alice and emphasizes a distinction from the mainstream Euro-American representations of 'mature' femininity. Nevertheless, Lavigne dresses in a more mature manner than Japanese performers, perhaps to avoid the accusation of 'infantilization', which would be perceived unfavourably in North American societies.

One might deduce that these videos highlight the unfavourability of young women to be dressed in an 'infantile', sweet look. This point is further endorsed by the tendency that North American female performers' Alice clips have to conclude with their departure from the 'wonderland' and a return to their normal, real selves. On the contrary, Japanese performers do not clearly leave the

wonderland. Kawase in 'Bloomin'!' loops back to the wonderland while we see
Mizuki and Kimura still dressed like Alice at the end. This might be reflective of
the conceptual difference. In North American culture, the wonderland and
performing a preadolescent 'girl' is like a dream that one needs to come out of
at the end. It is acceptable only if it is ephemeral and the individual returns to her
real, mature self. In Japan, even if there are certain criticisms attached to it, being
'infantile' can be prolonged.[120] Thus, adopting and appropriating the imagery of
Alice highlights cross-cultural differences in perceiving the aesthetic concept of
'infantilization'.

Furthermore, like the concepts of *kawaii* and *shōjo*, these three Japanese
singers' appropriations of Alice likely manifest their capabilities to modify, parody
or deliberately inflate the 'infantile' cuteness that their 'little girl' dresses connote.
By failing to see the diversity in a state of 'infantility', authors like Dworkin are
underestimating the complexity of women's subject position. This is because, in
contrast to its apparent docility, the *kawaii* aesthetic can be compatible with
senses of autonomy and agency, like the character of Alice herself. Indeed, the
concept of *kawaii* can operate as a revolt, although not a Wagnerian but rather a
subtle one.[121]

A delicate kind of revolt

What is striking about the Japanese concept of *kawaii* is, indeed, that it can be
interpreted as a 'delicate revolt' that softly and implicitly subverts established
stereotypes and cultural preconceptions. Kinsella, in her ground-breaking work
on Japanese *kawaii* culture, articulates this point:

> Cute fashion was . . . a kind of rebellion or refusal to cooperate with established
> social values and realities. It was a demure, indolent little rebellion rather than
> a conscious aggressive and sexually provocative rebellion of the sort that has
> been typical of western youth cultures. Rather than acting sexually provocative
> to emphasise their maturity and independence, Japanese youth acted pre-
> sexual and vulnerable in order to emphasise their immaturity and inability to
> carry out social responsibilities. Either way the result was the same.[122]

In this sense, the concept of *kawaii* can operate like a feminine masquerade in
Joan Riviere's terms.[123] According to McVeigh, women can use cuteness to their
own advantage by obtaining favours and attention from those hierarchically
above while their apparently 'non-threatening' manners might gain control over
those who are their subordinates.[124] This idea enables a reading that such a kind
of cuteness displayed by the Japanese performers in their music videos might be
telling of something more than a submissive, docile femininity. For example,

through crafting the Alice look, these three performers manifest an implicit parody of Japanese female 'idols', which is a conceptual embodiment of the *kawaii* and *shōjo* aesthetics in Japanese popular culture.[125] The most typical image associated with female pop idols, particularly in the 1970s and 1980s, is that of Miss Sweet and Innocent with a ballerina-like flared dress, an image largely believed to be manufactured and controlled by male producers.[126] The dominant image of 'idols', moreover, were those who do not expect or are not expected to contribute to any creative or production process of their music.[127]

This has led Japanese female pop musicians, let alone Japanese pop music itself, to be seen by both Japanese and non-Japanese critics as lacking in authenticity. For those critics, authenticity is largely predicated on a do-it-yourself aesthetic and emphasis on creative control.[128] However, paying particular attention to Miller's theory of 'feigned innocence', I would argue that the music videos of Mizuki, Kawase and Kimura narrate three stages of *kawaii* specifically as a means to exercise creative control. While Mizuki's Alice was still showing the influences of Japanese 'idol' images and her (or her managing agent's) attempt to move away from them, Kawase and Kimura had careers performing in rock bands prior to their solo careers, and wrote most of their own lyrics. They have established themselves as songwriters, not 'idols', and their creative control over their repertoires allow them to embrace and parody the cute aesthetics freely.

Three stages of subtle revolutions

Compared with Kimura and Kawase, Mizuki's version of Alice is perhaps the most straightforwardly cute. She was only fourteen years old and was one of the top 'idols' at the time that the music video was filmed. It was also the aftermath of the end of the sweet female 'idol' era, which occurred around 1989.[129] Given that the dominant image of Japanese idols is of performers who do not and are not expected to contribute to any creativity to the production of their music, her cuteness does not demonstrate subversive or rebellious aspects/intentions.[130] For this particular video clip, Mizuki herself later commented: 'The theme of this clip is *Alice's Adventures in Wonderland*. Why? Why Alice? Is it because my name is Alisa? Isn't it too simple? That was what I was thinking when shooting this clip', indicating the absence of her agency in creating this particular music video.[131] However, she was not merely a commodified object either.

In the video, she does not manifest a doll-like docility or inactivity. Instead, she propels the narrative, passing through famous fairy tales and the Shakespeare play *Romeo and Juliet*, making each story happier by slapping the dead Romeo awake, for instance. This sense of agency corresponds with her public image of a 'legendary girl' or an 'It Girl' at the time, which was further endorsed by the title of her debut song and her first feature film *Chōshōjo Reiko* (Reiko, the Super Girl,

1991).[132] This is largely attributed to her tall, slender physique with long limbs and a general aura of maturity, as well as her prior career as a fashion model, all of which inverted, if not subverted, the typical girl idol images of charming but ordinary girls next door, the image engraved in the 1980s.

Challenging the stereotyped image of Japanese female musicians, communication arts scholar Brian Cogan and Asian religion scholar Gina Cogan argue that these musicians do make their contributions 'in ways that they are not usually recognized'.[133] What they are referring to is the visual production and presentation.[134] This includes singing as well as creating, sustaining and circulating the visual image via appearing in music videos, interviews and fashion magazines. According to Cogan and Cogan, these musicians are simultaneously commodified objects and producers of 'a commodity that can be said to be authentic'.[135] According to the logic introduced by Cogan and Cogan, Mizuki contributed to the visual aspect of her commodified public image via her exceptionally beautiful looks, and her frequent appearances in music television programmes, television dramas, advertisements and fashion magazines.[136] Furthermore, Mizuki's face is captured close-up smiling shyly and self-consciously, facing the viewer directly as the video concludes. This Brechtian self-reflexivity can be interpreted as implying that Mizuki is not merely a passive object of the viewer's gaze, but is actually performing the role of Alice.[137] This underscores a parody of cuteness and hence the fabricated and performed nature of *kawaii*.

Kimura's version of Alice appears to accentuate the saccharine qualities more than Mizuki's. This is particularly evident in her mannerisms such as smiling and waving to the camera (audience), and clasping a teddy bear. This renders her almost thoroughly an object of the viewer's gaze. However, her intentional, performed nature of this *kawaii* aesthetics is suggested by the contrast made in her 'public' image. Unlike the sugary innocent images manifested in her 'Snowdome' video, she has in public established something of a cute yet cheeky, independent and boyish character.[138] 'Hyperfemininity' is not a quality she is usually associated with. A few months after the release of 'Snowdome', for instance, she performed the song in her concert tour but wore a black dinner jacket with a matching pair of trousers and a white shirt, like her male supporting musicians.

Kimura also emphasizes her contribution to her music. According to her, the music of 'Snowdome', which was one of the pieces composed for her by the Japanese rock/punk band Beat Crusaders, sounded like an 'idol' pop song. Since sweet 'idol' pop was not her usual style, she took up the challenge, choosing it and wrote lyrics that would suit the music, which also influenced the video clip.[139] Miller has pointed out that the performing nature of *kawaii*, or *burikko* (feigned innocence) in her case, is highlighted when done by those who are not customarily identified with those sorts of gestures or behaviours.[140] Thus, Kimula's performed nature of 'infantile' cuteness is highlighted.

The parodied nature of *kawaii* is further evolved in Kawase's version of Alice, which is more aloof compared to the former two. First of all, she was twenty-seven years old when she appeared as Alice in 'Bloomin'!'. At a glance, Kawase's performance of Alice does not seem overly camp. She appears to be considerably younger than her age, and is dressed as such. This indicates Kawase's intention to appear seriously like 'Alice', and hence no exaggerated, humorous or theatrical effects regarding her craft of the Alice look are obviously evident. A closer observation, however, reveals that her serious attempt itself reflects a cleverly placed self-awareness. Masayuki Matsumoto, the editor of music magazine *Marquee*, points out that the saccharine intensity of Tommy reflects Kawase's composed ability to craft and self-produce the exaggerated 'idolness'.[141] The term 'idolness' figuratively refers to hyperbolic and artificial sweetness and innocence whose manufactured nature is tacitly understood. Kawase herself mentions that the kitsch yet candy-coated world of Tommy is comprised of her roots and personal tastes, and reflects her own creative control.[142] Moreover, the constructed and performed nature of Kawase's Alice is further emphasized by Miller's theory that an accentuated *kawaii* look performed by 'those clearly beyond an age of innocence, unmasks the artifice of the manoeuvre' and neutralizes adult sexuality.[143] We can deduce, then that these performers' Alice looks demonstrate three different stages of *kawaii* aesthetic as a 'revolt'.

Whereas in Mizuki's version, *kawaii* shows a degree of inflection, a compromise between the expected cute 'idolness' and the desire to establish a more independent and distinguished identity, in Kimura's version, the *kawaii* concept illuminates her playfulness, which is made clear via the vivid comparison with her perky, independent public image. Kawase's rendition of *kawaii* enacted through Alice further demonstrates her own individuality and creative controls via the construction of the 'infantile' cute image without an explicit hint of camp sensitivity or sexuality. While the three musicians illustrate different stages of *kawaii* specifically as a means to exercise creative control, their Alice performances highlight one shared characteristic, that is, the combination of girlish styles and sober chic colours. I argue that this balancing act of cuteness and subdued aesthetics is effective in rendering their performances as 'delicate revolts' against the negative stereotypes of girlish femininity.

The equilibrium of pastel and dark shades

The *kawaii* aesthetics manifested in these videos are indeed kept at a considerably moderate level. Their dresses are delicately but not extensively ornate, and the colours are on the sombre side. Their preference for earthy colours is significant in light of the commonness of girls' clothing in pastels, often with lace. Sober colours did not contradict the trend of girls' dresses in Victorian England.[144] No matter if it connotes the sinister, the macabre, elegance, individual distinction, dignity, maturity, substance or probity, colours like black would not, however, be the best choice to display innocent girlishness.[145] Thus, in addition to their deliberate lack of (hyper)feminine qualities, the deployment of darker and sober colours in these three Japanese performers' Alice dresses endorses their intention to market themselves as having a 'twist' that makes them different from other, more straightforwardly sweet-looking performers. As a result, their dresses maintain an intricate balance between infantile cuteness, asexuality and a sense of independence, which, delicately and implicitly, points to a construction of girlish yet not necessarily passive or objectified mode of female appearance.

The three Japanese female performers may not be representative of Japanese women in general. Nor are all Japanese female performers devoid of eroticism. It is, however, striking to see that there exists a group of female performers who can embrace 'infantile' cuteness that points to a lack of mature, sexual allure although they are not necessarily puritanical in their real lives. Such representations demonstrate that the idea that 'fashion is not inevitably produced to render the wearer attractive to the opposite sex' and challenges the idea that ornate clothes function solely for men's erotic pleasures.[146] As Duits and van Zoonen point out, schizophrenic demands of the virgin–whore dichotomy tend to define women's clothing styles at either extreme of the decency continuum.[147] As a result, the cultural construction of women's fashion is unstable, and largely problematic. Ultimately, the girlish yet asexual, innocent yet autonomous 'cute' fashion displayed in these Japanese music videos possibly serves as an alternative to the established multiple binaries of aggressive sexualization and subservience in which young women tend to be represented, particularly in but not exclusive to Euro-American culture.

Conclusion

Through crafting the look of Alice, the three Japanese performers demonstrate a compatibility between *kawaii* fashion aesthetics and senses of agency and autonomy. Emphasizing sweetness, demureness and femininity without hinting at sexuality or seeking the objectifying male gaze serves to repudiate the stereotyped representation of cuteness as passive, compliant and powerless against the sexual objectification of women. I suggest that this is more effective than such approaches as 'porno-chic' or 'girl punks'. These two styles are seemingly defined, at least in part, through the 'othering' of more demure and perhaps 'normative' modes of femininity. These styles, as long as they exist as the antithesis of conventional femininity, therefore 'do not seem to disrupt but rather appear to endorse existing gender hierarchies'.[148] In contrast, the significance of Japanese *kawaii* and *shōjo* aesthetics as demonstrated by the

Japanese performers lie in their abilities to reaffirm 'infantile' cute and apparently saccharine fashion aesthetics and values (which tend to be denounced in Euro-American societies) as positive and desirable. The compatibility of autonomy and decorative girlish fashion will be further explored in the next chapter through the analysis of the Japanese film *Shimotsuma Monogatari* and the Japanese fashion trend of *Lolita*.

5
RIBBONS AND LACE: GIRLS, DECORATIVE FEMININITY AND ANDROGYNY

'There's one thing about you,' Maudie said. 'You always look ladylike.'
'Oh God,' I said, 'who wants to look ladylike?'

—JEAN RHYS, *Voyage in the Dark*, 1934.[1]

. . . for the aesthetics of the rococo, the more delicate a girl becomes,
the higher her value.

—*Shimotsuma Monogatari.*[2]

A girl of seventeen drives a scooter fast. In the blurred images, her white, delicately flounced dress flutters on wind. She then collides with a greengrocer's truck and soars high in the beautiful sky, a bunch of cabbages waltzing and whirling behind her. She falls gracefully in a fashion redolent of Alice falling down into the rabbit hole in Lewis Carroll's *Alice's Adventures in Wonderland*. This is what we encounter soon after the opening in the Japanese film *Shimotsuma Monogatari* (Shimotsuma Story or Kamikaze Girls, abbreviated as *Shimotsuma* 2004). Clair Hughes in her book *Dressed in Fiction* argues that '[t]raditionally, aspects of dress have been used to portray aspects of personality, particularly when a character first enters the story'.[3] A girl attired in a white, lace calf-length puff-sleeved dress, known as Japanese *Lolita* dress, with a pair of Vivienne Westwood's Rockin' Horse shoes, rides a scooter fast with a serious mien. If what Hughes argues is applicable to films, this sequence alone is enough to hint that *Shimotsuma* offers a portrayal of teenage girls that is full of juxtapositions and contradictory images. These are revolutionary and striking.

In the previous chapter, I argued that some Japanese female performers manifest the possibility of a detachment from the eroticism often associated with 'infantile' cute and apparently girlish appearances. In this chapter I pay attention to the established idea that female sartorial ornamentation is a stable signifier of dependency and subservience, the view made famous by architect Adolf Loos and sociologist Thorstein Veblen at the turn of the last century. This idea continues to the present day, most notably via feminist scholars. For them, women's concerns for appearance, including fashion, operates for the purpose of attracting and serving the objectifying male gaze. These ideas substantiate one facet of gender performative theory, articulated by Judith Butler, which considers gender as a construction created and sustained by series of performances including gestures and dress. The socially inscribed dress of 'femininity' creates, demarcates and distinguishes the gender category from 'masculinity', which is symbolically embodied by the austere, sober and supposedly more functional men's suit. To what extent does a 'girlish' and emphatically 'ornamental' fashion-look as typified by Japanese *Lolita* style, then, inevitably signify such unfavourable connotations? Is it instead a visual embodiment of Valerie Steele's view that '[h]istoricizing, glamorous fashion could be subversive, not nostalgic'?[4]

The functionalist idea that construes decorative femininity as symbolic of oppression has been both critiqued and challenged by scholars of dress, particularly since the 1970s. Works by Bonnie G. Smith (1981), Elizabeth Wilson (1985), Valerie Steele (1985) and Joanne Entwistle (2000) are but a few examples. Following these works, what I hope to achieve with this chapter is to offer an alternative to the somewhat monolithic idea that amalgamates decorative girlish fashion and unfavourable feminine passivity. I employ *Shimotsuma* and its predominantly positive depiction of *Lolita* fashion as an exemplary case study of this aim. This in turn reinforces another facet of the theory of gender performativity, that a young woman can 'perform' both 'masculine' and 'feminine' acts alternately, while being clad in the same white puff-sleeved dress adorned with flounces and ribbons (in the case of *Shimotsuma*). Thus, the film demonstrates the idea of performative gender even more effectively and credibly.

I begin the above operation with a general overview of *Lolita* fashion. I explain how this concept is a manifestation of a complex cultural commingling between European and Japanese cultures. The second section consists of a textual analysis of *Shimotsuma*. In particular, by examining what roles clothes play in the film, this section argues that fashion is much more than a mere embellishment to the narrative, and that the film's representation of *Lolita* fashion is therefore eloquent. The subversive qualities of *Shimotsuma* that problematize traditional negative views about decorative femininity are the focus of the third section. In the final section I aim to explore the socio-psychological analysis of 'androgyny', which the heroine's fluent demonstration of both 'masculine' and 'feminine' attributes arguably endorses. I seek to establish the idea that 'androgyny' does not necessarily have to be manifested through 'masculine' clothes, and that the ornamental and 'girlish' sartorial style could be equally effective in its performance.

The dress of a bisque doll princess: aspects of *Lolita* fashion

Japanese *Lolita* fashion, which was believed to emerge in the mid-to-late 1990s, is characterized by its self-consciously girlish style, often with the extravagant opulence of lace, flounces and ribbons. The style's origins remain largely undecided.[5] Nor is there any clear definition of *Lolita* style; rather, it functions as a general term for a number of subtly different trends.[6] The orthodoxy of the fashion style, however, consists of a highly elaborate, Victorian 'little girl' calf-length dress hooped with layers of pannier, frilly knee-length socks, and 'Mary Jane' or strap shoes including Westwood's Rockin' Horse ballerina. The look is completed with intricate headdresses or bonnets. This fashion, when practised in its 'full-on' form, is often associated with the physical restrictions the style imposes on the wearer. Akinori Isobe, the owner of the renowned *Lolita* fashion brand Baby, The Stars Shine Bright (hereafter abbreviated as Baby), once admitted that the opulent use of lace and frills makes his garments both heavy and impeding.[7] Echoing this impression, the actress Kyoko Fukada, who wears *Lolita* garments (including some actually designed by Baby) in *Shimotsuma*, commented that they were not as physically impeding as she had expected.[8]

For some who wear this style, *Lolita* is not merely a choice of clothing, but also defines their identity and lifestyle.[9] Their fashion and demure body language is closely associated with their romantic views of privileged young women in the idle, aristocratic elite social classes of eighteenth- and nineteenth-century Europe (Marie Antoinette of France and Alice in Lewis Carroll's two *Alice* books are most obvious and accessible examples). Yet to what extent does *Lolita* style embrace and appropriate historic European dress styles? The style's appropriation of European dress forms of the eighteenth and nineteenth centuries appears to be more conceptual than stylistic, embroidered with certain aesthetic essences of these periods. In this sense, it is a 'transtextual' style in which references to other texts or sources are deployed, and definitely not a straightforwardly accurate and monotonous replication of period dress.[10] In addition to the aesthetic sensibilities conceptualized and romanticized by *Lolita*, we shall also see how Japanese understandings of historic European dresses have been influenced by Japanese popular culture (e.g. girls' *manga*).

Embroidering the romantic past: European dress aesthetics and Japanese appropriations

Steele writes of *Lolita* fashion in her book *Japan Fashion Now*, noting '[t]he look as a whole is often said to resemble a nineteenth-century French doll or *jumeau*'.[11] Thus, the Japanese style has some historical references to period clothes.[12] This is despite the fact that the notable promulgation of European women's clothing forms in Japan did not occur until the early twentieth century, during the Taishō period (1912–26), when the 'modern girl' and 'garçonne' look emerged, and Western buildings and furniture styles also became prevalent in the country's urban centres.[13] Close observation of *Lolita* style reveals that its incorporation of European fashion aesthetics has not necessarily been concerned by historical or stylistic authenticity. The manner in which historical accuracy gives way to aesthetic preferences in *Lolita* style is representative of Walter Benjamin's philosophy of fashion. Ulrich Lehmann summarizes it thus: 'a particular style or stylistic element is taken from costume history and brought into present fashion to create reference and friction simultaneously, along with new commodities'.[14] *Lolita* incorporates the *ideas* of certain aesthetic elements from historical European dresses, but its actual style is considerably contemporary. *Lolita* fashion does, however, have a history.

As noted in the previous chapter, the intensive saturation of lace and frilly aesthetic sensitivity through Japanese pop culture in the 1970s and 1980s was a likely precursor to *Lolita* fashion. Japanese clothing brands such as Milk, Pink House (est. 1972) and Megumi Murano's Jane Marple (est. 1985) were founded during this period. These brands are considered part of the so-called Japanese DC (Designer and Character) brands, which boomed during the bubble years in the 1980s. DC brands, such as Rei Kawakubo's Comme des Garçons as well as Milk, have wider consumer appeal than *Lolita* style, and despite not identifying with fashion, their somewhat romantic, girlish aesthetics are shared by later *Lolita* fashion brands, such as Baby (est. 1988).

The link between *shōjo manga* and *Lolita* aesthetics is quite clearly indicated. Fumiyo Isobe, a designer and co-founder of Baby, for example, acknowledges the influences of Yumiko Oshima's girls' comic books such as *Banana Bread Pudding* (Banana Bread no Pudding, 1977–8) on her designs.[15] Such appropriation and restylization displays a degree of creativity and hence authority exercised by Japanese designers. Masuko Honda's analysis of a girlish aesthetic in Japan, typified by fluttering ribbons, or dresses of decorative lace and frills (*hirahira*), which are associated with senses of romanticism and latitude, also emphasizes a link between the concept of Japanese 'girlhood' and decorative sartorial items.[16] This in turn supports the view that transcultural appropriation of dress can be systematic and tactical.[17] How, then, have Japanese fashion designers sartorially translated and adopted such ideas?

Lolita dress often exudes an air of *robe à la française* style.[18] This court dress style was 'an open robe with box-pleated panels falling from the shoulder to form a train', hooped with panniers, and was a popular dress for upper-class women throughout the eighteenth century in Europe.[19] To emphasize this aspect of hooped petticoats, 'the skirt was open in front to reveal a decorative petticoat', and even an 'ordinary' *robe à la française* 'was highly decorated, made of patterned silks covered in ribbons, ruffles, furbelows, and lace'.[20] This is explicated in a *Lolita* dress, designed by Innocent World (est. 1998) with the name of 'Pompadour bustle skirt (dress)'.[21]

Its name alone connotes the rococo reference. Pompadour refers to Jeanne Poisson (1721–64), known as the Marquise de Pompadour, a famous mistress of French King Louis XV; she had 'come to be the personification of the rococo in costume with its curving serpentine lines and riotous decoration'.[22] Accordingly, the *échelle* of three detachable ribbons placed vertically on the bodice of this twilled cotton dress corresponds with 'the three-dimensional ornamentation of the dress that was an essential part of the rococo'.[23] Combined with the classical rose patterns and the *robe à la française* emulated skirt with a matching petticoat on which pale yellow lace trims separate the skirts into three parts, as if the petticoat were being in front, these qualities of the dress bear resemblances to the dress the Marquise wears in the famous portraits by François Boucher (1756). The back of the dress, however, is bustled. Although it was not an invention of the Victorian period, the bustle became a fashionable part of women's dress between 1882 and 1889.[24] According to Toby Slade, Japan's first attempt to incorporate European women's dress in the 1880s was unsuccessful largely due to the bustle style and its 'extreme deviation' from the body's natural shape.[25] Therefore, it is deducible that the bustle has a connotation of the late nineteenth-century European dress forms in Japan.

The bustle was often paired with a long skirt, and even influenced children's dress in the late Victorian period. From today's perspective, young girls' dress styles in this period have an air of maturity. Elizabeth Ewing described the dresses of young girls in Europe at the time as 'tight, cramping and devoid of youthfulness, down to the elaborate tight, buttoned boots or the even more elaborate ones made of satin and laced up over open fronts'.[26] As noted in the previous chapter, until the 1920s, age and class hierarchies of female dress style in Europe were largely maintained through the length of skirts. Only very young girls or lower-class women would wear short skirts, and skirts lengthened as the age of the wearer.[27] Thus, the short 'little girl' skirt emphasizes the 'infantile' qualities of this *Lolita* dress, and hence accentuates 'youthfulness' or 'girlishness'. This elucidates the *kawaii* aesthetics notable in Japan. Further significance of the 'Pompadour bustle dress' is added by the way in which amateur model Misako Aoki wears it in volume 13 of the magazine *KERA MANIAX* (Figure 5.1).

She is pictured wearing the dress over a white, flounced blouse named 'Ribbon Crown Tucked Blouse' and an organdie pannier.[28] Unlike the French

Figure 5.1 Amateur model Misako Aoki dressed in Innocent World's Pompadour bustle dress. *KERA MANIAX* 2009, 13, p. 16.

Photography: Tetsuji Shibasaki, Hair and make-up: Akio Namiki (Clara System), Text: Emi Uemura, Design: Akiyoshi Akira Design, Model: Misako Aoki. Courtesy of Mariko Suzuki/Jacke Media Japan.

court dress, this *Lolita* dress has no sleeves, and wearing it over a blouse might avoid the exposure of cleavage.

For more Victorian references, Victorian Maiden's 'Rose Lace Blouse Dress' offers a long-sleeved, bell-shaped, calf-length dress with tulle lace and a tucked yoke made of cotton lawn cloth. The tucked yoke and long sleeves of a blouse allude to the style of the Victorian era, particularly in the 1890s. Yet the outfits suggested by the brand include wearing a puff-sleeved dress over the very dress and layers of pannier under it in order to accentuate further a bell-shaped effect, again highlighting the style's 'appropriated' quality. Judging from its appearance, a *Lolita* pannier can be described more precisely as a hooped petticoat of the twentieth century rather than the authentic eighteenth-century French garment. Further adding to this mix of appropriation and 'trans-periodic' quality, one might argue that these *Lolita* dresses' silhouettes are stylistically closer to a 1950s American formal gown – as immortalized by the prom dress. While the American dress was popular at the same time in Japan, and again briefly in the late 1970s, *Lolita* style has rarely been considered in relation to American culture, either by *Lolita* brands or the community. Instead, the style is commonly correlated with historical Europe, reinforced by descriptive terms such as princess, maiden and ballerina. Indeed, Isaac Gagné notes in his study of *Lolita* style that 'the meaning of the fashion is to become a "princess"'.[29] Arguably, what is important for the style is the opulent feeling created through the emphatically hooped skirt, produced by wearing layers of filmy undergarments *à la* Marie Antoinette. In this sense, while the actual shape of the dress is considerably more contemporary, it aspires to the quintessence of rococo aesthetic sensibilities, namely 'frills, ribbons and flounce'.[30]

The authenticity of historical European dresses has also been negotiated in terms of practicability suited to our time. The calf-length dress, made of such fabrics as cotton or nylon, hooped with the (petticoat-like) pannier, is lighter, less restrictive and more affordable than a long, full-length velvet, silk or wool dress with a heavier crinoline would be. The use of panniers can create a more opulent, aristocratic feel, and for aesthetic reasons, the layers of cotton tulle or nylon sheer bear a striking resemblance to a bell-shaped ballet skirt.[31] *Lolita* style may therefore be a negotiation between the fashion aesthetics of early/modern Europe and the kind of functionality appreciated at the turn of the twenty-first century. Rather than being unfamiliar with European sartorial history, some Japanese designers have studied European dress history at university, and thus are able to reference strategically certain aspects of historical European dress, producing something new.[32] It indicates the degrees to which Japanese designers are able to make decisions and exercise creative control. Hence, transnational appropriation, as Margaret Maynard has said, can be systematic and tactical rather than 'chaotic'.

Another notable characteristic of *Lolita* style is its emphatic display of sweet, almost infantile, girlish aesthetics. *Lolita* adds a shade of girlish style favoured in Japan – notably a *kawaii* (cute) aesthetic – to a frilly European aristocratic dress form. Mixed with *kawaii* aesthetics, *Lolita* reinvents historical European dresses as something novel and girlish. The projection of the *kawaii* aesthetic as embodied by the shortened length of skirts, exemplifies a conscious, creative adoption of foreign cultural forms. The demure aesthetics of the style can evoke a sense of docility for those who are not familiar with this fashion. In that case, it is logical to question whether or not this opulently ornate, girlish fashion endorses female subservience and eroticization.

Decorative femininity: praises and criticism

Women's elaborate dresses in nineteenth-century Europe, by which *Lolita* style is partially inspired, have been perceived as symbolic of feminine oppression.[33] This is explicated in two ways: firstly, the economic dependency of bourgeoise women rendered them a property, a living index of the pecuniary strength of men, by being adorned in lavishly ornamental dresses. This has contributed to the assumption that such sartorial ornamentation was a stable signifier of female dependency and subservience.[34] Secondly, in order to attract such financially stable men, women were, it is believed, forced to rely on their physical allure, and their clothes would serve that purpose to the maximum degree.[35] As a result, the decorative woman was presumed to symbolize female subservience as well as the source of the man's erotic pleasure. We might wonder, then, whether or not *Lolita* style's opulent use of lace, ribbons and flounces, which both imposes a degree of physical restraint and makes the wearer an object of the spectator's gaze, endorses similar preconceptions. The question is made more pertinent by the dominantly girlish qualities of the fashion. This is because not only feminine fashion but also 'girlish femininity' itself has been perceived negatively, particularly but not exclusively in Anglophone cultures.

Girls, and the connected concept of 'girlhood' are frequently perceived as being associated with passivity and vulnerability.[36] The adolescent female body is both commodified and glorified as the ideal sexual body in popular culture at the same time the institutional spheres such as schools and family perceive the female body as 'a tainted body need of control'.[37] Media portrayal of adolescent girls moreover, often arouses social concerns relating to the promotion of sexual precocity in teenage girls, but such perspectives themselves are through the lens of the voyeuristic gaze of adults.[38] Consequently, the voices of girls with senses of agency and positive attitudes are frequently disregarded.[39] In order to claim a position of power, some girls even adopt overtly 'masculine and boyish' demeanours and 'differentiate' themselves from more 'girlish' or 'normatively feminine' girls who are regarded as dull and unfavourable.[40] It can be deduced from these ideas that despite the largely constructed nature of both genders, conventional 'masculinity', even if it is on the side of 'hypermasculine', tends to be seen as a 'natural' quality of human beings. By contrast, conventional 'femininity' is seen as 'gendered', and hence is 'crafted'. Indeed, the concept of being 'genderless' is itself often adjusted to one particular image of white, heterosexual and 'masculine'. Blindly seeking and attempting to apply this concept to any individuals who do not fit into that type can, therefore, result in undermining their senses of freedom and individuality.[41]

Although this kind of political interpretation of women's dress, particularly the ornate kinds, has been challenged in recent times, it is nevertheless still prevalent. Sheila Jeffreys, for instance, writes as recently as in 2005 that differences inscribed in what men and women wear demarcate sexual differences between the two genders, and women's clothes turn their wearer 'into toys to create sexual excitement in' men.[42] From the perspective that sees 'feminine' clothes as creating and recreating a conventional, negative image of 'femininity', *Lolita* style is a reification of unfavourable female passivity and objectification. However, most of those who indulge in this romantic sartorial aesthetics, regardless of their nationality, strongly deny these assumptions.[43] It is generally assumed that *Lolita* style is largely 'pre-sexual' despite the possibility of the style veering into the sexualized.[44] One of the shop staff at Baby in Japan who dresses in the style regularly, for instance, has said her initial motivation to dress in *Lolita* was a desire to wear cute, doll-like clothes.[45]

Elsewhere, I have argued that Japanese Lolitas 'tend to endorse the egoism and cruelty associated with childhood rather than its innocence, naiveté or submissiveness'.[46] Moreover, '[a]bstinence, girlishness, and virginity' – albeit qualities often considered sexually desirable in various societies – have characterized this style in late 1990s Japan, in contrast to the overt sexual connotations ascribed to Nabokov's novel, from which the name of the style was drawn.[47] My intention here is not to deny women's desire to attract admirers via fashion or appearance. It might, of course, appeal to certain fetishist tastes, and it is also possible for some women to deploy *Lolita* style to attract sexual attention, but this does not seem to be the aim for most *Lolita* wearers.[48]

Assuming these dresses merely endorsed feminine oppression is rather simplistic. Wilson argues that 'to understand all "uncomfortable" dress as merely one aspect of the oppression of women is fatally to oversimplify, since dress is not and never has been primarily functional and is certainly not natural'.[49] Moreover, 'what may be considered "functional" dress in one epoch or culture may not be so in another'.[50] Anne Hollander points out that '[c]omfort, which in clothing is a mental rather than a physical condition, was no more likely to be a matter of course in skimpy clothes than in voluminous ones'.[51] This means that the length of a skirt or the decorativeness of a dress might not, at least significantly, influence the utility of the clothing. Her view is rendered credible by what Entwistle has noted. Although generally overlooked, she writes, there is a degree of discomfort attached to 'the tight, fitted male clothes' as well.[52] Similarly, while voluminous, crinoline skirts and corsets of nineteenth-century Europe (by which *Lolita* style has been influenced) have been perceived by some as a sartorial incarnation of imposed female docility, women's senses of agency, not their passivity, are also evident even in women's fashion in this era.[53]

Repudiating the idea that wearing an ornate dress simply implies Victorian women's consent to submission, Steele argues that neither upper-class men nor women's clothes at the time in Europe were practical, as they were not designed for manual labour.[54] More significantly, the silhouette of such florid, embellished women's dresses 'might be interpreted as emphasizing the female presence in a way that male clothing singularly failed to do'.[55] Smith, in *Ladies of the Leisure Class* (1981), has also suggested that voluminous decoration of women's dresses in the mid-to-late 1800s might have given the wearers some degree of power and visibility.

> Full skirts, bodices, huge sleeves gave substance to female claims to importance by increasing their physical size to at least double that of men. Women wearing hoop skirts, crinolines, bustles, or trains filled the social space and made people aware of their presence.[56]

Steele and Smith highlight the view that senses of agency and autonomy were thus involved when women wore ornate dresses.[57]

Steele also emphasizes that the significant meanings ascribed to women's dress in the nineteenth century were far more complex, saying: 'Victorian fashion expressed neither the social and sexual repression of women nor male perceptions of them as primarily sexual beings.'[58] She argues that the Victorian woman's emulation of an ideal of beauty, even if it came with limitations, should be understood more 'as a personal choice or an aspect of women's self-development than as a part of their oppression as "sex objects"'.[59] This is because 'women dressed not only for men or against other women, but also for themselves'.[60] This means that Victorian women likely dressed in such a way because they believed the fashion would make them look and feel pretty. In other words, they would feel pleasant, or even cosy via the sensation of being 'well-dressed'.[61] The aesthetic value of clothing is one of the fundamental factors ruling our selection of clothes. Thus the aesthetic importance of clothing should not be underestimated. If comfort is seen as one of the functions of clothing, wearing clothes that match our aesthetic sensibilities would surely and significantly increase the functionality of the clothes. This preposition is quite plausibly applicable to *Lolita* fashion.

The sense of agency combined with a highly girlish fashion style has moreover been a notable characteristic in Japanese popular culture. Anthropologist Anne Allison points out that the assumption of a 'masculine' demeanour is required not only for male heroes but also for female heroes in American popular culture. According to her:

the preferred model of superheroism (in both fantasy and 'real' realms) remains strongly masculine in the United States and strongly biased against a female hero, particularly one who behaves in a feminine or girlie manner. There is also an implicit message that even if a superhero is a girl, she is expected to act, and even look, like a boy.[62]

In contrast, 'feminine', 'girlie' or 'cute' appearances are not necessarily incompatible with independent strong women in Japanese popular culture.[63] Allison's interpretation of the Japanese animated series *Sailor Moon*, for example, illustrates that in contrast to the singular, masculine model of American heroism, 'there are two different hero models operating, one male and one female' in Japanese culture.[64] It is my belief that Tetsuya Nakashima's film *Shimotsuma Monogatari* and its portrayal of a young woman who is almost totally dressed in *Lolita* fashion offer a visual rendition of this point.[65] Such a representation, it is argued, can serve as a largely positive and favourable alternative to the monolithic idea that perceives girlish/feminine appearances as endorsing passive objectification. I examine this film in the next section in order to substantiate this point.[66]

A *Lolita* girl in the countryside: dress and *Shimotsuma Monogatari*

Shimotsuma Monogatari (2004) is a film adaptation of Novala Takemoto's novel of the same title (2002). The film was a success at the box office and has established a somewhat cult status outside Japan. The story of the film can be briefly summarized in the following way. Momoko Ryūgasaki (played by pop idol and actress Fukada) is a seventeen-year-old schoolgirl, and a daughter of a failed *yakuza* and bar hostess. Although she lives in the rural Ibaraki Prefecture with her good-for-nothing father and his eccentric mother, Momoko dresses in the clothing of Baby, The Stars Shine Bright.[67] She identifies with French rococo culture, and despite the curious eyes of the locals, lives according to her rococo aesthetics (e.g. she refuses to ride a bicycle simply because it is against her aesthetic principles, and she carries a parasol whenever she is outside in order to avoid sunburn). One day, after falling into a financial crisis that prevents her from purchasing expensive Baby garments, she decides to sell off the cheap and illegal imitations of Versace goods her father had produced earlier. Her advertisement attracts the attention of Ichigo Shirayuri (played by fashion model and rock singer Anna Tsuchiya), a seventeen-year-old student and a member of an all-girls bikie gang (*yankee*) 'the Ponytails'.[68] Seemingly situated almost at the other end of *Lolita* fashion, *yankee* style is generally known for its brazen gaudiness, combined with working-class clothes, modified school uniforms and other styles.[69] Despite the fact that these two girls seem to be the exact opposite in character and in fashion taste, they somehow get closer as they spend time together, and embark on a journey to find a legendary embroiderer in the posh area of Daikanyama in Tokyo, in order to ask him to stitch a design on Ichigo's bikie garment (tokkōfaku).

From the very beginning, fashion propels the narrative in the film. Momoko's father produces and sells cheap, 'knock-off' merchandise, which bears the misspelled name of Versach, thus incurring the family's financial crisis and subsequent retirement to rural Shimotsuma. We learn that Momoko was born and raised in the industrial city of Amagasaki, which the film calls the 'track suits paradise' (*jāji tengoku*). The hideously made 'Versach' garments introduce Ichigo and Momoko, who are initially, mutually surprised by the former's *démodé sukeban* (female delinquent) sartorial style and the latter's frilly, 'infantile' fashion. Embroidery brings the two heroines closer; Ichigo's determination to find a legendary embroiderer in Daikanyama forces Momoko to spend time with her, while their friendship seriously develops when Ichigo requests Momoko to embroider the design on Ichigo's garment instead.[70] Momoko becomes anxious after being asked by the owner of Baby to embroider a design on a white lace *Lolita* dress. She reveals her vulnerability, only to be encouraged by Ichigo in a strong, loud voice. Clearly, clothing functions as an essential driving force of the narrative in *Shimotsuma*. In order to examine the significant meanings of *Lolita* fashion in this film, it is useful first to observe what roles dress in general plays in it, and how it is connected to the identity and ideology of the wearer.

Appearance says everything: dress and identity in *Shimotsuma Monogatari*

Do the clothes that Momoko and Ichigo don represent their 'true identities' or do they instead offer the two protagonists a means to play with their identities? In the era of postmodern thinking, we tend to assume that identity is a masquerade and has an essentially instable and fragmented nature. This means that rather than being inherent, 'one's identity is defined in terms of the image that one creates through one's consumption of goods, including the clothes one wears'.[71] Llewellyn Negrin argues that this is not an entirely accurate reading because '[r]ather than just being about the creation of a "look", the way one adorns oneself should reflect one's values and beliefs'.[72] In other words, one's style of appearance refers to 'the ideology of the wearer'.[73] Somewhat more cautiously, Wilson suggests that dress and demeanours may allow us to assume a false or disguised identity.[74] However, even our intention to don particular garments in order to disguise or adopt a false identity itself is a part of our identity. This is because it reflects and is intertwined with our desires and wills. Thus I argue that ultimately, dress is inextricable from our inner 'self'. Likewise, *Shimotsuma* predominantly endorses the idea of fashion/appearance as carrying 'the ideology of the wearer'. For example, in a sequence during their first encounter, Momoko is dressed up for a meeting with a new person, Ichigo. Beginning with a red velvet headdress trimmed with white lace, roses and red ribbons, she is attired in Baby's red velvet 'Elizabeth' dress with white flounce sleeves. As can be seen in Figure 5.2, its stomacher-like bodice has a lace and flounced yoke with the *échelle* of a red ribbon and white lace roses, while the bell-shaped, calf-length skirt has five tiers of white lace, revealing a pair of frilly high socks.

Ichigo surprises Momoko with her school uniform worn in a 1980s' *sukeban* style. With a short black jacket, which has rolled-up sleeves revealing a leopard-patterned lining, Ichigo's *sukeban* look consists of a white shirt with a loosely-knotted black tie, a very long black pleated skirt reaching to ankle level, kitsch

Figure 5.2 Momoko and Ichigo's first encounter.

From *Shimotsuma Monogatari* (2004), directed by Tetsuya Nakashima, produced by Yuji Ishida, Takashi Hirano and Satoru Ogura. Toho Co., Ltd, Japan.

red sunglasses and heavy make-up with particular attention to her drawn eyebrows, a typical characteristic of *yankee* style for women.[75] Ichigo is in turn surprised by learning that a girl who glitters with lace and ribbons is in fact seventeen years old, the same age as herself, saying: 'I figured only a child would wear that kind of frilly dress. But I shouldn't judge by appearance.' Momoko gently yet decidedly replies: 'But appearance says everything', reinforcing the idea that she conceives fashion/dress as reflective of identity.

Momoko does almost anything to continue to purchase her favourite Baby items, even after falling into financial crisis. This alone indicates her perception of *Lolita* fashion (and more precisely Baby garments) as something much more than merely inessential, consumable pieces of cloth detached from her identity or the self. As for Ichigo, her purple *tokkōfuku*) is represented as almost synonymous with her soul. In the sequence where Momoko offers to embroider a design on Ichigo's bikie garment after they had a quarrel, Ichigo accepts the offer, giving Momoko her garment. When Momoko asks Ichigo: 'Can you really trust me?', Ichigo, sitting astride her scooter in the rain, seriously replies: 'To entrust your bikie garment to someone means to entrust your soul to that person'.

Unlike their school peers, and despite their visible sartorial differences, Baby and *yankee* garments might also function as signifiers of the similarities between Momoko and Ichigo in *Shimotsuma*. Ichigo, like Momoko, has light-brown hair with rather embellished make-up, and rides a pink scooter, all of which undoubtedly renders her comparable to Momoko despite their clearly different sartorial preferences. Their commonalities are most evident in a sequence where the two girls are sitting face to face in the 'Forest of the Aristocrats' (*kizoku no mori*), a local tearoom. As Figure 5.3 indicates, Momoko's demure posture, illuminated by her pale pink classical dress with frilled yoke and machine-brocaded ribbon-type textile, her matching straw hat adorned with a gauzy ribbon and rose corsages are strikingly juxtaposed with Ichigo's casual posture. Ichigo's deportment corresponds well with her hip-hop-meets-*yankee* fashion consisting of a loose red track suit, a matching hooded sweatshirt and a black singlet. Despite these sartorial differences, the two girls are equally shown in a medium shot, which, significantly, implies their equality, making a clear contrast to the scene where Momoko is seen with her classmates, to which I shall return later.

This point endorses what Georg Simmel stated in *The Philosophy of Fashion*, that their fashion 'establishes uniformity within itself, as well as differentiation from outsiders'.[76]

Momoko's strong sense of independence impresses Ichigo, while Momoko begins to understand and respect Ichigo as an individual who strictly follows her own 'principles'. Both heroines express their stringent loyalty to their philosophies, and hence their individuality through (rather) minor clothing styles. This very

Figure 5.3 Momoko and Ichigo at 'Forest of the Aristocrats'.

From *Shimotsuma Monogatari* (2004), directed by Tetsuya Nakashima, produced by Yuji Ishida, Takashi Hirano and Satoru Ogura. Toho Co., Ltd, Japan.

practice, however, provides a sense of commonality, which draws the two girls visibly (if moderately) closer.

If clothes are interrelated with identities in *Shimotsuma*, what is the significance of the frilly and lace *Lolita* dress by which Momoko is so fervently captivated? Considering the functionalist analysis of dress, the emphasized girlishness and the frilly and lace ornamentation of *Lolita* fashion might suggest it endorses a passive, restricted girlish femininity. Ichigo's comparatively aggressive demeanour and rather unisex, loose-fitted silhouette of the *yankee* garments further accentuate the sweetness and girlish femininity of the style Momoko wears. Is Momoko a passive heroine who lacks a sense of autonomy/agency? Earlier in the film, Momoko claims: 'I've got a puny grip, I can't run fast or swim. But for the aesthetics of the rococo, the more delicate a girl becomes, the higher her value increases'. This principle echoes Veblen's perception of the 'Leisure Class' in which '[t]he more the style and construction of a person's clothes indicates a complete unsuitability for work. . . the greater would be [the] "reputability" of their wearer'.[77] Michael Carter in *Fashion Classics* notes that for Veblen, women's dress 'goes even farther in the way of demonstrating the wearer's abstinence from productive employment'.[78] On one level, *Lolita* fashion, in which Momoko is thoroughly attired, is a tailor-made embodiment of Veblen's philosophy of women's dress. What makes the film and its portrayal of Momoko subversive of such a political interpretation can be explained in two ways. Notably, Momoko's perception of rococo principles is largely a romanticized version of aristocratic aesthetics, and these do not pose any serious restriction of her sense of agency.

Sweet reveries of the rococo: the rococo dreams of Momoko

According to Momoko's narrating voiceover, her rococo aesthetics teach one that life is like candy, and that one should immerse oneself in a world of sweet dreams. For instance, Momoko explains that aristocratic ladies of the rococo period in eighteenth-century France had their waists laced as tightly as possible solely for aesthetic purposes. This would be regarded as a virtue even when they fainted due to dyspnea or suffocation. This almost 'idiotic' prioritization of aesthetics and apparent lack of functionality accords with *Lolita* fashion, although the latter displays some practical reinvention of period costumes. In fairness, we need to acknowledge that Momoko's understanding of rococo culture is a romanticized version of the cultural movement. The rococo movement became notable in France in the 1730s, fully bloomed in the 1740s and began to wilt with the flowering of the neo-classical movement in the late 1760s. Fashion and art historian Aileen Ribeiro remarks that the rococo is the 'most "feminine" period in the history of dress'[79] and 'was a princely and urban art form, which demonstrated a kind of opulence in taste sympathetic to absolute rule'.[80] According to Ribeiro:

> It was a style characterised by wit and fantasy, by playful ornamentation, asymmetry and three-dimensional decoration. . .In terms of costume, the new style exemplified every fantasy about the essence of the feminine; everything undulates and curves, from the tightly curled hairstyles (a popular style was named *tête de mouton*, like a sheep's fleece) decorated with a tiny, frivolous headdress called *pompon* (a few flowers, a scrap of lace, a glittering *tremblant* jewelled ornament which shivered as the wearer moved) to the dress itself, usually a *sacque* or a robe *à la française* with floating back drapery, and trimmed with ribbons and flowers in serpentine curves. With the aid of small hoops or hip pads, the silhouette formed a graceful pyramid.[81]

Thus, the qualities of the rococo movement can be summarized more or less as 'feminine', artificial and elegant, all of which correspond well with Momoko's understanding of rococo aesthetics. Unquestionably, however, the rococo is far more complex than that, for not only the aristocrats in eighteenth-century France enjoyed the blessing of the rococo movement. Although the movement was most strongly identified with the court (particularly with the mistresses of Louis XV, Madame de Pompadour and Madame Du Barry, to be followed in the next reign by the iconic Marie Antoinette), Steele has demonstrated that the influences and presence of urban society were also notable in the rococo movement.[82] Indeed, according to historian Stephen Jones, 'not only the aristocracy, but the prosperity of the upper middle classes also made them ideal patrons of the arts' during this period.[83] Moreover, Madame de Pompadour, a paragon of the rococo sensibilities, was a self-made aristocrat and patron of the arts, and both her tastes and life trajectory signified the subversion of hierarchal distinctions in class and gender.[84]

How did the rococo dresses differ from the dresses of peasant women? Social and cultural historian Daniel Roche's study of popular dress in eighteenth-century Paris gives a picture of what the labouring-class or peasant women in 1770 would have worn. According to him, women in this class were dressed in a fairly uniform way; many of them:

> wore petticoats (or skirts, for the distinction between *jupon* and *jupe* is not always clear) loose smock and shirt; a corset indicated the superior ways of servants, girls working in the world of fashion, or the wives of good artisans. There were camisoles, some slightly superior low-cut dresses, a few mantlets, not many cloaks, but they all wore stockings, a good number of checked aprons, and the pairs of pockets essential to good housewives.[85]

Momoko's idea of France of the rococo period as an opulently romantic, aristocratic aesthetic therefore comes only from the limited and idealized space of the aristocracy of the period. Further, superficiality at least, it seems that Momoko's own version of rococo aesthetics both enhances and reinforces the assumed correlation between women's ornate dress and their imposed subservience.

What is significant about *Shimotsuma Monogatari* is, however, that Momoko's dress does not operate to render her submissive or the object of the male gaze. I argue that three main factors contribute to this significance: the independence in the characterization of the heroine, the almost absence of romance in the narrative and the subsequent lack of objectifying male gaze, and Momoko's abilities to travel between both established 'masculine' and 'feminine' activities effortlessly without undergoing any sartorial metamorphosis. I examine these factors below, beginning with the independent personality of Momoko. As we have seen, one of the points that assigns a negative attribute to elaborate 'feminine' fashion is that such a fashion signifies female restriction. Yet despite *Lolita* fashion's signified impracticability and demure girlishness, Momoko's activities are neither fully restricted nor impeded. On the contrary, she demonstrates a considerably independent personality.

Frills for independence

As the director Tetsuya Nakashima himself comments, Momoko has achieved a status of 'independence'.[86] As described by Ichigo, 'Momoko always stands up for herself. She follows only her own rules.' According to this proclamation, her sense of independence is well observed in the school lunch sequence, where we see Momoko having her lunch alone in the classroom. First and foremost, Momoko is visually distinct from her peers. In the medium-close shot, she faces the window, whereas her classmates are having their lunch in groups, portrayed in the long shot behind Momoko. Her blondish ringlets, delicate make-up and even her pink heart-shaped lunchbox filled with colourful sweets mark her 'difference' from the uniformly black-haired, simple-looking and thus more conservative classmates. Since Momoko is presented in contrast to her classmates, the film's intention is clearly to affirm her alienation. This also positively highlights her independent mentality, as she is able to stand alone if necessary, in order to live by her own values and judgements.

Momoko's sense of independence and individuality does not originate from her actual rejection of conformity, but predominantly from her aesthetic principles. When Ichigo attempts to persuade Momoko to join her bikie gang, Momoko, refusing decidedly, states, 'I won't be a *yankee*, ride a bike, get in a fight or be in a group, and I won't be shedding this [*Lolita*] dress' because 'it [the *yankee*] just looks tasteless'. This implies that her activities, including her sense of individuality and independence, are largely predicated on her own aesthetic principles. Momoko's independence is, however, not as flawless as it appears. Towards the climax of the film, she reveals her weakness and vulnerability, seeking encouragement from others (notably Ichigo) rather than handling her anxieties by herself. As director Nakashima notes, she might immerse herself in *Lolita* style and strictly follow her romanticized rococo principles in order to avoid being hurt by interacting with other individuals.[87] In this interpretation, Momoko's adherence to the fashion style, and hence her 'conformity' to a (minority) fashion trend, symbolizes both her independence and her vulnerability. This intricacy manifested through the character of Momoko gainsays the one-dimensional image of dependent women who are opulent trophies of their male breadwinners while pointing to the 'power' such decorative girlish fashion holds. Her independent status is further highlighted by the almost entire absence of romantic narrative in the film. This is significant because the lack of romantic narrative alludes to the conclusion that Momoko's immaculately crafted 'look' does not operate primarily for the male gaze.

Valiant be the sweet maidens: girls propelling the narrative

Shimotsuma Monogatari challenges a common conception that romance is an essential aspect of culture concerning adolescent girls, let alone film.[88] Romantic heterosexual elements in *Shimotsuma* are, in contrast, largely absent. The only romantic element that involves the two protagonists is the episode of Ichigo's first love.[89] The comical visual elements of Ryūji (Sadao Abe), Ichigo's romantic interest, prevent him from being perceived as an attractive male character in a traditional sense by the audience. Those elements instead trivialize the romantic aspect in the film, with the exception of the sequence where Ichigo cries after learning that he is in fact the fiancé of Akimi (played by Eiko Koike), the respected leader of Ichigo's bikie gang. This sequence in turn highlights the bond between Momoko and Ichigo. From this moment, Momoko begins to understand and respect Ichigo as an individual who strictly follows her own principles, such as 'girls shouldn't cry in front of anybody'.

Like Ridley Scott's renowned film *Thelma and Louise* (1991), the activities of the two protagonists are predicated almost entirely on their mutual friendship and personal desires in *Shimotsuma*. This seemingly endorses the idea that at any age, people in Japan tend to find emotional stability in a range of more 'permanent' relationships than sexual relationships, such as friendships and group memberships, than Americans are believed to do.[90] In contrast to the portrayal of Ryūji, Ichigo frequently engages her status as a 'romantic hero'. Although neither intelligent nor clever, Ichigo is portrayed as violent, rough, ardent, straightforward, masculine and loyal. Her habits of spitting and head butting are unquestionably associated with men and conventional 'masculinity'. Ichigo also comes to Momoko's rescue when she is in trouble, first when she faints with bliss after meeting her 'god' Isobe (Yoshinori Okada), and more significantly, when Momoko is troubled by Isobe's request to stitch a rose pattern on his latest product sample.

The film's celebration of female camaraderie might carry different connotations for certain groups of lesbian, heterosexual female or heterosexual male audiences. Although such a reading is not completely absent, an analysis of the film as a lesbian romance does not seem to be mainstream. I believe this is predicated largely on the film's rather unsentimental portrayal of the female friendship, combined with its avoidance of (Momoko's) misandrist attitudes, which are present in the original novel, and the integrated nature of 'female friendship' in Japanese popular culture. It may be argued that the relative absence of heterosexual romance in *Shimotsuma*, just like the Japanese music videos analysed in Chapter 4, exonerates the two protagonists from obvious eroticization.

Momoko and Ichigo are the ones who are in charge of controlling and propelling the narrative, and they are the ones with whom the audience is most likely to identify. Applying Laura Mulvey's famous theory of the gaze, this enables the (female) audience to engage with Momoko and Ichigo in the ego-libido way – taking pleasures by empathizing with the protagonists in the film. In addition, since the two protagonists are young women, the female audience is not likely to be required to be involved in the process of 'masculinization' in order to derive pleasures from empathizing with the protagonists. According to this reading, *Shimotsuma Monogatari* refuses to allow Momoko and Ichigo to become objects of the camera's traditionally male gaze. In contrast to Simone de Beauvoir's contention that women's preoccupation with fashion and appearance symbolized their enslavement by the objectifying male gaze, Momoko is moreover portrayed as not preoccupied with attracting the gaze of men.[91]

Importantly, Momoko's *Lolita* fashion itself may be operating against eroticization. This is because ornaments such as frills and ribbons can simultaneously emphasize girlishness and draw attention away from the body of the wearer by concealing its shape.[92] This idea that ornate feminine dress diminishes eroticism is also applicable to films. As film studies scholar Stella Bruzzi argues of Jean Paul Gaultier's costumes in Pedro Almodóvar's *Kika* (1993), elaborate feminine fashion in cinema can 'diminish' heterosexual allure and sexual desirability of the wearer. This is because 'the more sensational clothes become, the less they signify the beauty and desirability of. . . the female characters who wear them. This contravenes directly the traditional interpretation of adornment as something which accentuates and complements the feminine'.[93] According to this logic, clothes in the film, let alone Momoko's highly ornate dresses, are not 'dictated by the fundamental desires of the opposite sex' as dress historian James Laver contended in his famous principles of Hierarch and Seduction (1950).[94]

It is, however, also possible to read *Lolita* dresses in a different, almost opposite way. Clothes can sexualize the body of the wearer, for instance, not only by revealing but also by hiding the body, and hence adding a sense of mystery.[95] Although contemporary Japanese culture locates sexuality in the body, nudity has not been important in the history of Japanese aesthetics. Traditionally, the nape (*unaji*) was an anatomical part of woman's body that exuded sensuality to the highest degree.[96] The kimono silhouette focused attention on the neck by wrapping the body and making a flat, straight look while de-emphasizing other body parts such as the breasts, waist and limbs.[97] In this sense, putting intricate layers between the gaze and the object hardly draws attention 'away' from the object, because if that object is understood as 'hidden', it might merely serve as a promise, or titillation. Considering these cultural complexities, I believe it is safe to contend that the ornate, girlish fashion in *Shimotsuma* is not a device to *intentionally* or *primarily* render the wearer an exclusive object of the objectifying gaze, although some viewers might find the fashion, or more precisely the image of Fukada in *Lolita* dress, to be erotically charged.

The romantic chemistry between the two female protagonists in this film, with Ichigo's apparent assumption of the 'masculine' role, displays a distinct influence of Japanese *shōjo* novels, which can be traced back to the early 1900s. It is worthwhile to observe this tradition in the present setting. This is because the film's modern take of this tradition sometimes inverts, and even subverts, assumed gender roles, and makes the film's depiction of youthful femininity even more complex.

A romantic camaraderie of girls

The romantic friendship between girls is an ongoing theme in Japanese girls' culture. Such relationships have been most obviously associated with *shōjo* literature in the early 1900s, with the author Nobuko Yoshiya (1896–1973) the main exponent of the genre, but they continue to be part of Japanese *shōjo manga* culture even today. These romantic relationships often involve two girls – one of them being tall, active, independent and handsome, while the other is petite, girlish, sweet and innocent.[98] To some extent, these girls represent idealized images of ideological 'masculinity' and 'femininity'. Until the 1990s, such relationships were depicted as short-lived, for these girls were soon integrated into heterosexual romance or, if the story ended tragically, the former girl died for the latter girl.[99]

Unlike the original novel, the friendship between the two protagonists in the film version of *Shimotsuma* is not as romantic and sensual as the one found in the novels of Yoshiya. It is, however, clear that the two protagonists exhibit notable aspects of the convention of 'masculine-feminine' girls. Visually, Momoko assumes the role of the 'feminine' girl in the tradition of romantic relationships between girls. She is portrayed as highly girlish with demure demeanour. Most of the time she is dressed entirely in *Lolita* fashion, which is a signifier of hyperbolic girlish femininity. This fashion matches her use of polite language in a softly spoken voice. The casting of Fukada, whose public image is often described as gentle and quiet, further enforces this image. In contrast, Ichigo, played by popular fashion model Anna Tsuchiya, is characterized by her (relatively) tall build with manly attitudes and frequent use of rough, masculine language, spoken in a deep, husky voice. All of these qualities signify her status as the 'masculine' girl in the tradition of girl-girl romantic friendship. What makes this film unique, however, is its play on this tradition, as the two protagonists' 'gender' roles are frequently switched.

Performing *masculin féminin*

It is significant that the film's two protagonists sometimes assert themselves through (reaffirming) traditionally feminine qualities and values, which are presented as positive and powerful (such as caring, girlish fashion and embroidery), while they also engage in activities traditionally associated with men (fist-fighting, spitting, reckless driving and gambling). In other words, Momoko and Ichigo assume conventionally 'masculine' and 'feminine', active and passive roles alternately.[100] This is particularly notable in the bonding scenes between the two girls, which are recurrent in *Shimotsuma*. In these sequences, the concept of bonding is nearly always interlaced with (traditionally) 'female' qualities. The concept of 'bonding' warrants special notice here: is it only a 'masculine' attribute?

Although female friendship and bonding, let alone bonding between men and women, are common in reality, female bonding is, unlike male bonding, still rarely depicted in mainstream Hollywood films, with the notable exception of *Thelma and Louise*.[101] This is because rather than showing female friendships, 'traditionally, films portray women mainly in terms of their relationship to men'.[102] Furthermore, most mainstream films that show female friendship are 'sentimental' films where women's friendship is depicted largely as a means of integrating them into society.[103] It must be noted that depictions of female friendship and bonding, particularly in relation to young women, are more common in contemporary Japanese cinema than they are in Hollywood.[104] Furthermore, as the commentary of the director suggests, the bond between Momoko and Ichigo in *Shimotsuma* is significantly less 'sentimental' than more stereotypical, sentimental girl friendships.[105] For this reason, Momoko and Ichigo's bonding likely has a 'masculine' tone even in Japanese culture.

The most significant of these 'masculine/feminine' juxtapositions is found in the climax sequence. We see Momoko clad in a simple, puff-sleeved, lace-trimmed white pinafore dress with decorative ribbon lacing on the bodice, wearing a white headdress, frilled high socks and a pair of white platform shoes similar to Vivienne Westwood's Rockin' Horse boots. As seen in Figure 5.4, she is driving her grandmother's scooter fast. Her mission is to rescue Ichigo, who is facing the danger of severe punishment by her fellow bikie members for not fully conforming to the gang's rules.

After seeing her, Ichigo valiantly confronts and fights the bikie members, who are uniformly clad in *tokkōfaku*, and is then seriously bashed by them. Momoko just stands there in utter amazement when Ichigo's blood splashes onto her and her white, frilly *Lolita* dress. She screams in a rather girlish fashion with her hands on her ears and cheeks. 'Shut up!' One of the bikie gangs throws Momoko into a large puddle. 'Momoko!' Ichigo shouts. Momoko, her entire body plastered with muddy water, rises with a sharp glare in a medium-close shot. Followed by a brief medium-long shot, the film offers a very close-up shot of Momoko's face, initially with her eyes lowered, then looking up and staring straight, displaying a furious mien. Against the exuberant elegance of Strauss's *The Blue Danube* and her softly spoken narration, which repeats, 'Ideally, I would have been born in France in the rococo period', Momoko reveals her aggression. She confronts the gang alone, first in a violent act by flourishing a metal baseball bat, then by using lies and manipulations, and eventually she saves Ichigo. Significantly, one scene after the fight sequence, we see Momoko return to her normal, girlish self. This highlights her smooth transformation from 'girlish' to 'masculine', and back to 'girlish'. The film ends with a close-up of the two girls smiling girlishly, with their faces covered with bruises, blood and mud – another juxtaposition of 'masculine'

Figure 5.4 Clad in a white *Lolita* dress, Momoko drives a scooter with a serious mien.
From *Shimotsuma Monogatari* (2004), directed by Tetsuya Nakashima, produced by Yuji Ishida, Takashi Hirano and Satoru Ogura. Toho Co., Ltd, Japan.

and 'feminine' qualities, while their physical closeness might signify their emotional closeness.

What draws my attention here is that Momoko's transformation from 'girlish' to 'masculine' and back to 'girlish' in the fistfight scene involves no sartorial metamorphosis. The significance of sartorial transformation is accentuated in the convention of American superhero genre, from *Superman* and *Spiderman* to the film *The Matrix* (1999).[106] This seemingly affirms the tradition of comic-book superheroes, for whom costume operates as 'a conductor for channelling powers',[107] and 'in which changing "into costume" functions as a "sign of inner change" from wimp to superhero'.[108] According to cultural historian Friedrich Weltzien, changing dress as a presentation of masculinity has traditionally been depicted within the context of fighting in this genre.[109] Manliness is therefore 'defined by the virtues of the warrior, at the same time tested and confirmed by violence'.[110] Following this logic, I deduce that Momoko's transformation in this sequence without any significant sartorial change apart from the stains of her dress with mud, water and blood elucidates her inner changelessness. This means that both 'girlish' and 'masculine' attributes are present in the character of Momoko.

If we recall what Butler has said about gender performativity, neither 'masculinity' nor 'femininity' is fixedly inscribed on one's body:

If the inner truth of gender is a fabrication and if a true gender is a fantasy instituted and inscribed on the surface of bodies, then it seems that genders can be neither true nor false, but are only produced as the truth effects of a discourse of primary and stable identity.[111]

Shimotsuma Monogatari and its portrayal of Momoko endorses Butler's theory in a less radical but perhaps more effective fashion. The absence of sartorial metamorphosis in *Shimotsuma* offers an alternative to the idea that 'gender' is defined and redefined through clothes, while Momoko's smooth crossing between the borders of the two gender categories substantiates the idea of the 'gender' boundary as both precarious and undefined.

Equally significant is *Shimotsuma*'s portrayal of a teenage girl dressed in a highly girlish fashion engaging in the conventionally 'masculine' activity of aggression.[112] This significance is further emphasised by such recent American films as Tim Burton's *Alice in Wonderland* (2010) and James Mangold's *Knight and Day* (2010). The principal female characters in these films, played by Mia Wasikowska and Cameron Diaz respectively, wear dresses with bell-shaped, more than calf-length skirts at times in the films. When they are seriously engaged with fighting, however, they undergo sartorial transformation either into a 'masculine' armour (in *Alice*) or a black, stylish trouser suit (in *Knight*). The implicit message that we might encode here is that despite the rather 'unrealistic' settings of these films, certain activities such as engaging in a fight while wearing highly 'feminine' or 'girlish' attires are next to unthinkable. This is particularly notable in *Alice* in the sequence where Alice, like the legendary Joan of Arc, wears a medieval or Renaissance-style armour in order to fight the dragon-like Jabberwocky. The medieval/Renaissance-style armour is integrated into the costume of American superheroes, which 'is reminiscent of imperial Roman armour but with apparent Renaissance influences'.[113] Thus, as Weltzien has argued, it can be a signifier of heroic masculinity. This raises the question: if a film is set in the world of nonsense where the heroine can shrink and grow tall or animals and other creatures can speak a human language, why can the heroine not defeat a monstrous creature while wearing the gauzy, blue or red dresses with flounces that she had on earlier in the film?

The equation of power, activity and authority with the concept of 'masculine', and inactivity with the concept of 'feminine' is arguably in operation here. In reality, heavy Renaissance armour could be more physically impeding than a filmy dress, but the discomfort associated with men's clothes has conveniently been overlooked.[114] Hence, these examples from American cinema uphold the validity of Allison's contention that in American popular culture, female heroes tend to dress and act in a 'masculine' fashion. On the contrary, as several authors have pointed out, even if with certain limitations, girlish/feminine appearances and traditionally 'masculine' attributes such as fighting are more compatible in

Japanese popular culture. With a young woman in a white gauzy dress who valiantly fights in order to save her friend, *Shimotsuma* is a vivid endorsement of this point.

It is simplistic to assume that these are only fictions, thus not mirroring reality in any ways. Crane and Bulman assert that the constructed ideals, biases or distortions demonstrated in cinema can themselves be part of the society/culture which first produced them.[115] 'Although the fantasy world of the cinema is obviously separate from the actual conditions of everyday life', writes sociologist Joanne Finkelstein:

> the intermingling of fashions with aesthetic injunctions about femininity and masculinity suggests that such images function mimetically. . . The close correspondence between women's fashions and cinematic depictions of femininity illustrates how the imagined and the imitated flow into one another.[116]

As these ideas affirm, the comparison between the American films and *Shimotsuma Monogatari* illustrate transcultural differences in conceiving the relationship between 'feminine' clothing forms and strong activity. Further affirmation of this point can be found in the fact that *Shimotsuma Monogatari* is not a single example of this kind in Japanese popular culture.

Kozueko Morimoto's *manga* series *Deka One-ko* (Detective One-ko or Wan-ko, 2008 to the present) is a new addition to this plethora of 'girlish' heroines dwelling in conventionally 'masculine' genres in Japanese popular culture. It centres around a newly recruited young female detective, Ichiko Hanamori, who is blessed with olfaction as acute as a police dog, a genetic inheritance from her father that enables her to solve crime cases.[117] She is dressed in a frilly dress all the time, which is stylistically not dissimilar to *Lolita* fashion. An earlier TV drama series *Fugō Keiji* (Multi-millionaire Detective, 2005–6), in which a young granddaughter of a multi-millionaire joins the police force, might have inspired the comic book series. The heroine Miwako, also played by Fukada, is dressed in a less frilly but equally opulent, 'feminine' fashion.[118] Although the author Morimoto has never described the heroine's style as *Lolita*, and perhaps it is not the genuine *Lolita* style in the strict sense, Ichiko's style is often named as *Lolita*.[119] When the story was adapted for the small screen in 2011, such renowned *Lolita* brands as Putumayo (est. 1987, *punk-Lolita*) and Angelic Pretty (est. 1979, *sweet-Lolita*) offered their clothes, further circulating the conception that this is the story of a female detective clad in *Lolita*-like fashion.[120] Like *Shimotsuma, Deka One-ko* further reinforces the idea that in Japanese popular culture, a young woman does not necessarily have to leave her opulent, highly 'girlish' clothes at home in order to engage in traditionally 'masculine' activities.

The manifestation of conventionally 'masculine' and 'feminine' attributes through the character of Momoko in *Shimotsuma* poses another question: does the characterization of Momoko, for whom the *Lolita* fashion is a fundamental component, delineate a sense of 'androgyny'? *Lolita* fashion, perhaps with the exception of the 'count (*ōji*)' style, accentuates 'hyper-girlish femininity'. *Lolita* fashion can moreover be understood as 'exclusively a culture for girls – boys are not allowed'.[121] All of this implies that Momoko could not be understood in terms of 'androgyny'. In the social-psychological definition of 'androgyny', however, the answer can be affirmative.

Refashioning the 'androgynous' look

Social-psychological analysis implies a possibility that the concept of 'androgyny' might be manifested through women with fairly 'feminine' appearances or men with comparatively 'masculine' appearances. By making distinctions from biological hermaphrodites, such an analysis conceptualizes androgyny as a psychological state. It refers 'to a specific way of joining the "masculine" and "feminine" aspects of a single human being'.[122] And this unison takes place largely in an idealistic way. For instance, Jungian analyst June Singer argued that:

> Men and women function in certain ways; each has masculine and feminine functioning capacities. In the process of living, these qualities, which for want of a better name we call 'masculine' and 'feminine,' are also convertible. The difference is that the conversions may proceed in a single direction as with our plane, or the conversions may move backwards and forwards, oscillating so swiftly that it is impossible to discern when 'masculine' functioning is in the superior position, and when 'feminine'.[123]

This is significant since '[t]he inner sexual duality has nearly always been taken for granted'.[124] Bem, who is noted for her influential work on androgyny, defines 'androgynous' individuals as possessing both stereotypically 'masculine' and 'feminine' qualities, unlike strongly sex-typed individuals.[125] Her research indicates that 'androgynous' individuals are able to 'engage freely in both masculine and feminine behaviours' and thus 'come to define a new and more human standard of psychological health'.[126] Such analysis of 'androgyny' does not by any means subvert the concept of gender. Rather, 'androgynous' individuals psychologically possess and display attributes of both gender categories without much conflict.

Although these psychological analyses of 'androgyny' date from the 1970s, they are still of considerable relevance for the conception of gender today. Carrie

Paechter, for instance, points out that we are unlikely to diverge from two main genders, despite the indefinable nature of gender. Each of us knows whether we are biologically male or female, or otherwise, something different or in between.[127] However, as argued by Bem and Singer, many individuals possess both conventionally 'masculine' and 'feminine' qualities. Thus it is important to treat masculinities and femininities 'only as aspects of identity, and . . . not insist that [identity] depends on them entirely, with one's sense of oneself as male or female as somehow secondary'.[128]

In simplest terms, 'androgyny' describes a psychological state that is not strongly or dominantly assigned to one category of gender. Bem also notes that '[d]efined as gender inappropriate for females, for instance, is the desire for autonomy and power; defined as gender inappropriate for males are feelings of vulnerability, dependency, and affection for same-sex others'.[129] I have demonstrated that all the qualities Bem noted are unified in the characters of Momoko and Ichigo. The emphasis of this 'androgynous' representation is highlighted by an established idea of androgynous appearance. When it is applied to describe clothing styles or the 'look', 'androgynous' appearance is, first and foremost, based on male clothes.[130] While the term androgyny means the combination of 'masculine' and 'feminine' traits (*andr*- from the word meaning man and *gyné* meaning woman in Greek), in modern times, the 'androgynous' look often means both men and women dressing in men's clothes. 'Female androgyny' as an aesthetically pleasing look, Hollander argues, may not aim to render women as looking fully 'masculine', but its appeal lies in women's assumption of a kind of beauty associated with the sexual uncertainty of the adolescent boy.[131] This means that the look of an adolescent boy is perceived as connoting sexual ambiguity, while that of an adolescent girl is not. In other words, the clothes that visibly connote 'girlishness' are highly gendered, and are not considered 'androgynous'. *Shimotsuma Monogatari*, on the other hand, endorses the ideas that despite the fixity in our biological gender, all of us have both conventionally 'masculine' and 'feminine' attributes. Hence, young women can display a sense of 'androgyny' while being fully clad in a highly ornate girlish fashion, without voluntarily embracing unwanted passivity or eroticization.

The film's portrayal of an adolescent girl in full activity, dressed in highly ornamental dresses, suggests that exquisitely frilled mini-dresses, platform shoes or a lace, white headdress are by no means less facilitative of movement, less worthy, less essential than more 'masculine' kinds of garments as preferred by functionalist ideas. This inverts utilitarian considerations where 'beauty became equated with or reduced to utility, the two being indistinguishable'.[132] Like the Victorian women in Steele's study, most women who wear *Lolita* style, both in film and in real life, do so by their own choice, for their own pleasures.[133] *Shimotsuma Monogatari* and its portrayal of *Lolita* fashion thus subverts the idea that women's fashion has a primary role to serve and please men's erotic pleasures. This in turn repudiates the preconceived equation of decorative girlish dresses with derogatory female passivity. It is fair to say that the film sheds positive light upon our understanding of the disparaged feminine clothing style.

Conclusion

Far from recreating the established idea that links female sartorial ornamentation with subservience and repression, *Shimotsuma Monogatari* offers a portrayal of an adolescent girl who is glittering with lace and flounces while also being active and autonomous. In this film, dress not only functions as a visual embellishment of the narrative, but also represents the identity of the wearer. It is, then, significant that unlike the tradition of the American comic book superhero or girl films, the heroines display both 'masculine' and 'feminine' gender attributes without undergoing any sartorial transformation. Girlish and ornamental dresses, in this sense, do not have to be devoid of significance, essentiality or substance. The emphasis of this film is particularly highlighted by the notion that films and dress can both reflect and shape the culture that creates them. In conclusion, my analysis of *Shimotsuma Monogatari* suggests that the film sheds positive light upon our understanding of the disparaged ornamental and 'girlish' sartorial style. This film offers us a new way to consider such emphatically girlish fashion styles with the extravagant opulence of ornamentation, and the aesthetic pleasures they manifest.

6
AN IVY BOY AND A PREPPY GIRL: STYLE IMPORT-EXPORT*

Taking great care of appearance is the first step of every fashion.
—KAZUO HOZUMI, *IVY Illustrated*, 1980.[1]

The narratives hitherto constructed of the analysis of contemporary Japanese clothing culture have two central intellectual concerns: firstly, clothes are important for both men and women, and secondly, modern styles of Japanese fashion manifest a process of transformation through the reinvention of tradition. By appropriating and reinventing traditional styles of European clothing, such fashion styles create new meanings. In this chapter, I shall try to unite these two concerns by looking at the 'Ivy style'.[1]

The Ivy style has occupied a special place in contemporary Japanese men's fashion since the 1960s. Because of its boyish yet classically elegant fashion aesthetics, the style seems to be appreciated particularly by those who locate themselves somewhere between boyhood and manhood. Culture and lifestyle magazine for mature men *Brutus*, for example, has a fashion issue devoted to preppy style (April 2012). In the magazine a chic beige suit of Prada and a black jacket, a double cuff shirt with a black bow-tie, and a plaid check trousers of Gucci are juxtaposed with Dolce & Gabbana's boyish set-up of a square mesh tank top and shorts with a pair of trainers. Two almost opposing characteristics are reflected in how the Ivy style is represented in contemporary Japan; the rugged boyishness associated with the image of Ivy Leaguers and dressed-down styling is combined with the suave charm of a suit and other clothing items connoting the classical past.

*An earlier version of this chapter appeared as 'Ivy in Japan: a regalia of non-conformity and privilege' in Patricia Mears (ed) *Ivy Style: radical conformist* (Yale University Press, 2012, pp. 175–85). I thank Ms Patricia Mears for her permission to include it here.

One of the enduring debates surrounding fashion is its definition. For Elizabeth Wilson and Ulrich Lehmann, among others, fashion is about change and novelty: 'Fashion is dress in which the key feature is rapid and continual changing of styles', writes Wilson. 'Fashion, in a sense, *is* change.'[2] In *Tigersprung*, Lehmann's view on fashion seems to correspond with Wilson's. He writes: 'sartorial fashion stands, almost by definition, for the absolutely new – for permanent novelty and constant, insatiable change'.[3] My aim here is not to delve into the question of 'What is fashion?'. The idea of change and novelty as a quintessence of fashion, however, does seem important when we look at the Ivy style in Japan.

Whether it is a navy blazer, a madras shirt with button-down collar or a pair of off-white cotton trousers, the familiar look of the Ivy style appears to refer to the past. Also, the Ivy style has continually appeared in Japanese fashion culture ever since it became popular in the early 1960s. We might ask: is the Ivy style a relic of the past? Or does it transcend history? The answer is more subtle than a simple yes or no. As former president of the venerated J. Press and maestro of the Ivy League style, Richard Press, says, the Ivy style's chief virtue is '[a] generational and historical continuity', which was in line with Japanese values.[4] When asked why Japanese fashion culture has such fondness for the style, Press's answer is: 'the sense of tradition is such a valid philosophy in Japan'.[5] Indeed, the history of the Ivy style in Japanese fashion culture, and its contemporary revival in particular, outlines both admiration for the past and the process of transformation.

I argue that the significance of the Ivy style embraced by Japanese fashion culture is its manifestation of the processes of cultural globalization and flows.[6] That is, it is an 'American' style adopted and localized in Japan. Through this cultural process of adoption and appropriation, the Ivy style has transformed into a fashion style with characteristics of often opposing concepts – past and innovation, unrefined boyishness and sophistication, and ruggedness and suavity. The style has become a sign that is ready to commingle with other similar yet different fashion concepts, resulting in the creation of novel styles, including ones for women, and travelling again outside Japan, notably 'back' to the United States. This process is particularly documented through Japanese fashion publications.

Through a Japanese lens

What makes the Ivy style significant is the influence of Japanese culture in the popularity of Ivy style today. The fashion writer David Colman, for instance, writes in relation to the modern day 'renaissance' of the Ivy style in the United States as follows: 'What makes today's prepidemic so fascinating is how it is, surprisingly enough, so Japanese. The look has its roots in the United States, to be sure. But the spirit, rigor and execution of today's prep moment is as Japanese as Sony.'[7]

Even the 'term "trad" itself is said to have been coined by the Japanese'.[8] Writer and artist W. David Marx goes even further by saying, '[s]ince the 1960s, Japan has been an important part of the story of the Ivy League Look, and during a few dark periods the island nation has played an important role in preventing the style from possible extinction.'[9] The popularity of Ivy style in Japan, and the Japanese fascination with the style, is immortalized in the form of *Take Ivy* (1965), a picture book that was presumably intended to serve as a style guide for Japanese youth of American Ivy League styles.[10] *Take Ivy* is often accredited with the preservation of the Ivy style in the United States. The images are striking for the way in which they capture the informality of collegiate life with a crisp representation of the clothing specifics. According to Valerie Steele, '[i]n 1965, Kensuke Ishizu commissioned photographer Teruyoshi Hayashida to travel to America and document the sartorial scene at Ivy League colleges. The result was *Take Ivy*, a book that has now achieved cult status among connoisseurs of traditional American menswear.'[11]

This 'bible' of Ivy League styles 'has always been extremely rare in the United States, a treasure of fashion insiders that can fetch more than $1,000 on eBay and in vintage book stores'.[12] Up until the recent reissue, the prevalence of the scanned images from *Take Ivy* online 'aroused renewed interest for its apparent prescience of preppy style'.[13] In a sense, it may not be a complete exaggeration to claim that today's Ivy style is founded on the Japanese romanticization and (mis)interpretation of the American style.[14] We might, then, wonder how the Japanese fascination with the Ivy style began and continues to operate.

Ivy goes to Japan

Up until the 1990s, the styles that evoke a degree of similarity to the Ivy style made almost continual appearances in the culture of Japanese clothing.[15] The history of Japanese Ivy style is often said to have begun with Kensuke Ishizu (1911–2005), who was the 'architect' of *Take Ivy*, and 'a kind of Ralph Lauren *avant la letter*'.[16] He founded the Ivy League-inspired clothing brand company VAN Jacket in 1951. Not only was Ishizu the owner of the company, but in his heyday he also designed VAN items and frequently wrote for *Otokono fukushoku* (later renamed *Men's Club*).[17] In addition to producing its original clothes, VAN Jacket also imported American fashion brands such as Gant and Spalding, with which it traded in the 1970s until the company declared bankruptcy in 1978.[18] "'Ivy Leaguers wear clothes with pride, not fashion" is the philosophy he ultimately distilled.'[19]

Rather than perceiving the Ivy League style as an entirely different, 'exotic' style, Ishizu articulated his belief that the style would be popular among Japanese men on the basis that there were some similarities between the two cultures. Ishizu located these similarities within the sartorial philosophy of Ivy Leaguers and the philosophy of male students in pre-World War II Japan. What Ishizu was referring to was the aesthetic of *bankara*, which involved 'intentionally dressing like a rustic, wearing a ragged and dirty kimono'.[20] Initially, *bankara*, in the late nineteenth century, was a reaction against *hikara* (Western chic) and the movement of Westernization, intentionally bringing back a style resembling the rough and dishevelled *rōnin* (drifter samurai) in order to make gentlemanly *hikara* men 'effeminate'.[21]

This concept became particularly well associated with schoolboys of old higher schools (*kyūsei kōkō*), which were exceptionally elite and exclusive institutions at the time. The kimono was replaced by 'a uniform modelled after Prussian military uniforms: a black high-collared jacket with brass buttons, trousers, and a cap with a brass badge'[22] (Figure 6.1).Their sartorial styles were often defined through the amalgam of privilege and self-inflicted shabbiness. Sociologist Yumiko Mikanagi describes it as follows:

> while *sanshu no jingi* (three sacred objects) – a black school cap decorated with white lines, a black cloak, and *hōba no geta* (clogs made from the Japanese big leaf magnolia) – symbolized students' privileged status, it was always worn torn and shabby as students cherished the *hēihabō* [literally shabby clothes and torn cap] style.[23]

By the time Ishizu was a young man, the tough, violent aspect of *bankara* was somehow downplayed and it instead blended with a new type of masculine ideal, which Mikanagi terms as 'self-cultivation (*kyōyōshugi*) masculinity'.

While preserving the *bankara* aesthetic by wearing their school uniforms often in a rugged and shabby condition, those elite schoolboys nevertheless emphasized 'the pursuit of knowledge in academic fields such as Western literature, culture, philosophy, and art'.[24] For Ishizu, the dandyism of Ivy League style and the rusticity of *bankara*, both of which were founded on a balancing act between the concepts of privileged sophistication and ruggedness, were two sides of the same coin. Thus, this cross-cultural affinity of male fashion aesthetics illustrates the claim made by Jan Nederveen Pieterse that interactions of cultures are founded on cultural affinities rather than on difference.[25]

VAN clothing, and hence the Ivy style, became popular in the mid-1960s in Japan. The covers of earlier issues of *Men's Club* are a visual testament of this.[26] The first issue of the men's lifestyle magazine *Heibon Punch* also featured Ayumi Ōhashi's illustration of Ivy style boys on its cover in 1964. Although strictly speaking different from the 'Ivy Boys', the fashionable youth who sauntered around Miyuki Street in the famous fashion district of Ginza, called

Figure 6.1 Bankara boys of old higher schools (*kyūsei kōkō*) in school uniform, c. 1930s. Photo from author's family collection.

Miyuki-Zoku (Miyuki Tribe), appeared, quite fleetingly, at the same time.[27] The tribe was divided primarily into two fashion groups. One group of the males wore dressed-down Ivy style clothes with particular emphasis on VAN items (including the brand's paper bag), and short, clean-cut hairstyles (Figure 6.2).

The other group, though fewer in number, wore the 'European continental' style with more flamboyant colours and styles like the ones designed by another fashion brand JUN (est. 1958). Their fashion inspiration might have been derived from the way James Bond, played by Sean Connery, wore his suit in *From Russia with Love* (1963).[28] From today's perspective, many of them dressed neat enough, and did not display excessive 'antisocial' behaviours, but they were caught and admonished by the police in September 1964, which marked the end of Miyuki Tribe. At that time Tokyo was preparing to host the Olympic Games, and it was allegedly part of the scheme to 'clean up' any culture that would look socially disruptive to the eyes of foreigners. Rather surprisingly, those Ivy-style clad young men and women were perceived as a moral threat by people from older generations.[29]

In the aftermath of the hippy movement, a revaluation of the Ivy style took place, and the style became associated with the readership of *Popeye*, a fashion

Figure 6.2 'Miyuki Zoku' in Tokyo, Japan. Fashion-conscious young Japanese people, called 'Miyuki Zoku', get together on Miyuki Dori Street in Tokyo's posh Ginza district. The photo was taken in the mid-1960s.

magazine for 'city boys' in the late 1970s and early 1980s. The typical look of Popeye boys, as they were called from this time, included a sporty European-branded polo shirt and a navy blazer, which became a fashion symbol of college boys at that time.[30] It was also in the late 1970s that the 'New Traditional' styles for women emerged in the Kobe district, and later in the Yokohama district. These styles were called 'Yokohama Traditional' or 'Hama-tra'.[31] The Hama-tra style is said to be inspired by the Northern American schoolgirl look, with a three-quarter-sleeved shirt, wrap-around skirt, a pair of flat shoes (both of which are preferably made by Fukuzo and Mihama, brands produced in Yokohama), and a Courrèges shoulder bag.[32] The style was believed to be either originated or popularized by the students of Ferris University, a 'privileged' all-women college in Yokohama, and this 'trad' style for young women was perceived as ideal in order to showcase 'innocent' and 'ladylike' femininity.

In the late 1980s and early 1990s, there was another fashion trend called 'Shibuya Casual' (abbreviated as 'Shibu-caji'), allegedly made popular by college and high school students in the upper-class areas of Tokyo (*yamanote*). The orthodoxy of the style, which was largely unisex, consisted of a navy blazer over a polo shirt, straight-fit jeans and a pair of loafers.[33] Perhaps the most striking aspect of the Shibu-caji style was its preference for American and European luxury brands. Despite the simple appearance, items such as a Ralph Lauren jacket and shirt, jeans made by Levi's, and a Louis Vuitton bag were 'musts'.[34] A cheaper, simpler version with the preference of black-and-white aesthetics called 'French-casual' emerged in the early 1990s with the particular emphasis on the items of agnès b., but this time led by a group of high school girls.[35]

The Ivy style is once again popular in the twenty-first century. This is particularly true for those who appreciate the neat and conservative (*kireime*) look and high-casual mode. This modern day revival of the Ivy style was particularly evident in the years between 2007 and 2008, and again in 2012 where Japanese men's fashion magazines concurrently featured the style (see for example, 'New Preppy Standard' edition of *Brutus*, April 2012; 'All About Rugged Trad' edition of *Free & Easy*, April 2012). The November 2007 issue of *Men's non-no* introduced the Ivy style with a tight silhouette, which the magazine called a 'Neo-Ivy style'. In the fashion spreads, the model Takeshi Mikawai is neatly and stylishly dressed, wearing a Cowichan sweater, a V-necked navy vest, a white shirt with button-down collar, black tie and a pair of striped trousers. Some of the pictures show Mikawai standing in front of an ivy-covered building, thus maintaining and visually emphasizing the link between fashion photography and the concept of Ivy League. We might wonder that the garments – or at least some of them – that Mikawai is wearing in the fashion spreads make him look more like a neat and elegant schoolboy than an 'uncouth' American Ivy League freshman in the early 1960s. What does this suggest? It seems that in Japanese fashion culture, Ivy style has become a sign, a symbol that is ready to commingle with other similar yet different styles or concepts. Indeed, the aesthetics of the 'Ivy' were amalgamated with other styles and have produced a number of similar fashions with a subtle nuance.

Dressing up for school: variations of the school style

A brief list of commingled styles includes 'college boy', a boyish look for grown-ups (*Popeye* November 2007); 'new preppy', with its white cricket sweater, striped shirt, narrow black tie and pair of off-white cotton trousers, all designed by UK brand Duffer of St. George, and worn in a dressed-down way (*Popeye*, September 2007); casual, yet elegant 'British traditional' (*Men's non-no*, December 2007); and 'French preppy' with its colourful Lacoste items visualizing the dual concept of sporty and elegance (*Fineboys*, April 2010). One style that we might find rather unusual is the 'dress preppy' style. This comprises Takeo Kikuchi's blue and yellow frilled or pale pink lace-embroidered shirts with white collar, or a simple coordination of a white shirt, grey narrow tie and navy cardigan, which are 'dressed up' with a pair of grey check trousers on which a brocade pattern is printed (*Popeye*, April 2007).

A style named 'school style' is another example of Japanese appropriation of the Ivy style. It is a 'blanket' term for styles including 'Ivy', 'preppy', 'European traditional' and 'schoolboy look'.[36] In the simplest term, the styles coming with the coordination of a shirt and narrow tie, jacket, letter sweater or pea coat could all be described as a school style. As we have seen in Chapter 3, the popularity of such a style in contemporary Japanese men's fashion scene is also indicated by Milkboy and its boyish yet edgy styles. The terms 'Ivy', 'preppy' and 'school' are also used in Japanese men's fashion magazines almost interchangeably. These styles are likely to be created with intentions to market and sell the fashion items rather than reflecting the actual fashion trend. One thing we can deduce from looking at these fashions, however, is that these styles combine sometimes opposing concepts of boyishness, casualness and neatness with a touch of elegance. In other words, the definite essence of the Japanese Ivy style is a rugged-suave look.

Arguably, one of the reasons for the perennial popularity and presence of the Ivy style in Japan is the style's detachment from class systems. In the United States, the Ivy style and the items associated with the fashion, such as a navy blazer, initially connoted an ideal dress identity for the army of traditionalist American men of the early post-war era.[37] In this sense, Ivy style was less about fashion and more about the regalia of privileged, conservative and conformist masculine identity. On the contrary, from the beginning, the Japanese Ivy style was marketed as a stylish, consumable fashion by such figures as Ishizu, *Men's*

Club and *Heibon Punch*. The significance of the Japanese Ivy style lies in the fact that such a privileged, suave male aesthetic has been recreated as everyday wear in Japan. It is fair to say that Japanese fashion culture has incorporated the insignia of elite Ivy Leaguers into their everyday style, making it available for virtually everyone who can afford it.

What is striking about the Japanese embrace of the Ivy style is not only its rescue of the style from possible extinction, but also its demonstration of subtly nuanced changes and transformations. While in 1965, *Take Ivy* defined Ivy Leaguers as uncouth dressers who 'don't bother looking neat for classes', today's Ivy style boys are, judging from the images represented in men's fashion publications, significantly more suave.[38] This process of Japanese adoption and appropriation of the Ivy style can be illustrated by the comparison between *Take Ivy* and another renowned Japanese publication, Kazuo Hozumi's *IVY Illustrated*. Hozumi, an established fashion illustrator and men's fashion expert, first created the distinct characters of big-eyed and round-faced 'Ivy Boy' and 'Ivy Girl' in the early 1960s, which were subsequently adopted by VAN Jacket to accompany its posters. His *IVY Illustrated* was, as he recollects later in 2003, originally intended as a manual for young men to learn how to dress in a systematic yet enjoyable way.[39]

Rugged suavity: *Take Ivy* and *IVY Illustrated*

Fashion critic Guy Trebay wrote in his *New York Times* article in 2010 that *Take Ivy* is '[p]art style manual for Japanese fans of American "trad" style and, somewhat inadvertently, an ethnographic study' of the Ivy Leaguers in the mid-1960s.[40] Its aim was quite obviously to capture and introduce the 'realistic' aspects of the subcultural lives of Ivy Leaguers in the early-to-mid 1960s. Published fifteen years after *Take Ivy*, Hozumi's *IVY Illustrated*, by contrast, revolves around idealized images of Ivy boys.

There are a number of differences outlined via a comparison between the two Japanese publications. *Take Ivy* tells the reader that Ivy boys do not 'bother looking neat for classes. They feel that they can get away with dressing casually as long as they don't look too shabby.'[41] This contrasts with the statement made in *IVY Illustrated*, which says, 'Ivy Boys take a great care of their appearance. A pleasant appearance is the first step of every fashion.'[42] There are subtle changes regarding the styles, too. *Take Ivy*, for instance, documents that during the week, Ivy Leaguers seldom wear ties and jackets, for it is trendy to dress casually on campus.[43] Even on Sunday, they would not wear a blazer. Instead, these young men would wear a tie with a cotton jacket, tweed jacket with a pair of jeans and so forth.[44]

Hozumi's *IVY Illustrated* says the opposite, for Ivy boys would wear a blazer even in the summer to dress up.[45] The Ivy Leaguers captured in *Take Ivy* are 'uncouth' dressers who, in their everyday lives, tend to dress for practicability rather than aesthetics. As we have seen, this is exactly what Ishizu thought the aesthetics of Ivy style and Japanese *bankara* shared in common. In contrast, Hozumi's version of Ivy boys are neatly dressed conservatives who respect tradition, and the foundations of their styles are appropriated forms of British Edwardian dandies.[46]

As noted in Chapter 3, along with the Ivy style, 'Neo-Edwardian' dandy style is a popular style frequently featured in contemporary men's fashion magazines like *Popeye* and *Men's non-no*, as well as street menswear labels like Milkboy. The male sartorial elegance that Neo-Edwardian dandy style carries closely associates with the Japanese conceptualization of the Ivy style. As a matter of fact, we see a striking resemblance between one of the styles offered by Hozumi, a winter style for Ivy boys featuring a navy blazer, grey flannel trousers, white shirt and regimental tie, and the 'Neo-Edwardian' dandy look in *Popeye* that is discussed in Chapter 3.[47] Only the navy blazer is replaced, by a black trench coat.

It may not be surprising to see a link that unites the Ivy style and historical European men's fashions. The Ivy style that Japanese fashion culture captured first of all in the 1960s and again in the 1980s, might have been, as writer Madoka Yamazaki has pointed out, a product of the admiration that White Anglo-Saxon Protestants (WASPs) had a European past.[48] It needs to be noted, however, that Ishizu too thinks the origin of the Ivy style could be traced to British men's fashion. For instance, when he entered university in 1929, Ishizu dressed in a British style: hand-woven tweed three-piece suit, oxford shirt, club tie and Burberry coat. He recalled this British fashion as perhaps signalling his first encounter with the Ivy League style.[49] The presence of fashion labels like Burberry Black Label demonstrates that the 'Edwardian Dandy' styles, once ascribed to certain social classes in England, have been claimed in contemporary Japan and Hong Kong as elegant yet affordable men's fashion. This further supports the hypothesis that clothing forms, which initially were carriers of clear social-class distinction, can be adopted and appropriated as a 'fashion', and become consumed by greater number of individuals in Japan.

The differences outlined via the comparison of these two Japanese publications indicate that *IVY Illustrated* is concerned more about an idealized and possibly 'appropriated' image of Ivy boys, which are integrated into the Japanese conception of the Ivy style today. In other words, Hozumi's Ivy boys are more likely an outcome of the fifteen years of fusion between American and Japanese cultures than a direct historical representation. Evidently, Hozumi's *IVY Illustrated* states that the spirit of 'Ivy' is to respect and appreciate traditions. Thus, as Hozumi writes, it would be desirable for Japanese Ivy boys and girls to wear the kimono at certain occasions such as at the summer festival, graduation ceremony and wedding.[50]

The further flow of Ivy is evident in Colman's perception of Ivy style. He calls the combination of a blue blazer, button-down collar, Bermudas and loafers the 'full-on Japanese prep' against the low-key version of the style with plain boat shoes, a faded Lacoste shirt with jeans or an off-white suit with a madras tie, the latter of which some American men still prefer. The 'full-on Japanese prep', according to Colman, requires 'the attitude to carry it off' in order to look good outside the Japanese context.[51] According to this view, the non-Japanese-oriented styles of 'Ivy' have been adopted and localized in Japan, and in turn, this blended style has been re-imported to the United States. While the famous J. Press, a most respected 'original' Ivy League clothier, was purchased by Onward Kashimaya of Japan in 1986 (in an amicable agreement, according to Richard Press) and now sells roughly six times as much as American-made J. Press merchandise there, it is not by any means a Japan-only phenomenon.[52] According to Patricia Mears, Ivy style is about 'the story of ostensible outsiders borrowing from and bettering the holy tartan', including the Italian-born Claudio Del Vecchio family owning Brooks Brothers, and Jewish creativities demonstrated via Band of Outsiders and Ralph Lauren, among others.[53] Nevertheless, this hints at both the popularity of preppy/Ivy style clothing in Japan and further flows of Ivy style. *Take Ivy* and *IVY Illustrated* are important for our understanding of the Ivy style in contemporary Japan, which often combines the ideas conceptualized by the two publications – 'uncouth' casualness and neat elegance. Equally significant in relation to this localizing process of the Ivy style in Japan is the strong presence of the 'Ivy' look for women.

Preppy girls

There is no written rule stating that Ivy style is boys-only, and there are versions of the style marketed at and taken up by women. In recent times, the character of Blair Waldorf in *Gossip Girl* is said to have contributed to the popularization of a conservative, preppy-chic look for young women, to note one example.[54] Despite this, men still occupy centre stage of Ivy style outside Japan. Perhaps reflecting this tendency, *Take Ivy* devotes a very limited space to the fashion of female students. It is therefore significant that six months after the illustrated work of Ivy boys, Hozumi published its 'gal' version. According to the author, the publication of the girls' version was to meet the demands of (female) readers, who wished to have style guides for young women.[55] Hozumi's illustrated book can be construed as symbolic of the strong presence of women within the Ivy style in Japan. The basic style for 'Ivy girls' as described in both *Take Ivy* and *IVY Illustrated* are similar. *Take Ivy* defines this style as a cotton dress, a plain blouse and a banal, mass-produced, pleated skirt,[56] and *IVY Illustrated* introduces a plain and simple, puff-sleeved cotton dress as the all-time favourite for Ivy gals.[57]

In both publications, neatness, simplicity and youthfulness are the key for Ivy girls' styles.

In modern times, the 'Ivy/preppy girl' style is commingled with the schoolgirl-like *kawaii* (cute) aesthetics in Japan. Chapter 4 demonstrated that certain kinds of *kawaii* aesthetics allow women to embrace the 'infantile' cute and almost saccharine fashion philosophy without hinting at obvious sexual allure. With the *kawaii* aesthetic, Japanese girl culture has reinvented such sartorial items as a beret, a blazer and a pair of argyle-patterned socks as cute and girlish fashion items. As recently as October 2010, *CUTiE*, a magazine for young women who prefer mainstream street fashion, offered the preppy style as a cute, schoolgirl style that would attract boys. Perhaps exploring the style more flamboyantly, the November 2010 issue of another fashion magazine for young women, *Zipper*, offered a modified preppy style. The imaginaries of these Japanese publications, particularly the latter, allude to further processes of change and to the continual remakings of the style. Now a preppy cardigan can be worn with a tiger-patterned miniskirt or a navy 'Ivy' blazer with a pair of Dr Martens.

Similar to what I argued of male fashionability and possible motivations in Chapter 3, the same aesthetic concept of 'Ivy (preppy)' can be interpreted as both chic and appealing to men (*CUTiE*) and a showcase of more flamboyant fashion senses (*Zipper*). This flexibility of 'preppy girl style' in Japan illustrates the theory of 'format' and 'product' as articulated by Keiko Okamura.[58] According to this theory, the Ivy style has now become a 'format' ready to create a 'product' that reflects further processes of cultural commingling, interaction and appropriation.

The styles for Ivy boys and Ivy girls are different in form. We have seen variations of the Ivy style offered by men's fashion magazines, some of which are colourful and ornate, but the Ivy style for boys still tends to be relatively conservative compared to the 'Ivy girl style'. For one thing, it does not include such items as a miniskirt or a beret, although the latter has been part of other styles for men. *Choki Choki*, a fashion and hairstyle magazine for salon-*kei* (salon-mode) conceptualizes this point. The 'Ivy/preppy styles' featured in *Choki Choki* include a navy fedora hat, a black leather jacket, a dark green letter sweater, a pair of checked trousers and a pair of second-hand red/brown shoes (November 2010, p. 85), a black cardigan, a narrow black tie with polka-dot pattern and red trainers (November 2010, p. 162), or a second-hand navy schoolboy jacket, a white cricket sweater, a pair of wide-silhouetted beige chino trousers and a pair of brown leather shoes (May 2011, p. 37). The sober simplicity of these 'Ivy styles' indicates that like other fashion cultures, Japanese fashion is not moving toward the extinction of gender distinctions. After all, as Steele has rightly said, men and women appear differently, and what they wear may reinforce or reflect gender roles.[59]

What the Japanese Ivy style illuminates, however, is the presence of a certain degree of similarity between the styles adopted by men and women, particularly their embrace of similar fashion aesthetics. Although it might be a utopian view, I suggest that the Japanese version of Ivy style seems to accept differences between men and women, and yet offers them almost equal opportunities to appreciate the same (or at least very similar) fashion aesthetics. As we have seen, this point is also supported by actual fashion brands like Milkboy as well. It is plausible that this is another testament of the notion that fashion is important for both men and women, and that gender distinctions might be – even if only in very subtle degrees – differently understood in contemporary Japanese culture.

Conclusion

Since its introduction by Kensuke Ishizu and his VAN Jacket brand in the 1950s, the Ivy style has achieved almost perennial popularity in Japanese fashion culture. Beginning with the now-classic *Take Ivy* through delightful *IVY Illustrated* to contemporary men's fashion magazines, subtly nuanced transformations in the Japanese Ivy style have been documented. Rather than being attached to a certain social class where the style was initially located, from the beginning, the Japanese Ivy style was marketed as stylish, consumable fashion. In Japanese fashion culture, the Ivy style has become a sign, a symbol that is ready to commingle with other similar yet different fashions or concepts, resulting in the production of a number of similar styles with a subtle nuance. It is fair to say that Japanese fashion culture has incorporated the unofficial uniform of elite Ivy Leaguers into their everyday style, making it available for virtually everyone who can afford it.

The Japanese version of the Ivy League style is a good example of a global crossing. A cultural form is accepted in a different cultural context, blended with 'local' characteristics, and then flows out again. Japanese adoption and appropriation of the Ivy League style, as we have seen, tells of a cultural process where 'American' clothing styles are blended with 'Japanese' aesthetic ideals and preferences. This cultural amalgam has in turn been re-imported to non-Japanese countries like the United States, thereby creating new meanings and new markets for this now perennial style.

The Japanese Ivy style also illustrates that not only men but also women take part in the style. This suggests that individuals of both genders may engage with fashion in very similar, if not identical, ways. Principally men and women in contemporary Japanese society dress and look differently. But the availability of 'Ivy/preppy style' for both men and women in Japanese fashion culture hints at the presence of almost equal opportunities to appreciate the similar fashion aesthetics. In this sense, the Ivy style is a notable interpretive illustration of fashion and change within a transnational world.

7

CONCLUDING JAPANESE FASHION CULTURES, CHANGE AND CONTINUITY

It is Ulrich Lehmann who articulates that fashion symbolizes 'permanent novelty and constant, insatiable change'.[1] While the definite meaning of fashion seems to be hard to grasp, changeable natures of fashion can be observed in the case studies we have seen in this book. Men's fashion magazine *Popeye* has since undergone a makeover and now focuses more on the aspects of culture and fashion while some magazines have ceased to exist. *Lolita* fashion still remains a minority one in Japan, but its visibility at an international level, however modest, seems growing. Brands like Baby and Angelic Pretty have opened their overseas stores in Paris, San Francisco and, for the latter, Shanghai, while the items of Innocent World can now be purchased in places like Stockholm, Bilthoven and New York, perhaps corresponding to where Japanese pop culture has become familiar and accessible. On the other hand, continual a resurgence of Ivy style and the presence of Milkboy, celebrating its fortieth birthday in 2014, along with the seemingly ever-unfading concept of *kawaii*, are indications of fashion being a process of transformation and continuity. Needless to say, the styles I have analysed in this book are only a small portion of clothing styles available in Japan. There are a number of different styles present for both men and women, and some of them are, for example, regarded as more revolving around romantic attraction while others might have creative twists, with the desire to attract admirers being lower in priority. The significance of the culture of Japanese clothing precisely lies in this diversity.

Since this book has focused only on a portion of contemporary Japanese popular culture and sartorial style, how individuals associate with these styles in their real lives must be pursued in another context. Further research on this issue will open a door to more critical and hence trustworthy conceptions of clothing as a cultural metaphor that is complete when animated by a body.

In the preceding chapters, I have identified some alternatives to the anachronistic yet persistent preconceptions about how men and women are assumed to engage with fashion. Such preconceptions adhere to the ideas that men dress for utility rather than for aesthetics, while women's motivations for fashion are predominantly geared to attract and please men. These 'distorted' conceptions have been firmly challenged by a series of theories in both dress scholarship and sociology that attest that motivations for dress, regardless of gender, can be more complex than that. Yet fragments of these preconceptions are still somewhat culturally ingrained, and persist in mainstream popular culture. My analyses of some select manifestations of mainstream Japanese popular culture, in relation to fashion, have, I hope, furthered those already established arguments. I have shown that not only women but also men dress for both the eyes of public and for themselves. I have demonstrated that a certain kind of 'infantile' cute aesthetics can be empowering. Finally, I have argued that an opulently decorated, girlish fashion does not necessarily need to be read as symbolic of female oppression and objectification. These points reinforce the contention made by Entwistle that we dress for different motivations depending on circumstances.[2] Our motivation for dress involves myriad factors rather than merely reflecting (often imposed) gender roles. Steele has convincingly articulated this point:

> For both men and women, whenever sex is an issue, so also is looking and being seen. Every woman who has ever been accosted on the street knows the temporary desire to be invisible, just as every person of either sex has posed in public, hoping to be regarded as attractive by his or her peers.[3]

Thus, as the principles of fashion house Milkboy has stated, taking care of one's appearance can be done to attract and please admirers as well as for one's own pleasure, reinforcing what I discussed in Chapter 3.

This book makes the final point that whether it was an Edwardian dandy, a Victorian upper-class girl, the rococo princess or the Ivy Leaguers in the 1960s, aesthetic essences of the romantic past are adopted, restyled and given new meanings in contemporary Japanese culture. This attests to the socio-cultural approaches that recognize the complexity of cultural globalization, where 'global' and 'local' cultures interact instead of one infiltrating the weaker others. Needless to say, the process of cultural globalization might not always operate in 'amicable' ways. There still exist issues of power and inequality, for example.[4] But as Roland Robertson has argued in relation to 'glocalization', the local is defined by the global, and 'when one considers them closely, they each have a local, diversifying aspect'.[5] Building on Nederveen Pieterse's theory of syncretism, I contend that cultural syncretism is a fusion of cultural forms in which two forms have changed and a 'third' cultural form has developed.[6]

This is what I hope my analyses of the selected clothing styles have elucidated. The Japanese incorporation of 'Neo-Edwardian' dandy styles into the field of mainstream men's fashion has two significant meanings. Namely, as the examples of Japanese men's fashion publications and the menswear brand Milkboy illustrate, such styles not only render these pleasantly suave and stylish aesthetics available at wider, everyday levels, but they also operate (consciously or otherwise) as an effective way to reinvent a mode of masculinity that works in contrast to the worn-out, dowdy 'salaryman'. I have shown how the imagery of Lewis Carroll's Alice and the dress of Victorian young misses are deployed by a group of Japanese young female performers in order to articulate 'infantile' cuteness, in a manner largely detached from the heterosexual economy. I have explained a synchronicity between the Victorian 'little girls' dresses' and a particular kind of Japanese *kawaii* aesthetic, and shown how it results in the detachment of eroticism from the representation of 'sweet' and 'girlish' sartorial styles. In addition, I have asserted that it also serves as an alternative to the established multiple binaries of sexualization, assertion and subservience in which women tend to be represented.

In similar fashion, Japanese *Lolita* style, which is quite ostensibly a style drawing strongly on the conceptualization of European historic dress aesthetics, can be read as a quintessential cultural amalgam. The film *Shimotsuma Monogatari* and its portrayal of the style attest to this. The teenage heroine, who is dressed almost thoroughly in the extravagantly opulent fashion, engages in both conventionally masculine and feminine activities quite fluently. This interpretation of the elaborate girlish fashion not only reinforces the established theories that argue against the preconception that accuses decorative femininity and its alleged impracticability of limiting women, but also reinforces the socio-psychological definition of androgyny. Such a definition of androgyny tells us that, contrary to the apparent fixity in our biological gender, most of us have both conventionally masculine and feminine attributes. Expressions of these 'gender' attributes, then, do not necessarily have to be connected to the traditional sartorial modes. This arguably inscribes new and, by and large, more innovative meanings, to historical, opulently decorated women's dresses.

Finally, the Japanese embrace of the 'Ivy style' within this theme illustrates that both men and women may engage with fashion in very similar, if not identical, ways. This is a testament to what the cultural and social-psychological analysis of gender has argued. While the presence of biological distinctions between men and women is incontestable, as human beings, these theoretical perspectives believe that such differences might be less significant than differences created by individuality. This book has demonstrated that principally men and women in contemporary Japanese society dress and look differently. But their motivations for dress, whether to impress and attract admirers, to serve their own pleasures or to manifest their 'revolt' against cultural preconceptions could be shared by individuals regardless of gender. To a certain degree, this brings men and women closer. Hollander expressed in 1994 that 'any true account of clothing must consider both sexes together', because '[f]ashion has affected both sexes equally, and nobody with eyes escapes it'.[7] My analyses of clothing and Japanese cultural texts attest that many of Hollander's wide-ranging perspectives on fashion and gender are still credible today, and equally so in Japanese fashion cultures.

NOTES

1. Introducing Japanese fashion, past and present

1 Phil Hammond, 'The Mystification of Culture: Western Perception of Japan', *Gazette*, 61(3–4), 1999, p. 312.

2 Koichi Iwabuchi, 'Complicit Exoticism: Japan and Its Other', *Continuum*, 8(2), 1994.

3 Oscar Wilde, 'The Decay of Lying: An Observation' in *Oscar Wilde Plays, Prose Writings and Poems* (London: David Campbell Publishers, 1991 [1891]) p. 94.

4 Alistair Phillips and Julian Stringer, 'Introduction', in A. Phillips and J. Stringer (eds), *Japanese Cinema: Texts and Contexts* (London and New York: Routledge, 2007), p. 14.

5 Diana Crane, *The Production of Culture: Media and the Urban Arts* (Newbury Park, London and New Delhi: SAGE Publications, 1992), p. 96.

6 Jan Nederveen Pieterse, *Globalization and Culture: Global Mélange* (Maryland: Roman & Littlefield Publishers, 2004), p. 46.

7 Margaret Maynard, *Dress and Globalization* (Manchester: Manchester University Press, 2004), p. 3.

8 Toby Slade, 'Clothing Modern Japan' (PhD Thesis, University of Sydney. 2006); Ken'ichiro Hirano, 'The Westernization of Clothes and the State in Meiji Japan', in K. Hirano (ed.), *The State and Cultural Transformation: Perspectives from East Asia* (Tokyo: United Nations University Press, 1993).

9 Keiko Okamura, *Gurohbaru shakai no ibunka-ron (Cross-cultural Theory in Global Societies)* (Kyoto: Sekaishiso-sha, 2003), pp. 137–49.

10 Kazuo Hozumi, *IVY Illustrated* (Tokyo: Aiiku-sha, 2003 [1980]), p. 132. Quote translated by Masafumi Monden.

11 Peter McNeil, 'Introduction: Late Medieval to Renaissance Fashion', in P. McNeil (ed.), *Fashion: Critical and Primary Sources*, Volume 1 (Oxford and New York: Berg Publishers, 2009), p. xxxiii.

12 Elizabeth Wilson, 'Fashion and Postmodern Body', in J. Ash and E. Wilson (eds), *Chic Thrills: A Fashion Reader* (Berkeley and Los Angeles: University of California Press, 1992), p. 5.

13 Wilson, 'Fashion and Postmodern Body', p. 6.

14 Ivan Morris, *The World of the Shining Prince: Court Life in Ancient Japan* (New York, Tokyo, London: Kodansha International, 1994 [1964]), pp. 194, 204.

15   Seiki Nagasaki, *Kasane no irome* (*The Combination of Colors in Layers: The Aesthetics of Color in the Heian Period*) (Kyoto: Seigensha, 2001 [1987]).

16   Lady Murasaki, *Genji Monogatari* (*The Tale of Genji*), trans. A. Waley, Volume 1 (London: George Allen & Unwin LTD, 1973 [1935]), p. 152.

17   Fusae Kawazoe, *Hikaru genji ga aishita ouchou brand hin* (*The dynastic brand artifacts Prince Genji loved*) (Tokyo: Kadokawa Gakugei Shuppan, 2008), p. 157.

18   A *hakama* is a long pleated divided skirt worn over the kimono. This description is largely based on Tengai Kosugi's novel *Makaze Koikaze* (1903), as cited in Melanie Czarnecki's 'Bad Girls from Good Families'.

19   Rebecca L. Copeland, 'Fashioning the Feminine: Images of the Modern Girl Student in Meiji Japan', *U.S.-Japan Women's Journal*, 30–1, 2006, p. 18.

20   Alisa Freedman, *Tokyo in Transit: Japanese Culture on the Rails and Road* (Stanford: Stanford University Press, 2011), p. 29.

21   Copeland, 'Fashioning the Feminine', p. 22.

22   Melanie Czarnecki, 'Bad Girls from Good Families: The Degenerate Meiji Schoolgirl', in L. Miller and J. Bardsley (eds), *Bad Girls of Japan* (New York: Palgrave Macmillan, 2005). The term 'high collar' (*haikara*) originally referred to a man's European shirt and the men who wore it at the turn of the twentieth century. It became jargon for describing individuals who were 'Westernized' or modern and chic. Today, the term is most often associated with schoolgirls who were dressed in the style similar to the one described here.

23   See, for example, Slade, 'Clothing Modern Japan'; Hirano, 'The Westernization of Clothes and the State in Meiji Japan'.

24   Llewyen Negrin, *Appearance and Identity: Fashioning the Body in Postmodernity* (New York: Palgrave Macmillan, 2008), p. 30.

25   Elizabeth Wilson, *Adorned in Dreams* (London: Virago, 1985), p. 117.

26   Vera Mackie, 'Transnational Bricolage: Gothic Lolita and the Political Economy of Fashion', *Intersections: Gender and Sexuality in Asia and the Pacific*, 20, April 2009.

27   Joanne Entwistle, *The Fashioned Body: Fashion, Dress and Modern Social Theory* (Cambridge: Polity Press, 2000), p. 140.

28   Judith Butler, 'Bodily Inscriptions, Performative Subversions', in S. Salih and J. Butler (eds), *The Judith Butler Reader* (Malden: Blackwell Publishers, 2004 [1990]), p. 114.

29   Butler, 'Bodily Inscriptions, Performative Subversions', p. 115.

30   Carrie Paechter, 'Masculine Femininities/Feminine Masculinities: Power, Identities and Gender', *Gender and Education*, 18(3), 2006; Drucilla Cornell, *At the Heart of Freedom: Feminism, Sex, and Equality* (Princeton: Princeton University Press, 1998), p. 80.

31   Joanne B. Eicher, 'Dress, Gender and the Public Display of Skin', in J. Entwistle and E. Wilson (eds), *Body Dressing* (Oxford and New York: Berg, 2001), p. 244.

32   Entwistle, *The Fashioned Body*, p. 141.

33   Sandra L. Bem, *The Lenses of Gender: Transforming the Debate on Sexual Inequality* (New Haven and London: Yale University Press, 1993), pp. 151, 148. It is significant that Valerie Steele and Marjorie Garber both note that this gendered scheme of colour is a recent historical cultural and construction, as boys would wear pink and girls blue before World War I (Garber, 1992: 1). See also V. Steele,

'Appearance and Identity', in C. B. Kidwell and V. Steele (eds), *Men and Women Dressing the Part* (Washington: Smithonian Institution Press, 1989), p. 6.

34 Anne Hollander, *Sex and Suits* (NY: Knopf, 1994), p. 33.

35 Entwistle, *The Fashioned Body*, p. 157.

36 Hollander, *Sex and Suits*, p. 40.

37 Hollander, *Sex and Suits*, p. 40.

38 Hollander, *Sex and Suits*, p. 40.

39 For more detailed accounts of Japanese history of dress, see Liza Dalby, *Kimono: Fashioning Culture* (London: Vintage, 2001 [1993]); Toby Slade, *Japanese Fashion: A Cultural History* (London and New York: Berg, 2009); Valerie Steele, *Japan Fashion Now* (New York: Yale University Press, 2010).

40 Liza Dalby, *Kimono: Fashioning Culture* (London: Vintage, 2001 [1993]), p. 28.

41 The Heian period lasted for approximately 390 years, from 794 to 1192.

42 Morris, *The World of the Shining Prince*, p. 194.

43 Norio Yamanaka, *The Book of Kimono* (Tokyo, New York and San Francisco: Kodansha International, 1982), pp. 34–5. A *hakama* is a long divided skirt worn over the kimono.

44 Dalby, *Kimono*, p. 39.

45 The Edo period lasted for more than 250 years, from 1603 to 1868.

46 Dalby, *Kimono*, p. 45.

47 Donald. H. Shively, 'Sumtuary Regulation and Status in Early Tokugawa Japan', *Harvard Journal of Asiatic Studies*, 25, 1964–5, p. 133.

48 Shively, Sumtuary Regulation, p. 123; Dalby, *Kimono*, p. 57.

49 Shively, Sumtuary Regulation, p. 134.

50 Shively, Sumtuary Regulation, p. 129.

51 Dalby, *Kimono*, p. 289.

52 The *obi* is a sash worn with the kimono. The width of women's *obi* increased as the length of the *kosode*'s sleeves grew longer in the Genroku period.

53 Dalby, *Kimono*, p. 289. Female actors were banned from appearing on the kabuki stage in 1629, due to concerns about moral decline.

54 Japan Youth Research Institute, 'Koukousei no seikatsu to ishiki ni kansuru chousa (*Survey of the lifestyles and consciousness of high school students*)', 2004 [http://www1.odn.ne.jp/%7Eaaa25710//research/index.html]. [Last accessed 18 May 2014]

55 Susan. J. Napier, 'Vampires, Psychic Girls, Flying Women and Sailor Scouts: Four faces of the Young Female in Japanese Popular Culture', in D. P. Martinez (ed.), *The World of Japanese Popular Culture* (Cambridge: Cambridge University Press, 1998), pp. 104–5.

56 Laura Miller, *Beauty Up: Exploring Contemporary Japanese Body Aesthetics* (Berkeley: University of California Press, 2006).

57 For the relationship between 1970s *manga* culture and (romanticized) Europe, see Keiko Takemiya, '1970 nendai no shōjo manga ni okeru geijutsusei e no shikō to sono mokuteki (1970s *shōjo manga*'s preference for artistry and its purpose)', *Bijutsu Forum 21* (Tokushū: Manga to manga, soshite geijutsu (special issue: Manga, Comics and Art), guest-edited by J. Berndt), 24, 2011, pp. 96–8. I thank Professor Jaqueline Berndt for suggesting this article.

58 Patricia Mears, 'Formalism and Revolution: Rei Kawakubo and Yohji Yamamoto', in V. Steele, *Japan Fashion Now* (New York: Yale University Press, 2010), p. 142.

59 Lise Skov, 'Fashion Trends, Japonisme and Postmodernism', in J. W. Treat (ed.), *Contemporary Japan and Popular Culture* (London: Cuzon, 1996), p. 151.

60 Leela Gandhi, *Postcolonial Theory: A Critical Introduction* (Sydney: Allen & Unwin, 1998), pp. 126–7.

61 David Morley and Kevin Robins, *Space of Identity: Global Media, Electronic Landscapes and Cultural Boundaries* (London: Routledge, 1995), p. 173.

62 Morley and Robins, *Space of Identity*, p. 173.

63 Iwabuchi, 'Complicit Exoticism'.

64 See, for example, Nederveen Pieterse, *Globalization and Culture*; Arjun Appadurai, 'Disjuncture and Difference in the Global Cultural Economy', in B. Robbins (ed.), *The Phantom Public Sphere* (Minneapolis: University of Minnesota Press, 1993).

65 Okamura, *Gurohbaru shakai*.

66 Ulf Harnnerz, 'The Cultural Role of the World Cities', in A. Cohen and K. Fukui (eds), *Humanizing the City?* (Edinburgh: Edinburgh University Press, 1993), p. 138.

67 Christopher Breward, *The Hidden Consumers: Masculinities, Fashion and City Life 1860–1914* (Manchester and New York: Manchester University Press, 1999), p. 17.

68 Peter McNeil, 'Art and Dress', in Lise Skov (ed.), *Berg Encyclopedia of World Dress and Fashion, Volume 8: West Europe* (Oxford and New York: Berg, 2010), pp. 522–7.

69 Elisabeth Bronfen, *Over Her Dead Body: Death, Femininity and the Aesthetic* (Manchester: Manchester University Press, 1992), p. 65.

70 Paul A. S. Harvey, 'Nonchan's Dream: NHK Morning Serialized Television Novels', in D. P. Martinez, *The World of Japanese Popular Culture, Shifting Boundaries and Global Cultures* (Cambridge and Melbourne: Cambridge University Press, 1998), p. 133.

71 Ulrich Lehmann, *Tigersprung: Fashion in Modernity* (Cambridge, MA: MIT Press, 2000), p. 299.

72 Crane, *The Production of Culture*, p. 106.

73 R. C. Bulman, *Hollywood Goes to High School: Cinema, Schools, and American Culture* (New York: Worth Publishing, 2005), p. 6.

74 Bulman, *Hollywood Goes to High School*, p. 6.

75 Anne Hollander, *Seeing Through Clothes* (New York: The Viking Press, 1978), p. 451.

76 Elizabeth Wilson, 'Magic Fashion', *Fashion Theory*, 8(4), p. 376.

77 Nederveen Pieterse, *Globalization and Culture*, p. 48.

78 Wilde, 'The Decay of Lying', p. 94.

2. Lost in a gaze: young men and fashion in contemporary Japan

1 Jane Austen, *Northanger Abbey* (London: Penguin Books, 1996 [1818]), p. 22.

2 The targeted readership of these publications is a heterosexual male. This is made obvious through the heterosexual discourse they deploy throughout. These magazines often run features with such titles as 'The styles that attract girls' or 'What fashion items girls like', and young women's perspectives on men's fashion styles are often incorporated. The absence of images or contents related to sexuality in many of these magazines including *Popeye* and *Men's non-no*, particularly in their fashion content, nevertheless may attract men regardless of their sexual orientations. In the strict sense of the term, narcissism means one's pathological attachment to or interest in one's own appearance. However, the word vanity, too, inevitably conveys negativity – excessive pride in or admiration of one's own appearance. In this chapter, narcissism or narcissistic concern is used to describe one's strong concern for appearance, which does not necessarily invoke negativity.

3 See, for example Laura Mulvey, 'Visual Pleasure and Narrative Cinema', in M. G. Durham and D. Kellner (eds), *Media and Cultural Studies: Key Works* (Oxford: Blackwell Publishers, 2001 [1975]); Susan Bordo, 'Beauty (Re)Discovers the Male Body', in Z. P. Brand (ed.), *Beauty Matters* (Bloomington: Indiana University Press, 2000); E. A. Kaplan, *Women and Film: Both Sides of the Camera* (New York and London: Methuen, 1983).

4 Laura Miller, *Beauty Up: Exploring Contemporary Japanese Body Aesthetics* (Berkeley: University of California Press, 2006).

5 John Clammer, 'Consuming Bodies: Constructing and Representing the Female Body in Contemporary Japanese Print Media', in L. Skov and B. Morean (eds), *Women, Media and Consumption in Japan* (Richmond, Surrey: Curzon Press, 1995), p. 210.

6 Mariko Morimoto and Susan Chang, 'Western and Asian Models in Japanese Fashion Magazine Ads: The Relationship with Brand Origins and International Versus Domestic Magazines', *Journal of International Consumer Marketing*, 21(3), 2009, p. 179.

7 According to Brian Moeran (2006: 229), more than fifty major new titles were launched in 2002 alone.

8 *Fashion Magazine: Men's Fashion Zassi Gaido (Men's Fashion Magazine Guide)*. (http://www.magazine-data.com/menu/oyazi.html). As of 18 May 2014, this website lists forty monthly men's magazines currently sold in Japan.

9 Brian Moeran, 'Elegance and Substance Travel East: Vogue Nippon', *Fashion Theory*, 10(1/2), 2006, p. 229.

10 Bunkyō-dō (http://bignet2.bunkyodo.co.jp/bignet2/magranking.asp?id=dajoh). Bunkyō-dō is currently one of the biggest chains of bookstores in Japan.

11 JMPA Magazine data: Dansei Life Design. Survey periods: 1 October 2011 to 30 September 2012. Available at http://www.j-magazine.or.jp/data_002/m2.html#002 [accessed 5 October 2013].

12 *Fineboys*, August 2007, pp. 121–8. According to the magazine, over 600 men participated in the survey. Since it is an informal survey and no information regarding survey methodology is provided, its credibility might be in question. However, it offers a picture of how the magazine's editors perceive and conceptualize their male readers.

13 Kensuke Ishizu, *Itsumo zero kara no shuppatsudatta (I always made my start from nothing)* (Tokyo: Nihon Tosho Centre, 2010), pp. 54–5.

14 The magazine was originally published bimonthly and now weekly.

15 Fabienne Darling-Wolf, 'The Men and Women of non-no: Gender, Race and Hybridity in Two Japanese Magazines', *Cultural Studies in Media Communication*, 23(3), 2006, p. 185.

16   Keiko Tanaka, 'The Language of Japanese Men's Magazines: Young Men Who Don't Want to Get Hurt', in B. Benwell (ed.), *Masculinity and Men's Lifestyle Magazines* (Oxford: Blackwell Publishing, 2003), p. 224.

17   Across Editorial Office (ed.), *Street Fashion 1945–1995* (Tokyo: Parco, 1995), p. 184.

18   Across Editorial Office, *Street Fashion*, pp. 200–2.

19   Germaine Greer, *The Beautiful Boy* (New York: Rizzoli, 2003), p. 7.

20   Christopher Breward, *The Hidden Consumers: Masculinities, Fashion and City Life 1860–1914* (Manchester and New York: Manchester University Press, 1999).

21   Breward, *The Hidden Consumers*, p. 50.

22   Christopher Breward, 'Mode of Manliness: Reflections on Recent Histories of Masculinities and Fashion', in G. Riello and P. McNeil (eds), *The Fashion History Reader: Global Perspectives* (London and New York: Routledge, 2010), pp. 301–2.

23   Peter McNeil, 'Introduction: Late Medieval to Renaissance Fashion', in P. McNeil (ed.), *Fashion: Critical and Primary Sources*, Volume 1 (Oxford and New York: Berg Publishers, 2009), p. xxxiii.

24   G. Bruce Boyer, *Elegance: A Guide to Quality in Menswear* (New York and London: W. W. Norton & Company, 1985), p. 48.

25   Joanne Entwistle, 'From Catwalk to Catalog: Male Fashion Models, Masculinity, and Identity', in H. Thomas and J. Ahmed (eds), *Cultural Bodies: Ethnography and Theory* (Malden and Oxford: Blackwell Publishing, 2004), p. 57.

26   See for example Alice Newbold, 'London Men Stake Their Place in the Fashion Spending Arena', *Telegraph*, 14 June 2012; Asher Moses, '"Ignored" Men Now in Fashion Online', *The Sydney Morning Herald*, 15 August 2012.

27   Joanne Entwistle, *The Fashioned Body: Fashion, Dress and Modern Social Theory* (Cambridge: Polity Press, 2000), p. 186.

28   Sean Nixon, 'Exhibiting Masculinity', in S. Hall (ed.), *Representation: Culture Representation and Signifying Practices* (London: Sage, 1997), p. 296. Needless to say, this 'androcentrism' also provides a demanding definition of 'a real woman'. As Bem (1993: 151) indicates, since it defines women 'in terms of their domestic and reproductive functions, women who are unable to have children almost inevitably experience a sense that they are not real women'.

29   John Beynon, *Masculinities and Culture* (Philadelphia: Open University, 2002), p. 15.

30   Sandra. L. Bem, *The Lenses of Gender: Transforming the Debate on Sexual Inequality* (New Haven and London: Yale University Press, 1993), p. 151.

31   Anne Hollander, *Sex and Suits* (New York: Knopf, 1994), p. 10.

32   Hollander, *Sex and Suits*, p. 11.

33   Christopher Breward, '"On the Bank's Threshold": Administrative Revolutions and the Fashioning of Masculine Identities at the Turn of the Century', *Parallax*, 3(2), 1997, p. 121.

34   Valerie Steele, 'Clothing and Sexuality', in C. B. Kidwell and V. Steele (eds), *Men and Women Dressing the Part* (Washington: Smithsonian Institution Press, 1989), p. 62.

35   Sean Nixon, *Hard Looks: Masculinity, Spectatorship and Contemporary Consumption* (New York: St. Martin's Press, 1996), p. 167.

36 Tim Edwards, 'Consuming Masculinities: Style, Content and Men's Magazines', in P. McNeil and V. Karaminas (eds), *The Men's Fashion Reader* (New York: Berg. 2009), p. 467; Federico Boni, 'Framing Media Masculinities: Men's Lifestyle Magazines and the Biopolitics of Men's Lifestyle Magazines and the Male Body', *European Journal of Communication*, 17(4), 2002, p. 469.

37 The policies of *Popeye*, when it was issued in 1976, included that the magazine would not include nude images (Shiine, 2008: 46).

38 Feona Attwood, '"Tits and Ass and Porn and Fighting": Male Heterosexuality in Magazines for Men', *International Journal of Cultural Studies*, 8(1), 2005, p. 85.

39 Miller, *Beauty Up*, p. 147.

40 Miller, *Beauty Up*, p. 127.

41 Susan. M. Alexander, 'Stylish Hard Bodies: Branded Masculinity in Men's Health Magazines', *Sociological Perspectives*, 46(4), 2003, p. 540. Her research is based on Mediamark Research (2002), and the age distribution is as follows: 23 per cent aged 18–24, 25 per cent aged 25–34, 23 per cent aged 35–44, 18 per cent aged 45–54, and 11 per cent aged 55+.

42 *Shadan-hōjin nihon zasshi-kyōkai* (Japan Magazine Organisation). The survey period was 1 October 2008 to 30 September 2009.

43 The *Men's non-no* website offers the profiles of its models. As of 18 May 2010, fifty-two models are currently hired by the magazine, forty-eight of whom offer their date of birth. The oldest model was thirty-four years old and the youngest seventeen.

44 For instance, *Leon* features Panzetta Girolamo, an Italian celebrity in his late forties living in Japan, as its 'muse' while Hiroshi Abe, who was the first exclusive model of *Men's non-no* in the 1980s, now appears regularly in *Uomo*. Abe is fifty years old as of July 2014.

45 Paul Hodkinson, 'Youth Cultures: A Critical Outline of Key Debates', in P. Hodkinson and W. Deicke (eds), *Youth Cultures: Scenes, Subcultures and Tribes* (New York: Routledge, 2007), p. 1.

46 Merry White, 'The Marketing of Adolescence in Japan: Buying and Dreaming', in L. Skov and B. Moeran (eds), *Women, Media, and Consumption in Japan* (Richmond, Surrey: Curzon Press, 1995), p. 225.

47 Roland Kelts, *Japanamerica: How Japanese Pop Culture Has Invaded the U.S.* (New York: Palgrave Macmillan, 2006), p. 164.

48 *JJ*, women's fashion magazine launched in 1975, became popular by using posh yet 'ordinary' female university students and young female office workers as its models. Such models made a stark contrast to *an an* and *non-no*, both of which predominantly used non-Japanese or Eurasian models at that time.

49 The majority of male figures appearing in magazines like *Choki Choki* are amateur models.

50 Joanne Entwistle, 'From Catwalk to Catalog: Male Fashion Models, Masculinity, and Identity', in H. Thomas and J. Ahmed (eds), *Cultural Bodies: Ethnography and Theory* (Malden and Oxford: Blackwell Publishing, 2004), p. 60.

51 Michael Carter, *Fashion Classics: From Carlyle to Barthes* (New York and Oxford: Berg, 2003), p. 67.

52 Llewyen Negrin, *Appearance and Identity: Fashioning the Body in Postmodernity* (New York: Palgrave Macmillan, 2008), p. 16.

53 *Fineboys*, April 2010, pp. 42–9.

54 *Fineboys*, April 2010, pp. 42–9.

55 *Men's non-no*, February 2008, pp. 142–55.

56 See, for example *Men's non-no*, May 2007, pp. 50–1; *Men's non-no*, January 2008, pp. 50–3.

57 Moeran, 'Elegance and Substance', p. 248.

58 Alexander, 'Stylish Hard Bodies', p. 541.

59 Moeran, 'Elegance and Substance', p. 245.

60 G. Kress and T. van Leeuwen, *Reading Images* (London and New York: Routledge, 1996), pp. 118–19.

61 Nixon, *Hard Looks*, p. 178.

62 Susan Bordo, 'Beauty (Re)Discovers the Male Body', in Z. P. Brand (ed.), *Beauty Matters* (Bloomington: Indiana University Press, 2000), p. 129.

63 Kress and van Leeuwen, *Reading Images*, pp. 124–6.

64 Hiroshi Abe, a now-famous actor, was crowned *non-no* Boyfriend (a male model position in *non-no*) and made his modelling debut in 1986, subsequently gracing the cover of *Men's non-no* forty-three consecutive times until December 1989 (*Men's non-no*, 2006: 160).

65 Alexander, 'Stylish Hard Bodies', p. 541.

66 Darling-Wolf, 'The Men and Women of *non-no*', p. 187.

67 Merry White, *Material Child* (Berkeley and London: University of California Press, 1993), p. 121.

68 *Shadan-hōjin nihon zasshi-kyōkai* (Japan Magazine Organisation).

69 As of 2010, *Popeye* and *Men's non-no* have female chief editors while *Fineboys* has a male editor-in-chief. Since mid-2012, *Popeye* also has a male editor-in-chief.

70 Bordo, 'Beauty (Re)Discovers the Male Body', p. 131.

71 Alexander, 'Stylish Hard Bodies', p. 541.

72 Alexander, 'Stylish Hard Bodies', p. 541.

73 Darling-Wolf, 'The Men and Women of *non-no*', p. 189.

74 *Fineboys*, March 2011, pp. 24–55.

75 Bordo, 'Beauty (Re)Discovers the Male Body', p. 135.

76 Alexander, 'Stylish Hard Bodies', p. 541.

77 Boni, 'Framing Media Masculinities', p. 472.

78 Nixon, 'Exhibiting Masculinity', p. 314.

79 Negrin, *Appearance and Identity*, p. 158.

80 Greer, *The Beautiful Boy*, p. 7.

81 Mulvey, 'Visual Pleasure and Narrative Cinema', p. 398.

82 Kaplan, *Women and Film*, p. 30.

83 Kaplan, *Women and Film*, p. 31.

84   Bordo, 'Beauty (Re)Discovers the Male Body', p. 142.

85   Kaja Silverman, 'Masochism and Subjectivity', *Framework*, 12, 1980.

86   Peter McNeil and Vicki Karaminas, 'Introduction', in P. McNeil and V. Karaminas (eds), *The Men's Fashion Reader* (Oxford and New York: Berg, 2009), p. 8.

87   Miller, *Beauty Up*, p. 155.

88   Tomoko Aoyama, 'Transgendering Shōjo Shōsetsu: Girls' Inter-text/Sex-uality', in M. McLelland and R. Dasgupta (eds), *Gender, Transgenders and Sexualities in Japan* (London and New York, Routledge, 2005), p. 50.

89   Aoyama, 'Transgendering Shōjo Shōsetsu', p. 50.

90   Tanaka, 'The Language of Japanese Men's Magazines', p. 233.

91   Kress and van Leewen, *Reading Images*, p. 130.

92   *Men's Club*, March 2010, pp. 132–9.

93   See for example *Leon*, September 2010, pp. 100–6.

94   The heterosexual context of *Leon* is largely constructed through the image of Girolamo Panzetta. He has created the public image of an amorous philanderer.

95   Julie Anne Springer, 'Art and the Feminine Muse: Women in Interiors by John White Alexander', *Woman's Art Journal*, 6(2), p. 4.

96   Anne Hollander, *Seeing Through Clothes* (New York: Avon Books, 1978), p. 412.

97   Chris Straayer, 'The Talented Poststructuralist: Heteromasculinity, Gay Artifice, and Class Passing', in P. Lehman (ed.), *Masculinity: Bodies, Movies, Culture* (New York: Routledge, 2001), p. 117.

98   Michael Warner, 'Homo-Narcissism; or, Heterosexuality', in J. A. Boone and M. Cadden (eds), *Engendering Men: The Question of Male Feminist Criticism* (New York and London: Routledge, 1990), p. 190.

99   Warner, 'Homo-Narcissism', p. 191.

100 Warner, 'Homo-Narcissism', p. 192.

101 Warner, 'Homo-Narcissism', p. 192.

102 Jacques Lacan, 'The Mirror-phase as Formative of the Function of the I', trans. J. Roussel, in S. Žižek (ed.), *Mapping Ideology* (London and New York: Verso, 1994 [1949]), p. 94.

103 Lacan, 'The Mirror-phase as Formative of the Function of the I', p. 94.

104 Warner, 'Homo-Narcissism', p. 194.

105 Warner, 'Homo-Narcissism', p. 198.

106 Warner, 'Homo-Narcissism', pp. 193, 198.

107 Valerie Steele, *Fashion and Eroticism: Ideals of Feminine Beauty from the Victorian Era to the Jazz Age* (New York and Oxford: Oxford University Press, 1985), p. 29.

108 Hollander, *Seeing Through Clothes*, p. 391.

109 Megumi Ushikubo, *Sōshoku-kei danshi [ojō-man] ga nihon wo kaeru (Herbivorous Men (Ladylike Man) Change Japan)* (Tokyo: Kōdansha +α shinsho, 2008), pp. 4–5.

110 Ushikubo, *Sōshoku-kei danshi*, p. 121.

111   *GQ Australia*, Spring/May 2010, p. 91.

112   Bordo, 'Beauty (Re)Discovers the Male Body', pp. 137–8; Negrin, *Appearance and Identity*, p. 158.

113   Bordo, 'Beauty (Re)Discovers the Male Body', p. 137.

114   Attwood, 'Tits and Ass and Porn and Fighting', p. 88.

115   Attwood, 'Tits and Ass and Porn and Fighting', p. 88.

116   Miller, *Beauty Up*, p. 155.

3. Boy's elegance: a liminality of boyish charm and old-world suavity

1   *Milkboy Staff's Blog*, 2013, available at http://ameblo.jp/mb-staff/page-67.html#main [accessed 7 October 2013]. The texts are translated by Masafumi Monden.

2   Michael Carter, *Fashion Classics: From Carlyle to Barthes* (Oxford: Berg, 2003), p. 116.

3   Michel Foucault, 'The Concern for Truth', in S. Lotringer (ed.), *Foucault Live (Interviews, 1966–84*, trans. J. Johnston (New York: Semiotext(e), 1989 [1984]), p. 298.

4   As in the previous chapter, narcissism or narcissistic concerns are used in this chapter to describe one's strong concerns for appearance, which does not necessarily invoke negativity or pathology.

5   Ken'ichiro Hirano, 'The Westernization of Clothes and the State in Meiji Japan', in K. Hirano (ed.), *The State and Cultural Transformation: Perspectives from East Asia* (Tokyo: United Nations University Press, 1993), p. 123.

6   Reader-models (*dokusha* models) are amateur models whose occupations are other than professional models (e.g. students, retail sales assistants and hairdressers).

7   Laura Miller, *Beauty Up: Exploring Contemporary Japanese Body Aesthetics* (Berkeley: University of California Press, 2006), p. 149.

8   Miller, *Beauty Up*, p. 149.

9   See, Meredith Jones, *Skintight: An Anatomy of Cosmetic Surgery* (New York: Berg, 2008), p. 41; Sharon Kinsella, 'Black Faces, Witches, and Racism Against Girls', in L. Miller and J. Bardsley (eds), *Bad Girls of Japan* (New York: Palgrave Macmillan, 2005), p. 147.

10   Yamato Shiine, *Popeye Monogatari (The Story of Popeye)* (Tokyo: Shincho-sha, 2008), p. 12.

11   For instance, the August 2007 issue of *Popeye* runs a short interview with Jun'ichi Okada, member of *V6*, a *Johnny*'s boy band, and five-paged fashion shoots.

12   See for example *Popeye*, January 2008, p. 50.

13   Arjun Appadurai, 'Disjuncture and Difference in the Global Cultural Economy', in B. Robbins (ed.), *The Phantom Public Sphere* (Minneapolis: University of Minnesota Press, 1993), pp. 271–2.

14   Mariko Morimoto and Susan Chang, 'Western and Asian Models in Japanese Fashion Magazine Ads: The Relationship with Brand Origins and International Versus

Domestic Magazines', *Journal of International Consumer Marketing*, 21(3), 2009, p. 178.

15 Morimoto and Chang, 'Western and Asian Models in Japanese Fashion Magazine Ads', p. 178.

16 This tendency is also supported by other men's magazines such as *men's egg* and *Choki Choki*. These magazines predominantly feature 'domestic' brand items and are full of Japanese amateur-models.

17 Miller, *Beauty Up*, 149.

18 Jones, *Skintight*, p. 41.

19 Megumi Fukumitsu, 'yase & usui danshi nanka ōishi' (Skinny and Thin Boys are Somehow Increased), *Asashi Shinbun Weekly*, 15 January 2007, pp. 38–41.

20 Fabienne Darling-Wolf, 'The Men and Women of *non-no*: Gender, Race and Hybridity in Two Japanese Magazines', *Cultural Studies in Media Communication*, 23(3), 2006, p. 186.

21 Based on my calculation of all the models with their height and weight listed in *Men's non-no* website. See http://www.mensnonno.jp/data/modelfile. These data are based on thirty-five models whose heights and weights are mentioned on the *Men's non-no* website. The tallest model is 192 cm with a weight of 63 kg, the shortest model is 170 cm and 52 kg, which is also the lightest as of May 2010. The heaviest model weighs 75 kg and their height is 189 cm [accessed 18 May 2010].

22 See, for example, the September 2007 issue of *Men's non-no*, pp. 128–33, and the April 2008 issue of *Fineboys*, pp. 134–6.

23 '*Tekido ni hikishimatta utsukushii*' describes particularly a male physique that is skinny but fit, and is often referred by these magazines as the ideal male physique.

24 Joanne Entwistle, 'From Catwalk to Catalog: Male Fashion Models, Masculinity, and Identity', in H. Thomas and J. Ahmed (eds), *Cultural Bodies: Ethnography and Theory* (Malden and Oxford: Blackwell Publishing, 2004), p. 60; Susan M. Alexander, 'Stylish Hard Bodies: Branded Masculinity In Men's Health Magazine', *Sociological Perspectives*, 46(4), 2003, p. 541.

25 Models.com, http://models.com/model_culture/50topmalemodels/index.cfm [last accessed 19 October 2013].

26 Alexander, 'Stylish Hard Bodies', p. 541.

27 Llewyen Negrin, *Appearance and Identity: Fashioning the Body in Postmodernity* (New York: Palgrave Macmillan, 2008), p. 158.

28 Entwistle, 'From Catwalk to Catalog', pp. 59–60.

29 Entwistle, 'From Catwalk to Catalog', p. 59.

30 Entwistle, 'From Catwalk to Catalog', p. 60.

31 Ministry of Health, Labour and Welfare, *The Survey Results of Health and Nutrition of the Nation for 2008, 2011*, p. 184.

32 See, for example: F. Boni (2002), 'Framing Media Masculinities: Men's Lifestyle Magazines and the Biopolitics of Men's Lifestyle Magazines and the Male Body', *European Journal of Communication*, 17(4), 2002, p. 472; S. Bordo, 'Beauty (Re)Discovers the Male Body', in Z. P. Brand (ed.), *Beauty Matters* (Bloomington: Indiana University Press, 2000), p. 186.

33   T. S. Freson and L. B. Arthur, 'Fashioning Men's Bodies: Masculinity and Muscularity', in A. Reilly and S. Cosbey (eds), *The Men's Fashion Reader* (New York: Fairchild Books, 2008), p. 339.

34   R. Martin, 'Robert Pattinson Wants you to Know He's Going to Get a Six Pack', *Marie Claire*, 13 September 2013.

35   See, for example famous male models like Mathias Lauridsen, and Garrett Neff who is renowned for his work with Calvin Klein. They have a boyish semblance and considerably masculine physique.

36   Beth Eck, 'Men are Much Harder: Gendered Viewing of Nude Images', *Gender & Society*, 17(5), pp. 691–710.

37   Anne Hollander, *Seeing Through Clothes* (New York: The Viking Press, 1978).

38   Lise Skov, 'Fashion Trends, Japonisme and Postmodernism', in J. W. Treat (ed.), *Contemporary Japan and Popular Culture* (London: Cuzon, 1996), p. 155.

39   The Heian Period lasted approximately 390 years, from AD 794 to 1192.

40   Ivan Morris, *The World of the Shining Prince: Court Life in Ancient Japan* (New York, Tokyo, London: Kodansha International, 1994 [1964]), p. 202.

41   *Fineboys*, October 2010, p. 82.

42   Many actors and singers publish photobooks in Japan. Photobooks of actresses, swimsuits models (gravure idols) and singers are predominantly targeted at the heterosexual male market, with images of the stars in swimsuits often included. The publication of photobooks of male celebrities is also on the increase, aimed primarily at the heterosexual female market.

43   Miller, *Beauty Up*, p. 151.

44   D&G is a slightly more casual line of the Dolce & Gabbana brand.

45   Gunther Kress and Theo van Leeuwen, *Reading Images* (London and New York: Routledge, 1996), pp. 118–19.

46   Alexander, 'Stylish Hard Bodies'; Boni, 'Framing Media Masculinities'.

47   *Popeye*, 'The Cowboy Way', April 2010, pp. 166–73.

48   Shaun Cole, 'Macho Man: Clones and the Development of a Masculine Stereotype', in P. McNeil and V. Karaminas (eds), *The Men's Fashion Reader* (Oxford and New York: Berg, 2009), p. 392.

49   Keiko Okamura, *Gurohbaru shakai no ibunka-ron* (*Cross-cultural Theory in Global Societies*) (Kyoto: Sekaishiso-sha, 2003), pp. 137–49.

50   Jan Nederveen Pieterse, *Globalization and Culture: Global Mélange* (Maryland: Roman & Littlefield Publishers, 2004); R. Robertson, 'Glocalization: Time-Space and Homogeneity-Heterogeneity' in M. Featherstone, S. Lash and R. Robertson (eds), *Global Maternities* (London: Sage Publications, 1994), p. 34; Appadurai, 'Disjuncture and Difference'.

51   Miller, *Beauty Up*, p. 127.

52   Jan Bardsley, 'The Oyaji Gets a Makeover: Guides for Japanese Salarymen in the New Millennium', in J. Bardsley and L. Miller (eds), *Manners and Mischief: Gender, Power, and Etiquette in Japan* (California: University of California Press, 2011), pp. 115–16.

53   Romit Dasgupta, 'Performing Masculinities? The "Salaryman" at Work and Play', *Japanese Studies*, 20(2), 2000, p. 193.

54 Examples include comic book (*manga*) series Kenshi Hirokane's series *Kachō Shima Kōsaku* (Section Chief Kōsaku Shima) and Kimio Yanagisawa's *Tokumei Kakarichō Tadano Hitoshi* (Mission Section Chief Hitoshi Tadano), both of which were later made into TV series and films.

55 Dasgupta, 'Performing Masculinities?', p. 199.

56 James Roberson, 'Fight!! Ippatsu!!: "Genki" Energy Drinks and the Marketing of Masculine Ideology in Japan', *Men and Masculinities*, 7, 2005, p. 369.

57 Megumi Ushikubo, *Sōshoku-kei danshi [ojō-man] ga nihon wo kaeru* (*Herbivorous Men* (*Ladylike Men*) *Change Japan*) (Tokyo: Kōdansha +α shinsho, 2008); Bardsley, 'The Oyaji Gets a Makeover', p. 133.

58 Ushikubo, *ojō-man,* 2008; Futoshi Taga, 'Rethinking Male Socialisation: Life histories of Japanese male youth', in K. Louie and M. Low (eds), *Asian Masculinities* (Abingdon: RoutledgeCurzon, 2003), p. 142.

59 S. Nixon, *Hard Looks: Masculinity, Spectatorship and Contemporary Consumption* (New York: St. Martin's Press, 1996), p. 189.

60 *Popeye*, May 2008, p. 78.

61 *Men's non-no*, April 2010, p. 149.

62 Ellen Moers, *The Dandy: Brummell to Beerbohm* (London: Secker & Warburg, 1960), p. 298.

63 Moers, *The Dandy*, p. 299.

64 Bardsley, 'The Oyaji Gets a Makeover', pp. 114–16.

65 Toby Slade, 'Clothing Modern Japan', PhD Thesis (University of Sydney, 2006); Hirano, 'The Westernization of Clothes', pp. 121–31.

66 Toby Slade, 'The Japanese Suit and Modernity', in P. McNeil and V. Karaminas (eds), *The Men's Fashion Reader* (Oxford and New York: Berg, 2009), p. 295.

67 Slade, 'The Japanese Suit and Modernity', p. 295.

68 Valerie Steele, *Japan Fashion Now* (New Haven and London: Yale University Press, 2010), p. 7. See also Peter N. Dale, *The Myth of Japanese Uniqueness* (New York: St. Martin's Press, 1986).

69 Nederveen Pieterse, *Culture and Globalization*, p. 72.

70 *Men's non-no*, March 2008, pp. 66–7.

71 Anne Hollander, *Sex and Suits* (New York: Knopf, 1994), p. 55.

72 Moers, *The Dandy*, p. 289.

73 Foucault, 'The Concern for Truth', p. 298.

74 Tiffany Godoy, *Style Deficient Disorder: Harajuku Street Fashion Tokyo* (San Francisco: Chronicle Books, 2007), p. 37. Harajuku is a district in Shibuya ward in Tokyo Prefecture, which has become known for youth fashion subcultures.

75 Kenji, 'History of Milkboy', email correspondence, October 2013.

76 Milkboy website, 'Our Brand and History', http://www.milkboy.net/about/index.html [accessed 28 September 2013].

77 Hitomi, cited in a Skype interview with Kenji of Milkboy's Design and Art Direction Team, 29 November 2013.

78 *Popeye*, December 2006, pp. 198–203.

79   Hitomi, cited by Kenji, Skype.

80   *spoon.*, August 2013, pp. 18–25.

81   *spoon.*, December 2013, pp. 14–31.

82   *Milkboy Staff's Blog*, http://ameblo.jp/mb-staff [accessed 2 November 2013].

83   Kenji, 'History of Milkboy', email correspondence, 1 October, 2013.

84   Kenji, Skype.

85   *spoon.*, August 2013, p. 29.

86   Ministry of Health, Labour and Welfare, *The Survey Results of Health and Nutrition of the Nation for 2008, 2009, 2010, and 2011*. The given percentages are calculated by averaging the results from these four years.

87   Anne Hollander, *Feeding the Eye* (Berkeley and Los Angeles: University of California Press, 2000), pp. 153, 157.

88   Hitome, cited by Kenji, Skype.

89   Kenji, Skype. I thank Mr Kenji for sharing an important story and information about Milk and Milkboy.

90   G. Bruce Boyer, *Elegance: A Guide to Quality in Menswear* (New York and London: W. W. Norton & Company, 1985), pp. 251–5.

91   *spoon.*, December 2013, p. 31.

92   Miller, *Beauty Up*, p. 127.

93   Ushikubo, *Sōshoku-kei danshi*, pp. 41, 44–5.

94   Ushikubo, *Sōshoku-kei danshi*, pp. 126–7.

95   Miller, *Beauty Up*; Bardsley, 'The Oyaji Gets a Makeover', p. 123.

96   *Fineboys*, October 2010, pp. 79–86.

97   *Men's non-no*, April 2010, pp. 62–9.

98   For example, the May 2011 edition of *Choki Choki* (pp. 71–8) runs a story titled: 'Build an attractive body that looks good even when unclothed! Pump up only the parts girls love', in which the magazine allegedly surveyed 100 young women about which part of a male body they are attracted to. The story then offers training methods for the five most popular areas: abdomen, arms, back, hip and chest.

 99   *Popeye*, April 2008, pp. 195–9.

100   Foucault, 'The Concern for Truth', p. 298.

101   Valerie Steele, *Fashion and Eroticism: Ideals of Feminine Beauty from the Victorian Era to the Jazz Age* (New York and Oxford: Oxford University Press, 1985), p. 142.

102   *Fineboys*, August 2007, pp. 152–5.

103   *Fineboys*, December 2010, pp. 82–3.

104   *Fineboys*, July 2007, p. 19.

105   Miller, *Beauty Up*, p. 127

106   Keiko Tanaka, 'The Language of Japanese Men's Magazines: Young Men Who Don't Want to Get Hurt', in B. Benwell (ed.), *Masculinity and Men's Lifestyle Magazines* (Oxford: Blackwell Publishing, 2003), p. 228.

107   See for example John Beynon, *Masculinities and Culture* (Philadelphia: Open University, 2002), p. 13; Bordo, 'Beauty (Re)Discovers the Male Body', p. 122; Sean

Nixon, 'Exhibiting Masculinity', in S. Hall (ed.), *Representation: Culture Representation and Signifying Practices* (London: Sage, 1997), p. 314; Miller, *Beauty Up*, p. 151.

108 Sandra. L. Bem, *The Lenses of Gender: Transforming the Debate on Sexual Inequality* (New Haven and London: Yale University Press, 1993), p. 151.

109 Feona Attwood, 'Tits and ass and porn and fighting': Male heterosexuality in magazines for men' *International Journal of Cultural Studies*, volume 8, issue 1, 2005, p. 85.

110 Hollander, *Sex and Suits*, p. 40.

111 Slade, The Japanese *Suit* and Modernity, p. 293.

112 Adrian Clark, 'editor' *Loaded Fashion*, Spring/Summer 2005, p. 25. *Loaded Fashion* was originally an offshoot of *Loaded*.

113 Miller, *Beauty Up*, p. 157.

114 Miller, *Beauty Up*, p. 157.

115 Ushikubo, *Sōshoku-kei danshi*, p. 88.

116 Elizabeth Wilson, 'Fashion and Postmodern Body', in, J. Ash and E. Wilson, (eds), *Chic Thrills: A Fashion Reader* (Berkeley and Los Angeles: University of California Press, 1992), p. 6.

117 Ushikubo, *Sōshoku-kei danshi*, pp. 126–8.

4. Glacé wonderland: cuteness, sexuality and young women

1 Hitomi, quoted and explained by Kenji of Milkboy during a *Skype* interview, 29 November 2013. I thank Kenji for sharing this important story.

2 The lyrics of the song were written by Tommy February, and the music was composed by Malibu Convertible. The Japanese parts of the lyrics were translated by the author.

3 In order to make distinctions, *Alice* stands for the children's story and Alice for the character.

4 Angela McRobbie, 'The Rise and Rise of Porno Chic', *The Times Higher Education*, 2 January 2004, http://www.timeshighereducation.co.uk/story.asp?storyCode=182087&sectioncode=26. [Last accessed 4 July 2014]

5 See for example Christiane R. Yano, *Pink Globalization: Hello Kitty's Track Across the Pacific* (Durham and London: Duke University Press, 2013). I thank Dr Emerald King for suggesting this reading.

6 *Numéro Tokyo*, 13, April 2008, p. 81.

7 Laura Miller, 'Cute Masquerade and the Pimping of Japan', *International Journal of Japanese Sociology*, No. Issue 1, 2011, p. 24.

8 Brian J. McVeigh, *Wearing Ideology: State, Schooling and Self-presentation in Japan* (Oxford and New York: Berg, 2000), p. 135.

9 Laura Miller, 'Perverse Cuteness in Japanese Girl Culture', paper presented at Japan Fashion Now Symposium at The Museum at Fashion Institute of Technology, 2010. I thank Professor Miller for sharing this paper; Inuhiko Yomota, *Kawaii-Ron (Theory of Cute)* (Tokyo: Chikuma Shobo, 2006).

10 Reiko Koga, *Kawaii no teikoku* (*The Empire of Kawaii*) (Tokyo: Seido-sha, 2009), pp. 134–5.

11 Sharon Kinsella, 'Cuties in Japan', in L. Skov and B. Moeran (eds), *Women, Media, and Consumption in Japan* (Richmond, Surrey: Curzon Press, 1995), p. 220.

12 Kinsella, 'Cuties in Japan', p. 229.

13 Merry White, *Material Child* (Berkeley and London: University of California Press, 1993), p. 129.

14 Koga, *Kawaii*, p. 56.

15 Roland Robertson (1995: 28) explains that the term 'glocal' is derived from the Japanese term *dochaku-ka*, 'originally the agricultural principle of adopting one's farming techniques to local conditions'.

16 Tiffany Godoy, *Style Deficient Disorder: Harajuku Street Fashion Tokyo* (San Francisco: Chronicle Books, 2007), p. 37.

17 Hitomi, cited in a Skype interview with Kenji of Milkboy, 29 November 2013.

18 Godoy, *Style*, p. 38.

19 Across Editorial Office (ed.), *Street Fashion 1945–1995* (Tokyo: Parco, 1995), pp. 152–3.

20 See, for example *non-no*, 15–16, 2010, pp. 18–22.

21 Kyoko Koizumi, *Panda no An-An* (Tokyo: Magazine House, 1997), pp. 112–13.

22 Kinsella, *Cuties*, p. 226.

23 Alessandro Gomarasca, 'Under the Sign of Kawaii', in F. Bonami and R. Simons (eds), *The Fourth Sex: Adolescent Extremes* (Milan: Charta, 2003), p. 262.

24 Hitomi Tsuchiya Dollase, 'Early Twentieth Century Japanese Girls' Magazine Stories: Examining Shojo Voice in Hanamonogatari (Flower Tales)', *Journal of Popular Culture*, 36(4), 2003, p. 733.

25 Koga, *Kawaii*, pp. 26–8.

26 *Utsukushiku ikiru: Nakahara Jun'ichi sono bigaku to shigoto* (*Live Beautifully: The Aesthetics and Works of Jun'ichi Nakahara*) (Tokyo: Heibon-sha, 1999), pp. 40, 45 and 54.

27 Yomota, *Kawaii-Ron*, pp. 33–6.

28 Donald Keene mentions irregularity, simplicity and perishability as the other three characteristics.

29 Donald Keene, 'Japanese Aesthetics', in N. G. Hume (ed.), *Japanese Aesthetics and Culture: Reader* (New York: State University of New York Press, 1995), p. 31.

30 Jaqueline Berndt, 'Considering Manga Discourse: Location, Ambiguity, Historicity', in M. MacWilliams (ed.), *Japanese Visual Culture* (Armonk, NY: M. E. Sharpe, 2008), p. 299.

31 Mizuki Takahashi, 'Opening the Closed World of Shōjo Manga', in M. W. Macwilliams (ed.), *Japanese Visual Cultures: Explorations in the World of Manga and Anime* (New York: M.E. Sharpe, 2008), p. 122.

32 Tomoko Aoyama, 'Transgendering Shōjo Shōsetsu: Girls' Inter-text/Sex-uality', in M. McLelland and R. Dasgupta (eds), *Gender, Transgenders and Sexualities in Japan* (London and New York: Routledge, 2005), p. 50.

33   Dollase, 'Early Twentieth Century Japanese Girls' Magazine Stories', p. 727.

34   Helen Kilpatrick, 'Envisioning the shôjo Aesthetic in Miyazawa Kenji's "The Twin Stars" and "Night of the Milky Way Railway"', *Portal: Journal of Multidisciplinary International Studies*, 9(3), 2012, p. 3.

35   Masuko Honda, 'The Genealogy of Hirahira: Liminality and the Girl', in Tomoko Aoyama and Barbara Hartley (eds), *Girl Reading Girl in Japan*, trans. T. Aoyama and B. Hartley (New York: Routledge, 2010 [1980]), p. 36.

36   Rebecca L. Copeland, *Lost Leaves: Women Writers of Meiji Japan* (Honolulu: University of Hawaii Press, 2000), p. 26.

37   Shuko Watanabe, *Shōjo-zō no tanjō – kindai nihon ni okeru 'shōjo' no keisei (The Birth of the Images of Shōjo – The Construction of Shōjo in Modern Japan)* (Tokyo: Shinsen-sha, 2007, pp. 112–14).

38   Sarah Frederick, 'Not That Innocent: Yoshiya Nobuko's Good Girls', in L. Miller and J. Bardsley (eds), *Bad Girls of Japan* (New York: Palgrave Macmillan, 2005), p. 67.

39   Frederick, 'Not That Innocent', p. 68.

40   Asako Takabatake, 'Takabatake kasho no kodomo no enitsuite no ikkou: arisu tono douitsusei wo megutte' (A thought on Kasho Takabatake's art works on children: About the kindred qualities with Alice), *Bigakujutushi ronshū*, 19 (2011), p. 73.

41   Karen Nakamura and Hisako Matsuo, 'Female Masculinity and Fantasy Spaces: Transcending Genders in the Takarazuka and Japanese Popular Culture', in J. E. Roberson and N. Suzuki (eds), *Men and Masculinities in Modern Japan: Dislocating the Salaryman Doxa* (New York: Routledge, 2002), p. 69; Aoyama, 'Transgendering Shōjo Shōsetsu', p. 53.

42   Watanabe, *Shōjo*, p. 59.

43   John Whittier Treat, 'Yoshimoto Banana Writes Home: The Shôjo in Japanese Popular Culture', in J. W. Treat (ed.), *Contemporary Japan and Popular Culture* (Honolulu: University of Hawaii Press, 1996), pp. 281–2.

44   Catherine Driscoll, *Girls: Feminine Adolescence in Popular Culture and Cultural Theory* (New York: Columbia University Press, 2002), p. 296.

45   Nakamura and Matsuo, 'Female Masculinity', p. 69.

46   Minako Saito, *Modern-Girl Ron (The Theory of Modern Girls)* (Tokyo: Bunshūb-bunko, 2003), first published 2000.

47   Melanie Czarnecki, 'Bad Girls from Good Families: The Degenerate Meiji Schoolgirl', in L. Miller and J. Bardsley (eds), *Bad Girls of Japan* (New York: Palgrave Macmillan, 2005), p. 61; Alisa Freedman, *Tokyo in Transit: Japanese Culture on the Rails and Road* (Stanford: Stanford University Press, 2010), p. 29.

48   Czarnecki, 'Bad Girls from Good Families', p. 61.

49   Miller, *Cute*, p. 24. Sanrio is the company that designs and manufactures products such as Hello Kitty.

50   Miller, *Cute*, p. 24.

51   Laura Miller, 'You are Doing Burikko!: Censoring/Scrutinizing Artificers of Cute Femininity in Japanese', in J. Shibamoto Smith and S. Okamoto (eds), *Japanese Language, Gender, and Ideology: Cultural Models and Real People* (New York: Oxford University Press, 2004).

52 Miller, 'You are Doing Burikko!', p. 148.

53 Sharon Kinsella, 'What's Behind the Fetishism of Japanese School Uniforms?', *Fashion Theory*, 6(2), 2002.

54 M. Kawado, 'Meiji no Ruisu Kyaroru' (Lewis Carroll in the Meiji Period), *Honyaku to rekishi*, 2 (2000), 30 September. See also Masafumi Monden, 'Being Alice in Japan: Performing a Cute, "Girlish" Revolt', *Japan Forum*, 26(2), 2014, p. 267.

55 Kawado, *Meiji no Ruisu Kyaroru*.

56 K. Sakakibara, *Alice no hon'yaku-shi 1899–2004* (*The History of Alice Translation*), n.d.

57 *Sō-en*, October 2007, pp. 26–47.

58 *Sō-en*, October 2007, p. 26.

59 Emily Temple Cute is a brand division of Shirley Temple. It was established in 1998 in order to cater for slightly older consumers.

60 Emily Temple Cute, *Wonderland* (Tokyo: Kadokawa Publishers, 2009).

61 Will Brooker, *Alice's Adventures* (New York and London: Continuum, 2005).

62 Brooker, *Alice's Adventures*, p. 145.

63 Driscoll, *Girls*, p. 43.

64 Sumiko Yagawa, *Fushigi no kuni no Alice* (*Alice's Adventures in Wonderland*) (Tokyo: Shincho-sha, 1994), p. 181.

65 Elizabeth Ewing, *History of Children's Costume* (London: B. T. Batsford Ltd, 1977), p. 96.

66 Brooker, *Alice's Adventures*, p. 143.

67 Brooker, *Alice's Adventures*, p. 105.

68 Jo Elwyn Jones and Francis J. Gladstone, *The Alice Companion: A Guide to Lewis Carroll's Alice Books* (New York: State University of New York Press, 1998), pp. 74–5.

69 Ewing, *Children's Costume*, p. 97.

70 For more detailed account of Alice as a symbol of Victorian adolescence, see Driscoll, *Girls*, pp. 42–6.

71 Japanese singers who have performed a song about *Alice* include: Yoshimi Iwasaki, *My Name is Alice* (1980); Seiko Matsuda, *Alice in Time-Land* (1984); Asami Kobayashi, *Lolita Go Home* (1984); Shoko Nakagawa, *Through the Looking-Glass* (2008).

72 *Oricon Style Website* [http://www.oricon.co.jp/prof/artist/198535/ranking/cd_single/].

73 *Marquee*, 71, 2009, pp. 50–1.

74 Although the differences are now blurring.

75 Kawase adapts the imagery of Alice again in 2009. In the music videos of her song *Wait For Me There* (from the album *I Kill My Heart*), she, as both Tommy Heavenly and February, is seen dressed almost exactly like Disney's Alice. Kawase dresses slightly differently in the February version and Heavenly version.

76 Carol Vernallis, *Experiencing Music Video: Aesthetics and Cultural Context* (New York: Columbia University Press, 2004), p. 3.

77 Vernallis, *Experiencing Music Video*, p. 101.

78 Anne Hollander, *Seeing Through Clothes* (New York: The Viking Press, 1978), p. 427.

79 Hollander, *Seeing Through Clothes*, p. 387.

80 Clare Rose, *Children's Clothes Since 1750* (London: B. T. Batsford Ltd, 1989), p. 131.

81 Hiromi Tsuchiya Dollase, 'Kawabata's Wartime Message in Beautiful Voyage (*Utsukushii tabi*)', in R. Hutchinson (ed.), *Negotiating Censorship in Modern Japan* (Abingdon and New York: Routledge, 2013), p. 80.

82 Rose, *Children's Clothes*, pp.126–7.

83 It should be noted that in Victorian times, working-class women and women at costume balls did wear short skirts. See Valerie Steele, *Fashion and Eroticism: Ideals of Feminine Beauty from the Victorian Era to the Jazz Age* (New York and Oxford: Oxford University Press, 1985), p. 114.

84 Roland Barthes, 'The Disease of Costume', in *Critical Essays*, trans. R. Howard (Evanston: Northwestern University Press, 1972), p. 46.

85 White, *Material Child*, pp. 123, 185; See also Laura Miller's comment in Patrick St Michel, 'For Japan's Justin Biebers, No Selena Gomezes Allowed', *The Atlantic*, 15 August 2012.

86 Toby Slade, *Japanese Fashion: A Cultural History* (Oxford and New York: Berg, 2009), pp. 115–16.

87 James Welker, 'From *The Cherry Orchard* to *Sakura no sono*: Translation and the Transfiguration of Gender and Sexuality in *Shōjo Manga*', in T. Aoyama and B. Hartley (eds), *Girl Reading Girl in Japan* (New York: Routledge, 2009), p. 168. See also Honda, *Hirahira*, p. 34.

88 Justin Wyatt, 'Weighing the Transgressive Star Body of Shelley Duval', in E. Meehan and E. R. Riordan (eds), *Sex and Money: Feminism and Political Economy in the Media* (Minneapolis: University of Minnesota Press, 2002), p.155.

89 It is noteworthy that Kimura has stated that her 'muse' is Twiggy. Indeed, Kimura has short hair, which is reminiscent of Twiggy's short, androgynous haircut, making a contrast to the long hair displayed by the other two performers.

90 White, *Material Child*, p. 172.

91 Jeffrey J. Arnett, 'The Sounds of Sex: Sex in Teens' Music and Music Videos', in J. D. Brown *et al.* (eds), *Sexual Teens, Sexual Media: Investigating Media's Influence on Adolescent Sexuality* (Mahwah: L. Erlbaum, 2002), p. 256.

92 Christenson and Roberts, 1998, cited in Arnett, 'The Sounds of Sex', p. 257.

93 L. M. Ward *et al.*, 'Contributions of Music Video Exposure to Black Adolescents' Gender and Sexual Schemas', *Journal of Adolescent Research*, 20(2), 2005, p. 144.

94 M. Tiggemann and A. S. Pickering, 'Role of Television in Adolescent Women's Body Dissatisfaction and Drive for Thinness', *International Journal of Eating Disorders*, 20(2), 1996, p. 200.

95 J. Anderson, cited in Martin, Brough and Orrego, *Get It On*, 2004.

96 S. Burman, cited in *Get It On*, 2004.

97 McRobbie, 'The Rise and Rise of Porno Chic'; Linda Duits and Liesbet van Zoonen, 'Headscarves and Porn-chic: Disciplining Girls' Bodies in the European Multicultural Society', *European Journal of Women's Studies*, 13(2), 2006, p. 112.

98   Feona Attwood, 'Pornography and Objectification: Re-reading "the Picture that Divided Britain"', *Feminist Media Studies*, 4(1), 2004, p. 14.

99   Amy Wilkins, 'So Full of Myself as a Chick: Goth Women, Sexual Independence, and Gender Egalitarianism', *Gender & Society*, 18(3), 2004, pp. 328–49; McRobbie, 'The Rise and Rise of Porno Chic'.

100   Lauraine Leblanc, *Pretty in Punk: Girls' Gender Resistance in a Boys' Subculture* (New Brunswick and London: Rutgers University Press, 2001).

101   Duits and van Zoonen, 'Headscarves and Porn-chic', p. 111.

102   Duits and van Zoonen, 'Headscarves and Porn-chic', p. 111.

103   Duits and van Zoonen, 'Headscarves and Porn-chic', p. 111.

104   Duits and van Zoonen, 'Headscarves and Porn-chic', p. 111.

105   For the criticism of *kawaii*, see, for example; Koga, *Kawaii*, pp. 206–7; Kimiko Akita, 'Cuteness: The Sexual Commodification of Women in the Japanese Media', in T. Carilli and J. Campbell (eds), *Women and the Media* (Lanham: University Press of America, 2005, pp. 44–57).

106   Anne Cooper-Chen and Miiko Kodama, *Mass Communication in Japan* (Ames: Iowa State University Press, 1997), p. 20.

107   Brian Cogan and Gina Cogan, 'Gender and Authenticity in Japanese Popular Music: 1980–2000', *Popular Music and Society*, 29(1), 2006, p. 82.

108   K. Schomer and Y. Chang, 'The Cult of Cute', *Newsweek*, 28 August 1995.

109   Deborah Merskin, 'Reviving Lolita? A Media Literacy Examination of Sexual Portrayals of Girls in Fashion Advertising', *American Behavioral Scientist*, 41(1), 2004, p. 123.

110   Brooker, *Alice's Adventures*, p. 90.

111   Brooker, *Alice's Adventures*, p. 72.

112   Brooker, *Alice's Adventures*, p. 64.

113   H. Haughton, 'Introduction', in *Alice's Adventures in Wonderland and Through the Looking-Glass*. London: Penguin. 1998, xli; Donald Serrell Thomas, *Lewis Carroll: A Portrait with Background* (London: John Murray, 1996), p. 365.

114   Thomas, *Lewis Carroll*, p. 8.

115   Appel, quoting Nabokov, *The Annotated Alice: Alice's Adventures in Wonderland and Through the Looking-Glass* (Harmondsworth: Penguin, 1970), p. 377.

116   Elizabeth Prioleau, 'Humbert Humbert: Through the Looking Glass', *Twentieth Century Literature*, 21(4), 1975, p. 434.

117   Mary A. Knighton, 'Down the Rabbit Hole: In Pursuit of Shōjo Alices from Lewis Carroll to Kanai Mieko', *US-Japan Women's Journal*, 40, 2011, pp. 59–89.

118   See for example Tom Petty and the Heartbreakers' *Don't Come Around Here No More* (1985, in which then 21-year-old actress Wish Foley played the role of Alice) and German industrial rock band Oomph!'s *Labyrinth* (2008). Japanese rock band Buck-Tick's music video to *Alice in Wonder Ground* (2007) also offers a more sophisticated yet similar depiction of Alice. In British duo Erasure's *Breath of Life* (1991), an adolescent, sylphlike Alice takes the role of the white rabbit.

119   *Sō-en*, October 2007, p. 41.

120 See, for example, White, *Material Child*, p. 126; McVeigh, *Wearing Ideology*, p. 146.

121 By Wagnerian I mean very loud.

122 Kinsella, *Cuties*, p. 243.

123 Joan Riviere, 'Womanliness as Masquerade', in A. Hughes (ed.), *The Inner World and Joan Riviere: Collected Papers: 1920–58* (London: Karnac Books, 1991 [1929]).

124 McVeigh, *Wearing Ideology*, p. 143.

125 The term 'idol' 'has a specific meaning in Japan different from the one that native English speakers know. Generally speaking, idols are young performers targeted at teenagers. In addition to their youthfulness, they usually sing bubble-gum pop and their physical attractiveness is a very important ingredient of their 'idolness'. See Philip Brasor and Masako Tsubuku, 'Idol Chatter: The Evolution of J-Pop', *Japan Quarterly*, 44(2), 1997, p. 55.

126 Cogan and Cogan, 'Gender and Authenticity', pp. 73–4.

127 Cogan and Cogan, 'Gender and Authenticity', p. 82.

128 Cogan and Cogan, 'Gender and Authenticity', p. 71.

129 Carolyn Stevens, *Japanese Popular Music: Culture, Authenticity, and Power* (London and New York: Routledge, 2008), p. 53.

130 Cogan and Cogan, 'Gender and Authenticity', p. 82.

131 Alisa Mizuki official website, http://www.avexnet.or.jp/alisa/special/history_dvd. [Last accessed 2 July 2014]

132 Alisa Mizuki official website, [Last accessed 17 May 2014].

133 Cogan and Cogan, 'Gender and Authenticity', p. 85.

134 Cogan and Cogan, 'Gender and Authenticity', p. 74.

135 Cogan and Cogan, 'Gender and Authenticity', p. 85.

136 Cogan and Cogan, 'Gender and Authenticity', p. 85.

137 Gunther Kress and Theo van Leeuwen, *Reading Images* (London and New York: Routledge, 1996), p. 126.

138 *SWITCH*, 23(8), 2005, p. 107.

139 *EYESCREAM*, February 2007, pp. 30–1.

140 Miller, *Burikko*, p. 155.

141 *Marquee*, 50, 2005, p. 17.

142 *Marquee*, 71, 2009, pp. 52–4.

143 Miller, *Burikko*, p. 156.

144 Ewing, *Children's Costume*, p. 94.

145 Hollander, *Clothes*, pp. 374, 380.

146 Stella Bruzzi, *Undressing Cinema: Clothing and Identity in the Movies* (London and New York: Routledge, 1997), p. xvii.

147 Duits and van Zoonen, 'Headscarves and Porn-chic,' p. 111.

148 Diane Reay, '"Spice Girls," "Nice Girls," "Girlies," and "Tomboys": Gender Discourses, Girls' Cultures and Femininities in the Primary Classroom', *Gender and Education*, 13(2), 2001, p. 163.

5. Ribbons and lace: girls, decorative femininity and androgyny

1   Jean Rhys, *Voyage in the Dark* (London: Penguin Books, 2000 [1934]), p. 10.

2   From the film dialogue, translated by Masafumi Monden.

3   Clare Hughes, *Dressed in Fiction* (Oxford and New York: Berg, 2006), p. 7.

4   Valerie Steele, *Gothic: Dark Glamor* (New Haven: Yale University Press, 2008), p. 73.

5   Masafumi Monden, 'The Nationality of Lolita Fashion', in F. Nakamura, M. Perkins and O. Krischer (eds), *Asia Through Art and Anthropology* (London and New York: Bloomsbury, 2013), p. 166.

6   For different styles of *Lolita*, see Monden, 'The Nationality of Lolita', pp. 166–7; K. A. Hardy Bernal, 'Japanese Lolita: Challenging Sexualized Style and the Little Girl Look', in S. Tarraant and M. Jolles (eds), *Fashion Talks: Undressing the Power of Style* (Albany: State University of New York Press, 2012), p. 118; Laura Miller, 'Cute Masquerade and the Pimping of Japan', *International Journal of Japanese Sociology*, 20, 2011, p. 21.

7   *Kyoko Fukada in Shimotsuma Story* (Tokyo: Pia, 2004), p. 110.

8   *Kyoko Fukada in Shimotsuma Story*, p. 112.

9   Tiffany Godoy, *Style Deficient Disorder: Harajuku Street Fashion Tokyo* (San Francisco: Chronicle Books, 2007), p. 144.

10 Vera Mackie, 'Transnational Bricolage: Gothic Lolita and the Political Economy of Fashion', *Intersections: Gender and Sexuality in Asia and the Pacific*, 20, April 2009.

11 Valerie Steele, *Japan Fashion Now* (New York: Yale University Press, 2010), p. 34.

12 It is significant that the childlike doll of the late nineteenth century and early twentieth century often led or acted as a trendsetter of contemporary fashion (Peers, 2004: 78).

13 Toby Slade, *Japanese Fashion: A Cultural History* (Oxford and New York: Berg, 2009), p. 101.

14 Ulrich Lehmann, 'Walter Benjamin', in V. Steele (ed.), *Berg Companion to Fashion* (London and New York: Berg, 2010), p. 69.

15 Street Mode Kenkyukai, 'History of Baby, The Stars Shine Bright', in *STREET MODE BOOK* (Tokyo: Graphic-sha, 2007), p. 66.

16 Masuko Honda, 'The Genealogy of Hirahira: Liminality and the Girl', in Tomoko Aoyama and Barbara Hartley (eds), *Girl Reading Girl in Japan*, trans. T. Aoyama and B. Hartley (New York: Routledge. 2010), pp. 28, 35. I thank Dr Lucy Fraser for making the link between Honda's theory and *Lolita* fashion.

17 Margaret Maynard, *Dress and Globalization* (Manchester: Manchester University Press, 2004), p. 22.

18 Baby, The Stars Shine Bright, official website: http://www.babyssb.co.jp/shopping/baby/onepiece/134317.html. [accessed 16 May 2012].

19 Peter McNeil, 'The Appearance of Enlightenment: Refashioning the Elites', in M. Fitzpatrick, P. Jones, C. Knellwolf and I. McCalmn (eds), *The Enlightenment World* (Oxfordshire and New York: Routledge, 2004), p. 384.

20 Valerie Steele, *Paris Fashion: A Cultural History* (Oxford and New York: Berg, 2nd ed., 1998), p. 35.

21 Innocent World, official website: http://innocent-w.jp/shopping/093709/index.html.

22 Aileen Ribeiro, 'Fashion in the Eighteenth Century: Some Anglo-French Comparisons', *Textile History*, 22(2), 1991, p. 331.

23 Aileen Ribeiro, *Dress in Eighteenth-Century Europe 1715–1789* (New Haven and London: Yale University Press, 2002 [1985]), p. 140.

24 Valerie Steele, *Fashion and Eroticism: Ideals of Feminine Beauty from the Victorian Era to the Jazz Age* (New York and Oxford: Oxford University Press, 1985), p. 65. The *robe à la polonaise* in the 1770s with the skirt bustled at the back was considered just as practical.

25 Slade, *Japanese Fashion*, p. 100.

26 E. Ewing, *History of Children's Costume* (London: B. T. Batsford Ltd. 1977), p. 96; Steele, *Victorian*, p. 114.

27 Clare Rose, *Children's Clothes Since 1750* (London: B. T. Batsford Ltd. 1989), pp. 126–7.

28 *KERA MANIAX*, 13, 2009, p. 16.

29 Isaac Gagné, 'Urban Princesses: Performance and "Women's Language" in Japan's Gothic/Lolita Subculture', *Journal of Linguistic Anthropology*, 18(1) (2008), p. 134.

30 Ribeiro, *Dress*, p. 136.

31 For the link between Japanese girls' culture and ballet costumes, see Masafumi Monden, 'Layers of the Ethereal', Fashion Theory 18(3), 2014, pp. 251–96.

32 Street Mode Kenkyukai, 'History of Baby, The Stars Shine Bright', p. 69.

33 Steele, *Victorian*, p. 3.

34 Thorstein Veblen, cited in Michale Carter, *Fashion Classics: From Carlyle to Barthes* (New York and Oxford: Berg, 2003), p. 48.

35 Simone de Beauvoir, *The Second Sex*, trans. H. M. Parshley (Middlesex: Penguin Books, 1975 [1949]), p. 543; James Laver, 1950, cited in Carter, *Fashion Classics*, p. 137.

36 See, for example Marnina Gonick, 'Between "Girl Power" and "Reviving Ophelia": Constituting the Neoliberal Girl Subject', *NWSA Journal*, 18(2), 2006, pp. 15–16.

37 P. J. Bettis and N. G. Adams, 'Landscape of Girlhood', in P. J. Bettis and N. G. Adams (eds), *Geographies of Girlhood: Identities In-between* (Mahwah: Lawrence Erlbaum Associates), 2005, p. 11.

38 Catharine Lumby, 'Watching Them Watching Us: The Trouble with Teenage Girls', *Continuum: Journal of Media & Cultural Studies*, 15(1), 2001, pp. 49–55.

39 Sharon R. Mazzarella and Norma O. Pecora, 'Girls in Crisis: Newspaper Coverage of Adolescent Girls', *Journal of Communication Inquiry*, 31(1), 2007, pp. 6–27.

40 Diane Reay, '"Spice Girls", "Nice Girls", "Girlies", and "Tomboys": Gender Discourses, Girls' Cultures and Femininities in the Primary Classroom', *Gender and Education*, 13(2), 2001.

41 Drucilla Cornell, *At the Heart of Freedom: Feminism, Sex, and Equality* (Princeton: Princeton University Press, 1998), p. 16.

42   Sheila Jeffreys, *Beauty and Misogyny: Harmful Cultural Practices in the West* (London and New York: Routledge, 2005), p. 87.

43   Suzanne Dorfield, 'Brisbane "Lolitas" Change Fashion Landscape', *The Age*, 5 November 2010; Masafumi Monden, 'Transcultural Flow of Demure Aesthetics: Examining Cultural Globalization through Gothic and Lolita Fashion', *New Voices*, 2, 2008, pp. 21–40; Momo Matsuura, *Sekai to Watashi to Lolita Fashion (The World, Lolita Fashion and I)* (Tokyo: Seikyu-sha, 2007).

44   Steele, *Japan*, p. 48.

45   Godoy, *Style*, p. 144.

46   Monden, 'Transcultural Flow of Demure Aesthetics', p. 28.

47   Godoy, *Style*, p. 135.

48   For more detailed accounts on ethnographic study of Lolitas, see Isaac Gagné, 'Bracketed Adolescence: Unpacking Gender and Youth Subjectivity through Subcultural Fashion in Late-Capitalist Japan' (Japan), and Sophia Staite, 'Femme Infantile: Australian Lolitas in Theory and Practice' (Australia), both in *Intersections: Gender and Sexuality in Asia and the Pacific*, 32, 2013. Available at http://intersections.anu.edu.au/issue32_contents.htm [last accessed 2 February 2014].

49   Elizabeth Wilson, *Adorned in Dreams: Fashion and Modernity* (London: I. B. Tauris, 1985), p. 224.

50   Llewyen Negrin, 'The Self as Image: A Critical Appraisal of Postmodern Theories of Fashion', *Theory, Culture & Society*, 16(3), 1999, p. 106.

51   Anne Hollander, *Seeing Through Clothes* (New York: The Viking Press, 1978), p. 339.

52   Joanne Entwistle, *The Fashioned Body: Fashion, Dress and Modern Social Theory* (Cambridge: Polity Press, 2000), p. 158.

53   Steele, *Victorian*, p. 3.

54   Steele, *Victorian*, p. 91.

55   Steele, *Victorian*, p. 91.

56   B. G. Smith, *Ladies of the Leisure Class* (Princeton: Princeton University Press, 1981), p. 79.

57   Smith, *Ladies of the Leisure Class*, p. 55.

58   Steele, *Victorian*, p. 4.

59   Steele, *Victorian*, p. 4.

60   Steele, *Victorian*, p. 143.

61   Steele, *Victorian*, pp. 93–4.

62   Anne Allison, 'Sailor Moon: Japanese Superheroes for Global Girls', in T. J. Craig (ed.), *Japan Pop!* (New York: M.E. Sharpe, 2000), p. 275.

63   See, for example, Allison, 'Sailor Moon'; Susan J. Napier, 'Vampires, Psychic Girls, Flying Women and Sailor Scouts: Four Faces of the Young Female in Japanese Popular Culture', in D. P. Martinez (ed.), *The World of Japanese Popular Culture* (Cambridge: Cambridge University Press, 1998), pp. 91–109.

64   Allison, 'Sailor Moon', p. 275.

65   For some participants of *Lolita* fashion, the film and Takemoto's original novel do not offer an accurate portrayal of the fashion. Some of them are also critical of these texts' stereotypical representation of a young woman who is devoted to *Lolita* fashion (see, for example; Matsuura, *Sekai*, pp. 14–15). The film has been received more favourably by *Lolitas* outside Japan. See Sophia Staite, 'Lolita: Atemporal Class Play with Tea and Cakes', MA Thesis (University of Tasmania, 2012), p. 51.

66 In this chapter, I focus mainly on the film version of *Shimotsuma Monogatari* because of its intricate position between mainstream and cult films. I believe the film is a significant example of a cult-theme brought into the mainstream cultural arena, and has acquired both popularity and recognition.

67 The Ibaraki Prefecture is located in the northeast of the Kantō region on Honshū island.

68 As Ikuya Satō (1991: 108) notes, the origin of the word *yankee*, which is used to describe delinquent youth in Japanese culture, is unknown, and a certain analogy between a *yankee* and a *bōsōzoku* (bikie gang) is sometimes assumed. That is the case in *Kamikaze Girls*.

69 Steele, *Japan*, p. 29.

70 One of the notable characteristics of *bōsōzoku* costumes is *tokkōfuku*, a jacket with long hems upon which a 'group name is usually sewn with gold or silver thread on the backs of *tokkōfuku* jackets. It may also be stitched into the upper sleeve or onto the upper left pocket' (Satō, 1991: 63). Such embroidery often used 'complicated Chinese characters with multiple meanings, much as American fraternity boys use Greek letters to create a sense of mystery and exclusivity' (Steele, 2010: 30). Steele (2010: 29) argues that 'their "outrageous paraphernalia" is intended primarily to enhance their tough image'.

71 Negrin, 'The Self as Image', p. 111.

72 Llewyen Negrin, *Appearance and Identity: Fashioning the Body in Postmodernity* (New York: Palgrave Macmillan, 2008), p. 30.

73 Negrin, *Appearance and Identity*, p. 31.

74 Elizabeth Wilson, 'Fashion and Postmodern Body', in J. Ash and E. Wilson (eds), *Chic Thrills: A Fashion Reader* (Berkeley and Los Angeles: University of California Press, 1992), pp. 8–9.

75 Ikuya Satō, *Kamikaze Biker: Parody and Anomy in Affluent Japan* (Chicago: University of Chicago Press, 1991), p. 110.

76 Georg Simmel, 'The Philosophy of Fashion', trans. K. H. Wolff in D. Frisby and M. Featherstone (eds), *Simmel on Culture* (London: Sage Publications, 1997 [1905]), p. 191.

77 Carter, *Fashion Classics*, p. 47.

78 Carter, *Fashion Classics*, p. 48.

79 Ribeiro, *Dress*, p. 165.

80 Ribeiro, *Dress*, p. 136.

81 Ribeiro, *Dress*, p. 53.

82 Steele, *Paris*, pp. 24–5.

83 Stephen Jones, *The Eighteenth Century* (Cambridge: Cambridge University Press, 1985), p. 17.

84 Melissa Hyde, *Making Up the Rococo: François Boucher and His Critics* (Los Angeles: Getty Publications, 2006), p. 92.

85   Daniel Roche, 'Popular Dress', in P. McNeil (ed.), *Fashion: Critical and Primary Sources the Eighteenth Century* (Oxford and New York: Berg. 2009), p. 90.

86   *Kamikaze Girls* US official website: www.kamikazegirls.net/interviews.html [accessed 24 April 2008].

87   Tetsuya Nakashima, 'Cinema', in *Men's non-no*, June 2006, p. 147.

88   See, for example; Catherine Driscoll, *Girls: Feminine Adolescence in Popular Culture and Cultural Theory* (New York: Columbia University Press, 2002); Gina Fournier, *Thelma and Louise and Women in Hollywood* (Jefferson: McFarland & Company, 2007), pp. 375–6.

89   Contrary to the original novel's depiction of Ryūji, he is portrayed (intentionally) as very comical if not ridiculous in the film. This is via visual elements such as his fashion sense and especially his highly exaggerated 'rockabilly' hairstyle.

90   Merry White, *Material Child* (Berkeley and London: University of California Press, 1993), p. 194.

91   de Beauvoir, *The Second Sex*, p. 543. The original novel portrays Momoko's dislike of boys and men at an almost 'pathological' level. This point is made clear in Mackie's analysis of the novel (2010). In the film this part is almost omitted completely.

92   Honda, *Hirahira*, p. 34. See also Mackie, 'Transnational Bricolage'.

93   Stella Bruzzi, *Undressing Cinema: Clothing and Identity in the Movies* (London and New York: Routledge, 1997), p. 14.

94   James Laver (1950), cited in Carter, *Fashion Classics*, p. 137.

95   Slade, *Japanese Fashion*, pp. 115–16.

96   I thank Dr Fuyubi Nakamura and Dr Olivier Krischer for suggesting this point.

97   Laura Miller, *Beauty Up: Exploring Contemporary Japanese Body Aesthetics* (Berkeley, Los Angeles and London: University of California Press, 2006), p. 78.

98   Yukari Fujimoto, *Watashi no ibasho wa doko ni aru no? Shojo manga ga utsusu kokoro no katachi* (*Where Do I Belong? The Shape of the Geart as Reflected in Girls' Comic Books*) (Tokyo: Gakuyo Shobo, 1998), pp. 177–89.

99   In many cases, these girls are long-separated sisters, and their romantic feelings are thus justified as sisterly affections.

100 My aim here is to use the terms 'masculinity' and 'femininity' as codes to describe certain attributes and activities that are conventionally believed to be, but are not necessarily, associated with either gender.

101 For further reading on the rarity of female bonding in mainstream Hollywood cinema, see Fournier, *Thelma and Louise*; Barry Keith Grant, *Film Genre: From Iconography to Ideology* (London: Wallflower Press, 2007), p. 81; Karen Hollinger, 'From Female Friends to Literary Ladies: The Contemporary Woman's Film', in S. Neal (ed.), *Genre and Contemporary Hollywood* (London: British Film Institute, 2002), pp. 77–90; Michael O'Shaughnessy, *Media and Society: An Introduction* (South Melbourne: Oxford University Press, 1999), p. 98.

102 O'Shaughnessy, *Media and Society*, p. 98.

103 Hollinger, 'From Female Friends', p. 79.

104 See, for example; Shun Nakahara's *Sakura no sono* (The Cherry Orchard, 1990), Nami Iguchi's *InuNeko* (Dogs and Cats, 2004), Nobuhiro Yamashita's *Linda Linda Linda* (2005) and Yuichi Sato's *Simsons* (2006).

105 DVD commentary included in *Shimotsuma Mnogatari* (2004).

106 C. Springer, 2005, p. 89 cited in Sarah Gilligan, 'Becoming Neo: Costume and Transforming Masculinity in the Matrix Films', in P. McNeil, V. Karaminas and C. Cole (eds), *Fashion in Fiction* (Oxford and New York: Berg, 2009), p. 154.

107 V. Karaminas, 2005, p. 6, cited in Gilligan, 'Becoming Neo', p. 153.

108 R. Reynolds, 1994, p. 32, cited in Gilligan, 'Becoming Neo', p. 153.

109 Friedrich Weltzien, 'Masque-ulinities: Changing Dress as a Display of Masculinity in the Superhero Genre', *Fashion Theory*, 9(2), 2005, p. 243.

110 Weltzien, 'Masque-ulinities', p. 243.

111 Judith Butler, 'Bodily Inscriptions, Performative Subversions', in S. Salih and J. Butler (eds), *The Judith Butler Reader* (Malden: Blackwell Publishers, 2004 [1990]), p. 111.

112 Needless to say, aggression is not restricted to men in reality. Yet it is often (stereotypically) perceived as 'masculine' particularly in contemporary popular culture.

113 Weltzien, 'Masque-ulinities', p. 238.

114 Entwistle, *The Fashioned Body,* p. 158.

115 Diane Crane, *The Production of Culture: Media and the Urban Arts* (Newbury Park, CA: Sage Publications, 1992); Robert C. Bulman, *Hollywood Goes to High School: Cinema, Schools, and American Culture* (New York: Worth Publishing, 2005).

116 Joanne Finkelstein, *After a Fashion* (Carlton South, Victoria: Melbourne University Press, 1996), p. 36.

117 One-ko is a pun. It is a slang for a dog in Japanese while the name of the heroine, Ichiko, is written as 一子, which can be pronounced as wan(一is one in Japanese)-ko (子). One-ko is thus her nickname in the story.

118 In the original novel of Yasutaka Tsutsui, published in 1978, the principal character was a young man, not a young woman.

119 Morimoto writes in the first volume that she merely wanted to create a heroine who is dressed in a frilly dress, and wanted to place her in the least likely workplace where men would feel uneasy about working with such a female colleague.

120 *Sō-en*, February 2011, p. 35.

121 Kumiko Uehara, interviewed by Valerie Steele, March 2010, in Steele, *Japan*, p. 38.

122 Julie Singer, *Androgyny: Toward a New Theory of Sexuality* (New York: Anchor Press, 1976), p. 22.

123 Singer, *Androgyny*, p. 27.

124 Elémire Zolla, *The Androgyne: Reconciliation of Male and Female* (New York: Cross Road, 1981), p. 15.

125 Sandra L. Bem, 'Sex Role Adaptability: One Consequence of Psychological Androgyny', *Journal of Personality and Social Psychology*, 31(4), 1975, pp. 634–43.

126 Bem, 'Sex Role Adaptability', pp. 635, 643.

127 Carrie Paechter, 'Masculine Femininities/Feminine Masculinities: Power, Identities and Gender', *Gender and Education*, 18(3), p. 254; Cornell, *At the Heart of Freedom*, p. 80.

128 Paechter, 'Masculine Femininities', p. 261.

129 Sandra L. Bem, *The Lenses of Gender: Transforming the Debate on Sexual Inequality* (New Haven and London: Yale University Press, 1993), p. 146.

130 Negrin, *Appearance and Identity*, p. 148; Anne Hollander, *Feeding the Eye* (Berkeley and Los Angeles: University of California Press, 2000), p. 157.

131 Hollander, *Feeding the Eye*, pp. 153, 157.

132 Negrin, 'The Self as Image', p. 102.

133 Steele, *Victorian*, p. 143.

6. An Ivy boy and a preppy girl: style import-export

1 For more reading on the Ivy style, see Patricia Mears (ed.), *Ivy Style: Radical Conformist* (New York: Yale University Press, 2012).

2 Elizabeth Wilson, *Adorned in Dreams* (London: Virago, 1985), p. 3.

3 Ulrich Lehmann, *Tigersprung: Fashion in Modernity* (Cambridge, MA: MIT Press, 2000), p. 9.

4 Richard Press, an interview with Christian Chensvold, in Mears, *Ivy Style: Radical Conformist*, p. 90.

5 Press, *Ivy Style*, p. 80.

6 Roland Robertson, 'Glocalization: Time-Space and Homogeneity-Heterogeneity', in M. Featherstone, S. Lash and R. Robertson (eds), *Global Maternities* (London: Sage Publications, 1994), p. 34; Jan Nederveen Pieterse, *Globalization and Culture: Global Mélange* (Maryland: Roman & Littlefield Publishers, 2004).

7 David Colman, 'The All-American Back From Japan', *The New York Times*, 17 June 2009 (http://www.nytimes.com/2009/06/17/fashion/18codes. html?pagewanted=print) [last accessed 6 April 2014].

8 J. Pompeo, 'Trad Men', *The New York Observer*, 8 September 2009 (http://www. observer.com/2009/fashion/trad-men) [last accessed 6 April 2014].

9 W. David Marx, 'The Man Who Brought Ivy To Japan', *Ivy Style*, 31 August 2010. (http://www.ivy- style.com/the-man-who-brought-Ivy-to-japan.html).

10 T. Hayashida, S. Ishizu, T. Kurosu and H. Hasegawa, *Take Ivy* (New York: powerHouse Books, 2010 [1965]), p. 66.

11 Valerie Steele, *Japan Fashion Now* (New York: Yale University Press, 2010), p. 13.

12 Colman, 'The All-American'.

13 Colman, 'The All-American'.

14 Madoka Yamazaki, 'Preppi to iu koto' (About Being a Preppy), *en-Taxi*, 31 (2010), p. 162.

15 Keita Fukasawa 'Men's ni manabu Trad kouza' (The Lecture on Trad Style Learning through Men's Fashion), *Numéro Tokyo*, 41 (November 2010), pp. 64–5.

16 Colman, 'The All-American'.

17 Kensuke Ishizu, *Itsumo zero kara no shuppatsudatta* (*I Always Made My Start from Nothing*) (Tokyo: Nihon Tosho Centre, 2010), p. 66.

18 Ishizu, *Itsumo zero*, pp. 77–8.

19 Leonard Koren, *New Fashion Japan* (Tokyo: Kodansha International, 1984), p. 78.

20 Ken'ichiro Hirano, 'The Westernization of Clothes and the State in Meiji Japan', in K. Hirano (ed.), *The State and Cultural Transformation: Perspectives from East Asia* (Tokyo: United Nations University Press, 1993), p. 128.

21 Yumiko Mikanagi, *Masculinity and Japan's Foreign Relations* (Boulder and London: First Forum Press, 2011), p. 28. As Mikanagi (2011: 26) writes, *bankara* is 'a play on the word *haikara*, with "ban" meaning barbarous'.

22 Steele, *Japan Fashion Now*, p. 9.

23 Mikanagi, *Masculinity and Japan's Foreign Relations*, p. 45.

24 Mikanagi, *Masculinity and Japan's Foreign Relations*, p. 29.

25 Pieterse, *Culture and Globalization*, p. 72.

26 The cover images of *Men's Club* from 1954 to 1964 are available from *Ishizu Kensuke daihyakka* (Encyclopedia of Kensuke Ishizu), available at http://www.ishizu.jp/gallery3/work3/w11_3/w11main3_2.html [last accessed 6 February 2014].

27 Yoichi Akagi, *Heibon Punch 1964* (Tokyo: Heibon-sha, 2004), pp. 112–13.

28 Across Editorial Office (ed.), *Street Fashion 1945–1995* (Tokyo: Parco, 1995), pp. 86–8.

29 Across Editorial Office (ed.), *Street Fashion*, p. 88.

30 Across Editorial Office (ed.), *Street Fashion*, p. 184.

31 Kobe is the capital city of Hyōgo Prefecture on the southern side of the main island of Honshū, Island. Yokohama is the capital city of Kanagawa Prefecture, located about 30 km from central Tokyo.

32 Kazuo Hozumi, *IVY Illustrated: Gals* (Tokyo: Aiiku-sha, 2003 [1980]), p. 174.

33 Across Editorial Office (ed.), *Street Fashion*, p. 216.

34 Across Editorial Office (ed.), *Street Fashion*, p. 216.

35 Across Editorial Office (ed.), *Street Fashion*, pp. 228–9.

36 *Fineboys*, December 2007, p. 13.

37 Daniel D. Hill, *American Menswear: From the Civil War to the Twenty-first Century* (Texas: Texas Tech University Press, 2011), p. 215.

38 Hayashida *et al.*, *Take Ivy*, p. 66.

39 Kazuo Hozumi, *IVY Illustrated* (Tokyo: Aiiku-sha, 2003 [1980]), p. 188.

40 Guy Trebay, 'Prep, Forward and Back', *The New York Times*, 23 July 2010 (http://www.nytimes.com/2010/07/25/fashion/25Prep.html) [last accessed 6 April 2014].

41 Hayashida *et al.*, *Take Ivy*, p. 66.

42 Hozumi, *Ivy*, p. 134.

43 Hayashida *et al.*, *Take Ivy*, p. 58.

44 Hozumi, *Ivy*, p. 126.

45 Hozumi, *Ivy*, p. 49.

46 Hozumi, *Ivy*, p. 10.

47 See for example *Popeye*, December 2006, p. 96.

48   Yamazaki, 'Preppi', p. 162.

49   Ishizu, *Itsumo zero*, p. 21.

50   Hozumi, *Ivy*, p. 51.

51   Colman, 'The All-American'.

52   Colman, 'The All-American'.

53   Mears, *Ivy Style*, p. 158.

54   Both in and outside Japan, American traditional styles for women tend to be called 'preppy' rather than 'Ivy'.

55   The Ivy style for 'gals', according to Hozumi, is the one embraced by students of the 'Seven Sisters', seven liberal arts colleges in the Northeastern United States. They are Barnard College, Bryn Mawr College, Mount Holyoke College, Radcliffe College, Smith College, Vassar College and Wellesley College. Historically these are women's colleges. For references to fashion, femininity and Radcliffe students, see Deirdre Clemente, '"Prettier Than They Used to Be": Femininity, Fashion, and the Recasting of Radcliffe's Reputation, 1900–1950', *The New England Quarterly*, 82(4), 2009, pp. 637–66.

56   Hayashida *et al.*, *Take Ivy*, p. 126.

57   Hozumi, *Ivy*, p. 39.

58   Keiko Okamura, *Gurohbaru shakai no ibunka-ron* (*Cross-cultural Theory in Global Societies*) (Kyoto: Sekaishiso-sha, 2003), pp. 137–49.

59   Valerie Steele, *Fashion and Eroticism: Ideals of Feminine Beauty from the Victorian Era to the Jazz Age* (New York and Oxford: Oxford University Press, 1985), p. 246.

7. Concluding Japanese fashion cultures, change and continuity

1   Ulrich Lehmann, *Tigersprung: Fashion in Modernity* (Cambridge, MA: MIT Press, 2000), p. 9.

2   Joanne Entwistle, *The Fashioned Body: Fashion, Dress and Modern Social Theory* (Cambridge: Polity Press, 2000), p. 186.

3   Valerie Steele, *Fashion and Eroticism: Ideals of Feminine Beauty from the Victorian Era to the Jazz Age* (New York and Oxford: Oxford University Press, 1985), p. 247.

4   Chris Barker, *Television, Globalization and Cultural Identities* (Buckingham and Philadelphia: Open University Press, 1999), p. 43.

5   Roland Robertson, 'Glocalization: Time-Space and Homogeneity-Heterogeneity', in M. Featherstone, S. Lash and R. Robertson (eds), *Global Maternities* (London: Sage Publications, 1994), p. 34.

6   Jan Nederveen Pieterse, *Globalization and Culture: Global Mélange* (Maryland: Roman & Littlefield Publishers, 2004), pp. 72–3.

7   Anne Hollander, *Sex and Suits* (New York: Knopf, 1994), pp. 6, 11.

REFERENCES

i. Books and articles

Across Editorial Office (ed.), *Street Fashion 1945–1995*, Tokyo: Parco, 1995.

Akagi, Y. *Heibon Punch 1964*, Tokyo: Heibon-sha, 2004.

Akita, K. 'Cuteness: The Sexual Commodification of Women in the Japanese Media', in T. Carilli and J. Campbell (eds), *Women and the Media*, Lanham: University Press of America, 2005.

Alexander, S. M. 'Stylish Hard Bodies: Branded Masculinity In Men's Health Magazines', *Sociological Perspectives*, 46(4) (2003), pp. 535–54.

Allison, A. 'Sailor Moon: Japanese Superheroes for Global Girls', in T. J. Craig (ed.), *Japan Pop!*, New York: M.E. Sharpe, 2000.

Aoyama, T. 'Transgendering Shōjo Shōsetsu: Girls' Inter-text/Sex-uality', in M. McLelland and R. Dasgupta (eds), *Gender, Transgenders and Sexualities in Japan*, London and New York, Routledge, 2005.

Appadurai, A. 'Disjuncture and Difference in the Global Cultural Economy', in Bruce Robbins (ed.), *The Phantom Public Sphere*, Minneapolis: University of Minnesota Press, 1993.

Arnett, J. J. 'The Sounds of Sex: Sex in Teens' Music and Music Videos', in J. D. Brown *et al.* (eds), *Sexual Teens, Sexual Media: Investigating Media's Influence on Adolescent Sexuality*, Mahwah: L. Erlbaum, 2002.

Attwood, F. 'Pornography and Objectification: Re-reading "the Picture that Divided Britain"', *Feminist Media Studies*, 4(1) (2004), pp. 7–22.

Attwood, F. '"Tits and Ass and Porn and Fighting": Male Heterosexuality in Magazines for Men', *International Journal of Cultural Studies*, 8(1) (2005), pp. 83–100.

Bardsley, J. 'The Oyaji Gets a Makeover: Guides for Japanese Salarymen in the New Millennium', in J. Bardsley and L. Miller (eds), *Manners and Mischief: Gender, Power, and Etiquette in Japan*, California: University of California Press, 2011.

Barker, C. *Television, Globalization and Cultural Identities*, Buckingham and Philadelphia: Open University Press, 1999.

Barthes, R. 'The Disease of Costume', in *Critical Essays*, trans. R. Howard, Evanston: Northwestern University Press, 1972.

Bem, S. L. 'Sex Role Adaptability: One Consequence of Psychological Androgyny', *Journal of Personality and Social Psychology*, 31(4) (1975), pp. 634–43.

Bem, S. L. *The Lenses of Gender: Transforming the Debate on Sexual Inequality*, New Haven and London: Yale University Press, 1993.

Berndt, J. 'Considering Manga Discourse: Location, Ambiguity, Historicity', in M. MacWilliams (ed.), *Japanese Visual Culture*, Armonk, NY: M. E. Sharpe, 2008.

Bettis, P. J. and Adams, N. G. 'Landscape of Girlhood', in P. J. Bettis and N. G. Adams (eds), *Geographies of Girlhood: Identities In-between*, Mahwah: Lawrence Erlbaum Associates, 2005.

Beynon, J. *Masculinities and Culture*, Philadelphia: Open University, 2002.

Boni, F. 'Framing Media Masculinities: Men's Lifestyle Magazines and the Biopolitics of Men's Lifestyle Magazines and the Male Body', *European Journal of Communication*, 17(4) (2002), pp. 465–78.

Bordo, S. 'Beauty (Re)Discovers the Male Body', in Z. P. Brand (ed.), *Beauty Matters*, Indiana Bloomington: University Press, 2000.

Boyer, G. B. *Elegance: A Guide to Quality in Menswear*, New York and London: W. W. Norton & Company, 1985.

Brasor, P. and Tsubuku, M. 'Idol Chatter: The Evolution of J-Pop', *Japan Quarterly*, 44(2) (1997), pp. 55–65.

Breward, C. '"On the Bank's Threshold": Administrative Revolutions and the Fashioning of Masculine Identities at the Turn of the Century', *Parallax*, 3(2) (1997), pp. 109–23.

Breward, C. *The Hidden Consumers: Masculinities, Fashion and City Life 1860–1914*, Manchester and New York: Manchester University Press, 1999.

Breward, C. 'Mode of Manliness: Reflections on Recent Histories of Masculinities and Fashion', in G. Riello and P. McNeil (eds), *The Fashion History Reader: Global Perspectives*, London and New York: Routledge, 2010.

Bronfen, E. *Over Her Dead Body: Death, Femininity and the Aesthetic*, Manchester: Manchester University Press, 1992.

Brooker, W. *Alice's Adventures: Lewis Carroll in Popular Culture*, New York and London: Continuum, 2005.

Bruzzi, S. *Undressing Cinema: Clothing and Identity in the Movies*, London and New York: Routledge, 1997.

Bulman, R. C. *Hollywood Goes to High School: Cinema, Schools, and American Culture*, New York: Worth Publishing, 2005.

Butler, J. 'Bodily Inscriptions, Performative Subversions', in S. Salih and J. Butler (eds), *The Judith Butler Reader*, Malden: Blackwell Publishers, 2004 [1990].

Carter, M. *Fashion Classics: From Carlyle to Barthes*, New York and Oxford: Berg, 2003.

Clammer, J. 'Consuming Bodies: Constructing and Representing the Female Body in Contemporary Japanese Print Media', in L. Skov. and B. Morean (eds), *Women, Media and Consumption in Japan*, Richmond, Surrey: Curzon Press, 1995.

Clark, A. 'Editor', *Loaded Fashion*, Spring/Summer (2005), p. 25.

Clemente, D. ' "Prettier Than They Used to Be": Femininity, Fashion, and the Recasting of Radcliffe's Reputation, 1900–1950', *The New England Quarterly*, 82(4) (2009), pp. 637–66.

Cogan, B. and Cogan, G. 'Gender and Authenticity in Japanese Popular Music: 1980–2000', *Popular Music and Society*, 29(1) (2006), pp. 69–90.

Cole, S. 'Macho Man: Clones and the Development of a Masculine Stereotype', in P. McNeil and V. Karaminas (eds), *The Men's Fashion Reader*, Oxford and New York: Berg, 2009.

Colman, D. 'The All-American Back From Japan', *The New York Times*, 17 June 2009 (http://www.nytimes.com/2009/06/17/fashion/18codes.html).

Cooper-Chen, A. and Kodama, M. *Mass Communication in Japan*, Ames: Iowa State University Press, 1997.

Copeland, R. L. *Lost Leaves: Women Writers of Meiji Japan*, Honolulu: University of Hawaii Press, 2000.

Copeland, R. L. 'Fashioning the Feminine: Images of the Modern Girl Student in Meiji Japan', *US-Japan Women's Journal*, 30–1 (2006), pp. 13–35.

Cornell, D. *At the Heart of Freedom: Feminism, Sex, and Equality*, Princeton: Princeton University Press, 1998.

Crane, D. *The Production of Culture: Media and the Urban Arts*, Newbury Park, CA: Sage Publications, 1992.

Czarnecki, M. 'Bad Girls from Good Families: The Degenerate Meiji Schoolgirl', in L. Miller and J. Bardsley (eds), *Bad Girls of Japan*, New York: Palgrave Macmillan, 2005.

Dalby, L. *Kimono: Fashioning Culture*, London: Vintage, 2001 [1993].

Darling-Wolf, F. 'The Men and Women of *non-no*: Gender, Race and Hybridity in Two Japanese Magazines', *Cultural Studies in Media Communication*, 23(3) (2006), pp. 181–99.

Dasgupta, R. 'Performing Masculinities? The "Salaryman" at Work and Play', *Japanese Studies*, 20(2) (2000), pp. 189–200.

David Marx, W. 'The Man Who Brought Ivy To Japan', *Ivy Style*, 31 August 2010 (http://www.Ivy-style.com/the-man-who-brought-Ivy-to-japan.html).

Davis, F. *Fashion, Culture, and Identity*, Chicago: University of Chicago Press, 1992.

de Beauvoir, S. *The Second Sex*, trans. H. M. Parshley, 1949. Middlesex: Penguin Books, 1975.

Dollase, H. T. 'Early Twentieth Century Japanese Girls' Magazine Stories: Examining Shojo Voice in Hanamonogatari (Flower Tales)', *Journal of Popular Culture*, 36(4) (2003), pp. 724–55.

Dollase, H. T. 'Kawabata's Wartime Message in Beautiful Voyage (Utsukushii tabi)', in R. Hutchinson (ed.), *Negotiating Censorship in Modern Japan*, Abingdon and New York: Routledge, 2013.

Dorfield, S. 'Brisbane "Lolitas" change fashion landscape', *The Age*, 5 November 2010 (http://www.theage.com.au/lifestyle/fashion/brisbane-lolitas-change-fashion-landscape-20101105-17grh.html). [Accessed 1 December 2010]

Driscoll, C. *Girls: Feminine Adolescence in Popular Culture and Cultural Theory*, New York: Columbia University Press, 2002.

Duits, L. and van Zoonen, L. 'Headscarves and Porn-chic: Disciplining Girls' Bodies in the European Multicultural Society', *European Journal of Women's Studies*, 13(2) (2006), pp. 103–17.

Durham, M. G. *Lolita Effect: The Media Sexualization of Young Girls and What We Can Do About It*, Woodstock and New York: The Overlook Press, 2008.

Eck, B. A. 'Men are Much Harder: Gendered Viewing of Nude Images', *Gender & Society*, 17(5) (2003), pp. 691–710.

Edwards, T. 'Consuming Masculinities: Style, Content and Men's Magazines', in P. McNeil and V. Karaminas (eds), *The Men's Fashion Reader*, New York: Berg, 2009.

Eicher, J. B. 'Dress, Gender and the Public Display of Skin', in J. Entwistle and E. Wilson (eds), *Body Dressing*, Oxford and New York: Berg, 2001.

Entwistle, J. *The Fashioned Body: Fashion, Dress and Modern Social Theory*, Cambridge: Polity Press, 2000.

Entwistle, J. 'From Catwalk to Catalog: Male Fashion Models, Masculinity, and Identity', in H. Thomas and J. Ahmod (eds), *Cultural Bodies: Ethnography and Theory*, Malden and Oxford: Blackwell Publishing, 2004.

Ewing, E. *History of Children's Costume*, London: B. T. Batsford Ltd, 1977.

Finkelstein, J. *After a Fashion*, Carlton South, Victoria: Melbourne University Press, 1996.

Foucault, M. 'The Concern for Truth', in S. Lotringer (ed.), *Foucault Live* (*Interviews, 1966–84*). trans. J. Johnston. New York: Semiotext(e), 1989 [1984].

Fournier, G. *Thelma and Louise and Women in Hollywood*, Jefferson: McFarland & Company, 2007.

Frederick, S. 'Not That Innocent: Yoshiya Nobuko's Good Girls', in L. Miller and J. Bardsley (eds), *Bad Girls of Japan*, New York: Palgrave Macmillan, 2005.

Freedman, A. *Tokyo in Transit: Japanese Culture on the Rails and Road*, Stanford: Stanford University Press, 2011.

Freson, T. S. and Arthur, L. B. 'Fashioning Men's Bodies: Masculinity and Muscularity', in A. Reilly and S. Cosbey (eds), *The Men's Fashion Reader*, New York: Fairchild Books, 2008.

Fujimoto, Y. *Watashi no ibasho wa doko ni aru no? Shojo manga ga utsusu kokoro no katachi* (*Where Do I Belong? The Shape of the Heart as Reflected in Girls' Comic Books*), Tokyo: Gakuyo Shobo, 1998.

Fukasawa, K. 'Men's ni manabu Trad kouza' (The Lecture on Trad Style Learning through Men's Fashion), *Numéro Tokyo*, 41 (November 2010), pp. 64–5.

Fukumitsu, M. 'Yase & usui danshi nanka ōishi' (Skinny and thin boys are somehow increased), *Asashi Shinbun Weekly*, 15 January (2007), pp. 38–41.

Gagné, I. 'Urban Princesses: Performance and "Women's Language" in Japan's Gothic/Lolita Subculture', *Journal of Linguistic Anthropology*, 18(1) (2008), pp. 130–50.

Gagné, I. 'Bracketed Adolescence: Unpacking Gender and Youth Subjectivity through Subcultural Fashion in Late-Capitalist Japan', *Intersections: Gender and Sexuality in Asia and the Pacific*, 32 (2013). Available at http://intersections.anu.edu.au/issue32/gagne.htm. [Last accessed 2 February 2014]

Gandhi, L. *Postcolonial Theory: A Critical Introduction*, Sydney: Allen & Unwin, 1998.

Garber, M. *Vested Interests: Cross-dressing and Cultural Anxiety*, New York: HarperPerennial, 1992.

Gilligan, S. 'Becoming Neo: Costume and Transforming Masculinity in the Matrix Films', in P. McNeil, V. Karaminas and C. Cole (eds), *Fashion in Fiction*, Oxford and New York: Berg, 2009.

Godoy, T. *Style Deficient Disorder: Harajuku Street Fashion Tokyo*, San Francisco: Chronicle Books, 2007.

Gomarasca, A. 'Under the Sign of Kawaii', in F. Bonami and R. Simons (eds), *The Fourth Sex: Adolescent Extremes*, Milan: Charta, 2003.

Gonick, M. 'Between "Girl Power" and "Reviving Ophelia": Constituting the Neoliberal Girl Subject', *NWSA Journal*, 18(2) (2006), pp. 1–23.

Grant, B. K. *Film Genre: From Iconography to Ideology*, London: Wallflower Press, 2007.

Greer, G. *The Beautiful Boy*, New York: Rizzoli, 2003.

Hammond, P. 'The Mystification of Culture: Western Perception of Japan', *Gazette* 61(3–4) (1999), pp. 311–25.

Hardy Bernal, K. A. 'Japanese Lolita: Challenging Sexualized Style and the Little Girl Look', in S. Tarraant and M Jolles (eds), *Fashion Talks: Undressing the Power of Style*, Albany: State University of New York Press, 2012.

Harnnerz, U. 'The Cultural Role of the World Cities', in A. Cohen and K. Fukui (eds), *Humanizing the City?* Edinburgh: Edinburgh University Press, 1993.

Harvey, P. A. S. 'Nonchan's Dream: NHK Morning Serialized Television Novels', in D. P. Martinez, *The World of Japanese Popular Culture, Shifting Boundaries and Global Cultures*, Cambridge and Melbourne: Cambridge University Press, 1998.

Hayashida, T., Ishizu, S., Kurosu, T., and Hasegawa, H. *Take Ivy*, New York: powerHouse Books, 2010 [1965].

Hill, D. D. *American Menswear: From the Civil War to the Twenty-first Century*, Texas: Texas Tech University Press, 2011.

Hirano, K. 'The Westernization of Clothes and the State in Meiji Japan', in K. Hirano (ed.) *The State and Cultural Transformation: Perspectives from East Asia*, Tokyo: United Nations University Press, 1993.

Hodkinson, P. 'Youth Cultures: A Critical Outline of Key Debates', in P. Hodkinson and W. Deicke (eds), *Youth Cultures: Scenes, Subcultures and Tribes*, New York: Routledge, 2007.

Hollander, A. *Seeing Through Clothes*, New York: The Viking Press, 1978.

Hollander, A. *Sex and Suits*, New York: Knopf, 1994.

Hollander, A. *Feeding the Eye*, Berkeley and Los Angeles: University of California Press, 2000.

Hollinger, K. 'From Female Friends to Literary Ladies: The Contemporary Woman's Film', in S. Neal (ed.), *Genre and Contemporary Hollywood*, London: British Film Institute, 2002.

Honda, M. 'The Genealogy of Hirahira: Liminality and the Girl', in Tomoko Aoyama and Barbara Hartley (eds), *Girl Reading Girl in Japan*, trans. T. Aoyama and B. Hartley, New York: Routledge, 2010 [1980].

Hozumi, K. *IVY Illustrated: Gals*, Tokyo: Aiiku-sha, 2003 [1980].

Hughes, C. *Dressed in Fiction*, Oxford and New York: Berg, 2006.

Hyde, M. *Making Up the Rococo: François Boucher and His Critics*, Los Angeles: Getty Publications, 2006.

Ishizu, K. *Itsumo zero kara no shuppatsudatta* (*I Always Made my Start from Nothing*), Tokyo: Nihon Tosho Centre, 2010.

Iwabuchi, K. 'Complicit Exoticism: Japan and Its Other', *Continuum*, 8(2) (1994), pp. 49–82.

Jeffreys, S. *Beauty and Misogyny: Harmful Cultural Practices in the West*, London and New York: Routledge, 2005.

Jones, J. E. and Gladstone, J. F. *The Alice Companion: A Guide to Lewis Carroll's Alice Books*, New York: State University of New York Press, 1998.

Jones, M. *Skintight: An Anatomy of Cosmetic Surgery*, New York: Berg, 2008.

Jones, S. *The Eighteenth Century*, Cambridge: Cambridge University Press, 1985.

Kaplan, E. A. *Women and Film: Both Sides of the Camera*, New York and London: Methuen, 1983.

Kawado, M. 'Meiji no Ruisu Kyaroru' (Lewis Carroll in the Meiji Period), *Honyaku to rekishi*, 2, 30 September (2000). Available from http://homepage3.nifty.com/nada/alice01.html [accessed 23 July 2012].

Kawazoe, F. *Hikaru genji ga aishita ouchou brand hin* (*The Dynastic Brand Artefacts Prince Genji Loved*), Tokyo: Kadokawa Gakugei Shuppan, 2008.

Keene, D. 'Japanese Aesthetics', in N. G. Hume (ed.), *Japanese Aesthetics and Culture: Reader*, New York: State University of New York Press, 1995 [1988].

Kelts, R. *japanamerica: How Japanese Pop Culture Has Invaded the U.S.*, New York: Palgrave Macmillan, 2006.

Kidwell, C. B. and Steele, V. (eds). *Men and Women: Dressing the Part*, Washington: Smithsonian Institution Press, 1989.

Kilpatrick, H. 'Envisioning the shôjo Aesthetic in Miyazawa Kenji's "The Twin Stars" and "Night of the Milky Way Railway', *Portal: Journal of Multidisciplinary International Studies*, 9(3) (2012), pp. 1–26.

Kinsella, S. 'Cuties in Japan', in L. Skov and B. Moeran (eds), *Women, Media, and Consumption in Japan*, Richmond, Surrey: Curzon Press, 1995.

Kinsella, S. 'What's Behind the Fetishism of Japanese School Uniforms?', *Fashion Theory*, 6(2) (2002), pp. 215–37.

Kinsella, S. 'Black Faces, Witches, and Racism Against Girls', in L. Miller and J. Bardsley (eds), *Bad Girls of Japan*, New York: Palgrave Macmillan, 2005.

Knighton, M. A. 'Down the Rabbit Hole: In Pursuit of Shōjo Alices from Lewis Carroll to Kanai Mieko', *US-Japan Women's Journal*, 40 (2011), pp. 59–89.

Koga, R. *Kawaii no teikoku* (*The Empire of Kawaii*), Tokyo: Seido-sha, 2009.

Koizumi, K. *Panda no An-An*, Tokyo: Magazine House, 1997.

Koren, L. *New Fashion Japan*, Tokyo: Kodansha International, 1984.

Kress, G. and van Leeuwen, T. *Reading Images*, London and New York: Routledge, 1996.

Lacan, J. 'The Mirror-phase as Formative of the Function of the I', trans. J. Roussel, in S. Žižek (ed.), *Mapping Ideology*, London and New York: Verso, 1994 [1949].

Leblanc, L. *Pretty in Punk: Girls' Gender Resistance in a Boys' Subculture*, New Brunswick and London: Rutgers University Press, 2001.

Lehmann, U. *Tigersprung: Fashion in Modernity*, Cambridge, MA: MIT Press, 2000.

Lehmann, U. 'Walter Benjamin', in V. Steele (ed.), *Berg Companion to Fashion*, London and New York: Berg, 2010.

Loos, A. 'Ladies' Fashion', in *Spoken into the Void: Collected Essays 1897–1900*, trans. J. O. Newman and J. H. Smith, Cambridge and London: The MIT Press, 1982 [1898, 1902].

Lumby, C. 'Watching Them Watching Us: The Trouble with Teenage Girls', *Continuum: Journal of Media & Cultural Studies*, 15(1) (2001), pp. 49–55.

Mackie, V. 'Transnational Bricolage: Gothic Lolita and the Political Economy of Fashion', *Intersections: Gender and Sexuality in Asia and the Pacific*, 20 (April 2009) (http://intersections.anu.edu.au/issue20/mackie.htm). [Last accessed 4 July 2014]

Mackie, V. 'Reading Lolita in Japan', in T. Aoyama and B. Hartley (eds), *Girl Reading Girl in Japan*, London and New York: Routledge, 2010.

Martin, R. 'Robert Pattinson Wants You to Know He's Going To Get A Six Pack', *Marie Claire*, 13 September 2013 (http://www.marieclaire.co.uk/news/celebrity/544347/robert-pattinson-wants-you-to-know-he-s-going-to-get-a-six-pack.html#index=1) [accessed 19 October 2013].

Matsuura, M. *Sekai to Watashi to Lolita Fashion* (*The World, Lolita Fashion and I*), Tokyo: Seikyu-sha, 2007.

Maynard, M. *Dress and Globalization*, Manchester: Manchester University Press, 2004.

Mazzarella, S. R. and Pecora, N. O. 'Girls in Crisis: Newspaper Coverage of Adolescent Girls', *Journal of Communication Inquiry*, 31(1) (2007), pp. 6–27.

McNeil, P. 'The Appearance of Enlightenment: Refashioning the Elites', in M. Fitzpatrick, P. Jones, C. Knellwolf and I. McCalmn (eds), *The Enlightenment World*, Oxford and New York: Routledge, 2004.

McNeil, P. 'Introduction: Late Medieval to Renaissance Fashion', in P. McNeil (eds), *Fashion: Critical and Primary Sources*, Volume 1, Oxford and New York: Berg, 2009.

McNeil, P. 'Art and Dress', In Lise Skov (ed.), *Berg Encyclopedia of World Dress and Fashion, Volume 8: West Europe*, Oxford and New York: Berg, 2010.

McNeil, P. and Karaminas, V. 'Introduction', in P. McNeil and V. Karaminas (eds), *The Men's Fashion Reader*, Oxford and New York: Berg, 2009.

McRobbie, A. 'The Rise and Rise of Porno Chic', *The Times Higher Education*, 2 January 2004 (http://www.timeshighereducation.co.uk/story.asp?storyCode=182087&sectioncode=26). [Last accessed 4 July 2014]

McVeigh, B. J. *Wearing Ideology: State, Schooling and Self-presentation in Japan*, Oxford and New York: Berg, 2000.

Mears, P. 'Formalism and Revolution: Rei Kawakubo and Yohji Yamamoto', in V. Steele (ed.), *Japan Fashion Now*, New York: Yale University Press, 2010.

Mears, P (ed.). *Ivy Style: Radical Conformist*, New York: Yale University Press, 2012.

Merskin, D. 'Reviving Lolita? A Media Literacy Examination of Sexual Portrayals of Girls in Fashion Advertising', *American Behavioral Scientist*, 48(1) (2004), pp. 119–29.

Mikanagi, Y. *Masculinity and Japan's Foreign Relations*, Boulder and London: First Forum Press, 2011.

Miller, L. 'You are Doing Burikko!: Censoring/Scrutinizing Artificers of Cute Femininity in Japanese', in J. Shibamoto Smith and S. Okamoto (eds), *Japanese Language, Gender, and Ideology: Cultural Models and Real People*, New York: Oxford University Press, 2004.

Miller, L. *Beauty Up: Exploring Contemporary Japanese Body Aesthetics*, Berkeley: University of California Press, 2006.

Miller, L. 'Perverse Cuteness in Japanese Girl Culture', paper presented at Japan Fashion Now Symposium at The Museum at Fashion Institute of Technology, unpublished, 2010.

Miller, L. 'Cute Masquerade and the Pimping of Japan', *International Journal of Japan*, 20(1) (2011), pp. 18–29.

Moeran, B. 'Elegance and Substance Travel East: Vogue Nippon', *Fashion Theory*, 10(1/2) (2006), pp. 225–58.

Moers, E. *The Dandy: Brummell to Beerbohm*, London: Secker & Warburg, 1960.

Monden, M. 'Transcultural Flow of Demure Aesthetics: Examining Cultural Globalization through Gothic and Lolita Fashion', *New Voices*, 2 (2008), pp. 21–40.

Monden, M. 'Japanese Men's Fashion Magazines', in J. Eicher (ed.), *Berg Encyclopaedia of World Dress and Fashion*, 2012. Online exclusive available at http://dx.doi.org/10.2752/BEWDF/EDch6511.

Monden, M. 'The Nationality of Lolita Fashion', in F. Nakamura, M. Perkins and O. Krischer (eds), *Asia Through Art and Anthropology*, London and New York: Bloomsbury, 2013.

Monden, M. 'Being Alice in Japan: performing a cute, "girlish" revolt', *Japan Forum*, 26(2) (2014), pp. 265–85.

Monden, M. 'Layers of the Ethereal: A Cultural Investigation of Beauty, Girlhood and Ballet in Japanese *shōjo manga*', *Fashion Theory*, 18(3) (2014), pp. 251–96.

Morimoto, M. and Chang, S. 'Western and Asian Models in Japanese Fashion Magazine Ads: The Relationship with Brand Origins and International Versus Domestic Magazines', *Journal of International Consumer Marketing*, 21(3) (2009), pp. 173–87.

Morley, D. and Robins, K. *Space of Identity: Global Media, Electronic Landscapes and Cultural Boundaries*, London: Routledge, 1995.

Morris, I. *The World of the Shining Prince: Court Life in Ancient Japan*, New York, Tokyo and London: Kodansha International, 1994 [1964].

Moses, A. '"Ignored" Men now in Fashion Online', *Sydney Morning Herald*, August 2012.

Mulvey, L. 'Visual Pleasure and Narrative Cinema in Durham', in M. G. Durham and D. Kellner (eds), *Media and Cultural Studies: Key Works*, Oxford: Blackwell Publishers, 2001 [1975].

Nagasaki, S. *Kasane no irome* (*The Combination of Colors in Layers: The Aesthetics of Color in the Heian Period*), Kyoto: Seigensha, 2001 [1987].

Nakamura, K. and Matsuo, H. 'Female Masculinity and Fantasy Spaces: Transcending Genders in the Takarazuka and Japanese Popular Culture', in J. E. Roberson and N. Suzuki (eds), *Men and Masculinities in Modern Japan: Dislocating the Salaryman Doxa*, New York: Routledge, 2002.

Nakashima, T. 'Cinema', in *Men's non-no*, June 2006, p. 147.

Napier, S. J. 'Vampires, Psychic Girls, Flying Women and Sailor Scouts: Four Faces of the Young Female in Japanese Popular Culture', in D. P. Martinez (ed.), *The World of Japanese Popular Culture*, Cambridge: Cambridge University Press, 1998.

Nederveen Pieterse, J. *Globalization and Culture: Global Mélange*, Maryland: Roman & Littlefield Publishers, 2004.

Negrin, L. 'The Self as Image A Critical Appraisal of Postmodern Theories of Fashion', *Theory, Culture & Society*, 16(3) (1999), pp. 99–118.

Negrin, L. *Appearance and Identity: Fashioning the Body in Postmodernity*, New York: Palgrave Macmillan, 2008.

Newbold, A. 'London Men Stake Their Place in the Fashion Spending Arena', *Telegraph*, 14 June 2012.

Nixon, S. *Hard Looks: Masculinity, Spectatorship and Contemporary Consumption*, New York: St. Martin's Press, 1996.

Nixon, S. 'Exhibiting Masculinity', in S. Hall (ed.), *Representation: Culture Representation and Signifying Practices*, London: Sage, 1997.

Okamura, K. *Gurohbaru shakai no ibunka-ron* (*Cross-cultural Theory in Global Societies*), Kyoto: Sekaishiso-sha, 2003.

O'Shaughnessy, M. *Media and Society: an Introduction*, South Melbourne: Oxford University Press, 1999.

Paechter, C. 'Masculine Femininities/Feminine Masculinities: Power, Identities and Gender', *Gender and Education*, 18(3) (2006), pp. 253–63.

Pease, B. *Men and Gender Relations*, Croydon: Tertiary Press, 2002.

Peers, J. *The Fashion Doll From Bébé Jumeau to Barbie*, Oxford and New York: Berg, 2004.

Phillips, A. and Stringer, J. 'Introduction', in A. Phillips and J. Stringer (eds), *Japanese Cinema: Texts and Contexts*, London and New York: Routledge, 2007.

Pompeo, J. 'Trad Men' *The New York Observer*, 8 September 2009 (http://www.observer.com/2009/fashion/trad-men).

Prioleau, E. 'Humbert Humbert: Through the Looking Glass', *Twentieth Century Literature*, 21(4) (1975), pp. 428–37.

Reay, D. '"Spice Girls", "Nice Girls", "Girlies", and "Tomboys": Gender Discourses, Girls' Cultures and Femininities in the Primary Classroom', *Gender and Education*, 13(2) (2001), pp. 153–66.

Ribeiro, A. 'Fashion in the Eighteenth Century: Some Anglo-French Comparisons', *Textile History*, 22(2) (1991), pp. 329–45.

Ribeiro, A. *Dress in Eighteenth-Century Europe 1715–1789*, New Haven and London: Yale University Press, 2002 [1985].

Riviere, J. 'Womanliness as Masquerade', in A. Hughes (ed.), *The Inner World and Joan Riviere: Collected Papers: 1920–58*, London: Karnac Books, 1991 [1929].

Roberson, J. 'Fight!! Ippatsu!!: "Genki" Energy Drinks and the Marketing of Masculine Ideology in Japan', *Men and Masculinities*, 7 (2005), pp. 365–84.

Robertson, R. 'Glocalization: Time-Space and Homogeneity-Heterogeneity', in M. Featherstone, S. Lash and R. Robertson (eds), *Global Maternities*, London: Sage Publications, 1994.

Roche, D. 'Popular Dress', in P. McNeil (ed.), *Fashion: Critical and Primary Sources the Eighteenth Century*, Oxford and New York: Berg, 2009.

Rose, C. *Children's Clothes Since 1750*, London: B. T. Batsford Ltd, 1989.

Saito, M. *Modern-Girl Ron* (*The Theory of Modern Girls*), Tokyo: Bunshūb-bunko, 2003 [2000].

Sakakibara, K. *Alice no hon'yaku-shi 1899–2004* (*The History of Alice Translation*) (http://homepage3.nifty.com/nada/alice01.html).

Satō, I. *Kamikaze Biker: Parody and Anomy in Affluent Japan*, Chicago: University of Chicago Press, 1991.

Schomer, K. and Chang, Y. 'The Cult of Cute', *Newsweek*, 28 August 1995.

Shiine, Y. *Popeye monogatari* (*The Story of Popeye*), Tokyo: Shincho-sha, 2008.

Shively, D. H. 'Sumptuary Regulation and Status in Early Tokugawa Japan', *Harvard Journal of Asiatic Studies*, 25 (1964–5), pp. 123–64.

Silverman, K. 'Masochism and Subjectivity', *Framework*, 12 (1980), pp. 2–9.

Simmel, G. 'The Philosophy of Fashion', trans. K. H. Wolff, in D. Frisby and M. Featherstone (eds), *Simmel on Culture*, London: Sage Publications, 1997 [1905].

Singer, J. *Androgyny: Toward a New Theory of Sexuality*, New York: Anchor Press, 1976.

Skov, L. 'Fashion Trends, Japonisme and Postmodernism', in J. W. Treat (ed.), *Contemporary Japan and Popular Culture*, London: Curzon, 1996.

Slade, T. 'Clothing Modern Japan', PhD Thesis, University of Sydney, 2006.

Slade, T. 'The Japanese Suit and Modernity', in P. McNeil and V. Karaminas (eds), *The Men's Fashion Reader*, Oxford and New York: Berg. 2009.

Slade, T. *Japanese Fashion: A Cultural History*, Oxford and New York: Berg, 2009.

Smith, B. G. *Ladies of the Leisure Class*, Princeton: Princeton University Press, 1981.

Springer, J. A. 'Art and the Feminine Muse: Women in Interiors by John White Alexander', *Woman's Art Journal*, 6(2) (1985), pp. 1–8.

St Michel, P. 'For Japan's Justin Biebers, No Selena Gomezes Allowed' *The Atlantic*, 15 August 2012 (http://www.theatlantic.com/entertainment/archive/2012/08/for-japans-justin-biebers-no-selena-gomezes-allowed/261181). [Last accessed 8 February 2014]

Staite, S, A. 'Lolita: Atemporal Class-Play with Tea and Cakes', MA Thesis, University of Tasmania, 2012.

Staite, S. 'Femme Infantile: Australian Lolitas in Theory and Practice', *Intersections: Gender and Sexuality in Asia and the Pacific*, 32 (2013). Available at http://intersections.anu.edu.au/issue32/staite.htm. [Last accessed 2 February 2014]

Steele, V. *Fashion and Eroticism: Ideals of Feminine Beauty from the Victorian Era to the Jazz Age*, New York and Oxford: Oxford University Press, 1985.

Steele, V. *Paris Fashion: A Cultural History*, Oxford and New York: Berg, 2nd ed., 1998.

Steele, V. *Gothic: Dark Glamor*, New Haven: Yale University Press, 2008.

Steele, V. *Japan Fashion Now*, New York: Yale University Press, 2010.

Stevens, C. S. *Japanese Popular Music: Culture, Authenticity, and Power*, London and New York: Routledge, 2008.

Straayer, C. 'The Talented Poststructuralist: Heteromasculinity, Gay Artifice, and Class Passing', in P. Lehman (ed.), *Masculinity: Bodies, Movies, Culture*, New York: Routledge, 2001.

Taga, F. 'Rethinking Male Socialisation: Life Histories of Japanese Male Youth', in K. Louie and M. Low (eds), *Asian Masculinities*, Abingdon: RoutledgeCurzon, 2003.

Takabatake, A. 'Takabatake kasho no kodomo no enitsuite no ikkou: arisu tono douitsusei wo megutte' (A thought on Kasho Takabatake's art works on children: About the kindred qualities with Alice), *Bigakujutushi ronshū*, 19 (2011), pp. 55–80.

Takahashi, M. 'Opening the Closed World of Shōjo Manga', in M. W. Macwilliams (ed.), *Japanese Visual Cultures: Explorations in the World of Manga and Anime*, New York: M. E. Sharpe, 2008.

Takemiya, K. '1970 nendai no shōjo manga ni okeru geijutsusei e no shikō to sono mokuteki' (1970s *shōjo manga*'s preference for artistry and its purpose), *Bijutsu Forum 21* (Tokushū: *Manga to manga, soshite geijutsu* (special issue: Manga, Comics and Art), guest-edited by J. Berndt), 24 (2011), pp. 96–8.

Tanaka, K. 'The Language of Japanese Men's Magazines: Young Men Who Don't want to Get Hurt', in B. Benwell (ed.), *Masculinity and Men's Lifestyle Magazines*, Oxford: Blackwell Publishing, 2003.

Thomas, D. S. *Lewis Carroll: A Portrait with Background*, London: John Murray, 1996, p. 365.

Tiggemann, M. and Pickering, A. S. 'Role of Television in Adolescent Women's Body Dissatisfaction and Drive for Thinness', *International Journal of Eating Disorders*, 20(2) (1996), pp. 199–203.

Treat, J. W. 'Yoshimoto Banana Writes Home: The Shōjo in Japanese Popular Culture', in J. W. Treat (ed.), *Contemporary Japan and Popular Culture*, Honolulu: University of Hawaii Press, 1996.

Trebay, G. 'Prep, Forward and Back', *The New York Times*, 23 July 2010 (http://www.nytimes.com/2010/07/25/fashion/25Prep.html).

Ushikubo, M. *Sōshoku-kei danshi [ojō-man] ga nihon wo kaeru* (*Herbivorous Men (Ladylike Men) Change Japan*), Tokyo: Kōdansha +α shinsho, 2008.

Utsukushiku ikiru: Nakahara Jun'ichi sono bigaku to shigoto (*Live Beautifully: The Aesthetics and Works of Jun'ichi Nakahara*), Tokyo: Heibon-sha, 1999.

Vernallis, C. *Experiencing Music Video: Aesthetics and Cultural Context*, New York: Columbia University Press, 2004.

Ward, L. W. *et al.*, 'Contributions of Music Video Exposure to Black Adolescents' Gender and Sexual Schemas', *Journal of Adolescent Research*, 20(2) (2005), pp. 143–66.

Warner, M. 'Homo-Narcissism; or, Heterosexuality', in J. A. Boone and M. Cadden (eds), *Engendering Men: The Question of Male Feminist Criticism*, New York and London: Routledge, 1990.

Watanabe, S. *Shōjo-zō no tanjō –kindai nihon ni okeru 'shōjo' no keisei* (*The Birth of the Images of Shōjo – The Construction of Shōjo in Modern Japan*), Tokyo: Shinsen-sha, 2007.

Welker, J. 'From *The Cherry Orchard* to *Sakura no sono*: Translation and the Transfiguration of Gender and Sexuality in *shōjo manga*', in T. Aoyama and B. Hartley (eds), *Girl Reading Girl in Japan*, New York: Routledge, 2009, pp. 160–73.

Weltzien, F. 'Masque-ulinities: Changing Dress as a Display of Masculinity in the Superhero Genre', *Fashion Theory*, 9(2) (2005), pp. 229–50.

White, M. *Material Child*, Berkeley and London: University of California Press, 1993.

White, M. 'The Marketing of Adolescence in Japan: Buying and Dreaming', in L. Skov and B. Moeran (eds), *Women, Media, and Consumption in Japan*, Richmond, Surrey: Curzon Press, 1995.

Wilde, O. 'The Decay of Lying: An Observation', in *Oscar Wilde Plays, Prose Writings and Poems*, London: David Campbell Publishers, 1991 [1891].

Wilkins, A. C. 'So Full of Myself as a Chick: Goth Women, Sexual Independence, and Gender Egalitarianism', *Gender & Society*, 18(3) (2004), pp. 328–49.

Wilson, E. *Adorned in Dreams*, London: Virago, 1985.

Wilson, E. 'Fashion and Postmodern Body', in J. Ash and E. Wilson (eds), *Chic Thrills: A Fashion Reader*, Berkeley and Los Angeles: University of California Press, 1992.

Wilson, E. 'Magic Fashion', *Fashion Theory*, 8(4) (2004), pp. 375–85.

Wyatt, J. 'Weighing the Transgressive Star Body of Shelley Duval', in E. Meehan and E. R. Riordan (eds), *Sex and Money: Feminism and Political Economy in the Media*, Minneapolis: University of Minnesota Press, 2002.

Yagawa, S. *Fushigi no kuni no Alice (Alice's Adventures in Wonderland)*, Tokyo: Shincho-sha, 1994.

Yamanaka, N. *The Book of Kimono*, Tokyo, New York and San Francisco: Kodansha International, 1982.

Yamazaki, M. 'Preppi to iu koto' (About Being a Preppy), *en-Taxi*, 31 (2010), p. 162.

Yano, C. R. *Pink Globalization: Hello Kitty's Trek Across the Pacific*, Durham and London: Duke University Press, 2013.

Yomota, I. *Kawaii-Ron (Theory of Cute)*, Tokyo: Chikuma Shobo, 2006.

Zolla, E. *The Androgyne: Reconciliation of Male and Female*, New York: Crossroad, 1981.

ii. Surveys and reports

Japan Youth Research Institute. *koukousei no seikatsu to ishiki ni kansuru chousa (Survey of the Lifestyles and Consciousness of High School Students)*, available at http://www1.odn.ne.jp/%7E-aaa25710//research/Index.html. 2004. [Last accessed 18 May 2014]

The Ministry of Health, Labour and Welfare in Japan. *Kokumin kenkō/eiyō chōsa no gaikō (The Survey Results of Health and Nutrition of the Nation)*. 2006, 2007, 2008, 2009, 2010, 2011.

iii. Websites and blogs

Alisa Mizuki: http://avex.jp/alisa/special/history_dvd. [Last accessed 4 July 2014]

Baby, The Stars Shine Bright: http://www.babyssb.co.jp/shopping/baby/onepiece/134317.html. [Last accessed 16 May 2012]

Bignet: Bunkyō-dō website: http://bignet2.bunkyodo.co.jp/bignet2/magranking.asp?id=dajoh. [Last accessed 30 September 2013]

Innocent World: http://innocent-w.jp. [Last accessed 4 July 2014]

Ishizu Kensuke daihyakka (Encyclopedia of Kensuke Ishizu): http://www.ishizu.jp.

Ivy Style: http://www.Ivy-style.com. [Last accessed 8 April 2012]

Kamikaze Girls: www.kamikazegirls.net. [Last accessed 24 April 2008, no longer available]

Men's non-no: www.mensnonno.jp. [Last accessed 8 May 2010]

Milkboy Staff's Blog: http://ameblo.jp/mb-staff. [Last accessed 27 October 2013]

Models.com: http://models.com/rankings/ni/Top50Men. [Last accessed 19 October 2013]

Oricon Style: http://www.oricon.co.jp/prof/artist/198535/ranking/cd_single.
Shadan-hōjin nihon zasshi-kyōkai (Japan Magazine Organisation):
    http://www.j-magazine.or.jp. [Last accessed 1 October 2010]
Victorian Maiden: www.victorianmaiden.com. [Last accessed 3 June 2011]

iv. Photo books and catalogues

Emily Temple Cute, *Wonderland*. Tokyo: Prevision. 2009.
Koike, Teppei, *kiss me, kiss me*. Tokyo: Shufu to seikatsu sha. 2006.
Kyoko Fukada in Shimotsuma Story. Tokyo: Pia. 2004.
Street Mode Kenkyukai, 'History of Baby, The Stars Shine Bright', in *STREET MODE BOOK*. Tokyo: Graphic-sha. 2007, p. 66.

v. Films

Alice in Wonderland. Walt Disney Pictures, directed by Tim Burton, starring Johnny Depp, Mia Wasikowska, Helena Bonham Carter. 2010, USA.
Knight and Day. Twentieth Century Fox Film Corporation, directed by James Mangold, starring Tom Cruise, Cameron Diaz, Peter Sarsgaard. 2010, USA.
Orphée. Andre Paulve Film, Films du Palais Royal, directed by Jean Cocteau, starring Jean Marais, François Périer, María Casares, Marie Déa. 1950, France.
Plein Soleil (Purple Noon). Robert et Raymond Hakim, Paris Film, directed by René Clément, starring Alain Delon, Marie Laforêt, Maurice Ronet. 1960, France and Italy, based on the novel by Patricia Highsmith, 1955.
Shimotsuma Monogatari (Kamikaze Girls). Toho, directed by Tetsuya Nakashima, starring Kyoko Fukuda, Anna Tsuchiya, based on the novel by Novala Takemoto. 2004, Japan.
Taxi Driver. Columbia Pictures Corporation, directed by Martin Scorsese, starring Robert De Niro, Jodie Foster, Cybill Shepherd. 1976, USA.
Thelma and Louise. MGM, directed by Ridley Scott, starring Susan Sarandon, Geena Davis, Harvey Keitel. 1991, USA.

vi. Music video clips

February, Tommy. 'Bloomin'!'. 2003.
Kimura, Kaela. 'Snowdome'. 2007.
Lavigne, Avril. 'Alice'. Dir. Dave Meyers. 2010.
Mizuki, Alisa. 'Eden no machi' (Town of Eden). 1991.
Oomph!. 'Labyrinth'. 2008.
Perry, Katy. 'California Gurls'. Dir. Mathew Cullen. 2010.
Stefani, Gwen. 'What You Waiting For?'. Dir. Francis Lawrence. 2004.
Tom Petty and the Heartbreakers. 'Don't Come Around Here No More'. Dir. Jeff Stein. 1985.

vii. Television programmes and commercials

Deka One-ko (Detective One-ko). Japan. Nippon Television. Starring Mikako Tabe, Yuya Tegoshi, Ikki Sawamura. 2011.

Fugo Keiji (Millionaire Detective). First Season. Japan. Televi-Asahi. Starring Kyoko Fukada, Shinji Yamashita, Isao Natsuyagi. 2005.

Martin, M., Brough, B. and Orrego, P. *Get It On* (Documentary), Canada, Chuma Television, 2004.

viii. Novels

Austen, Jane. *Northanger Abbey*. London: Penguin Books. 1996 [1818].

Carroll, Lewis. *Alice's Adventures in Wonderland and Through the Looking-Glass*. London: Penguin. 1998.

Carroll, Lewis. *Alice's Adventures in Wonderland and Through the Looking-Glass*. London: Vintage Books. 2007 [1865, 1871].

Carroll, Lewis. *The Annotated Alice: Alice's Adventures in Wonderland and Through the Looking-Glass*. Harmondsworth: Penguin. 1970, p. 377.

Lady Murasaki, *Genji Monogatari* (*The Tale of Genji*), trans. A. Waley, volume 1, London: George Allen & Unwin Ltd. 1973 [1935].

Rhys, Jean. *Voyage in the Dark*. London: Penguin Books. 2000 [1934].

Takemoto, Novala. *Shimotsuma Monogatari* (*Kamikaze Girls*). Tokyo: Shōgakkan. 2004 [2002].

ix. Japanese *Manga* (comic books)

Morimoto, Kozueko. *Deka One-ko* (*Detective One-ko*). Volumes 1–8, Tokyo: Kōdan-sha. 2008–present.

Oshima, Yumiko. *Banana Bread no Pudding* (*Banana Bread Pudding*). Tokyo: Hakusen sha. 1995 [1977–8].

x. Periodicals

an an (2010)
Brutus (2012)
CanCam (2007, 2010)
Choki Choki (2010–11)
CUTiE (2010)
EYESCREAM (2007)
Fineboys (2006–11)
GQ Australia (2010)
KERA MANIAX (2007–10)

Marquee (2005–10)
Men's non-no (2006–11)
non-no (2007, 2010)
Numéro Tokyo (2008, 2010)
Popeye (2006–11)
Sō-En (2004–10)
spoon (2013)
SWITCH (2005)
Zipper (2006–10)

INDEX